THE MORAL LIFE OF MAN

The Moral Life of Man

Its Philosophical Foundations

JACOB KOHN

Dean, Graduate School and Associate Professor of Theology
University of Judaism at Los Angeles

Rabbi Emeritus, Congregation Sinai

PHILOSOPHICAL LIBRARY
NEW YORK

COPYRIGHT 1956 BY
PHILOSOPHICAL LIBRARY
15 EAST 40TH STREET, NEW YORK

PRINTED IN THE UNITED STATES OF AMERICA

DEDICATED

IN LOVE AND GRATITUDE

TO THE MEMORY OF

AUGUSTA

ACKNOWLEDGMENTS

The author wishes to acknowledge his indebtedness to Simon Greenberg, Vice-Chancellor of the Jewish Theological Seminary of America and Director of the University of Judaism, for his deep interest first in the series of lectures upon which the manuscript of this book was ultimately based, and secondly for his careful and critical reading of the manuscript itself. My colleague, Israel Chodos, the Rabbi of Congregation Sinai, has earned my sincere gratitude for the sympathy and urgency he has always displayed for the completion of this volume as well as for his valuable suggestions concerning the form of the text itself, which have proved so helpful. Rabbi Max Vorspan both as a student in the Graduate School and later as Registrar of the University of Judaism has been a source of constant help and encouragement.

A word of thanks is likewise due to my son Gustave K. Kohn, Chief Research Chemist of the California Spray Chemical Corporation, for having carefully perused the section entitled "Beyond Causation" and for proposing certain corrections which were later embodied in the complete text. He was likewise helpful in calling my attention to articles appearing from time to time in various scientific periodicals and which he thought might prove relevant to some of the problems dealt with in these pages.

Above all, my devoted and efficient secretary, Miss Colette Sigal, has made a major contribution at all stages in the development of the manuscript. She first undertook responsibility for the mimeographed outlines of the separate lectures which, during a period of almost two years, were each week placed in the hands of students. In the last few months, in addition to certain other secretarial duties for the University of Judaism, she gave time, thought and enthusiasm to the preparation of the book far beyond the line of duty.

January 1956

CONTENTS

CHAPTER I

OBLIGATION 1
The Two Categories, 1. — The Category of Obligation or Duty, 2. —The Importance of Status in Defining Obligation, 3. — Limitation Upon Free Will Imposed by Obligation, 6 — The Growing Burden and Complexity of Human Obligation, 8. — Rebellion as Instinctive, 9. The Assumption that Religion is Always the Opiate and Soporific, 13. — The Lesson From History, 14. — Obligations in Conflict, 21. — Transference of Obligation to Moral Principles and Generalizations, 22. — Examples from Rabbinic Literature, 25. — (I) The Shema and the Commandments, 25. — (II) The Golden Rule in its Positive and Negative Aspects, 26. — (III) Thou shalt love thy neighbor as thyself, 27. — (IV) The Individual, 28. — (V) The Six hundred and thirteen commandments, 29. — (VI) Which a man shall do, and by which he shall live, 31. — (VII) Goodness and the Holy Spirit, 33. — Ethical Ideals — What is and What Ought to Be, 34.

CHAPTER II

THE GOOD 38
Good and Evil, 38. — The Sensuality of Man, 39. — On the Spiritual Level, 40. — The Human Spirit—A Definition of Spirituality, 41. — Egoism and Altruism, 45. — The Second Transference, 47. — The Highest Obligation and the Perfect Good, 49. — Can We Experience Perfection, 50. — The Perfect Truth, 53. — Messianic Vision and Perfect Goodness, 55. — The Reality of Progress and the Primacy of Evil, 56. — A Definition of Progress, 66. — Progress, Peace, and Democracy, 67. — Tradition and Progress, 68. —

CHAPTER III

MORAL FREEDOM 73
The Problem of the Freedom of the Will, 73. — Character as a Determining Factor in Human Behavior, 74. — God's Omniscience and Man's Freedom, 77. — Spinoza's Denial of Freedom, 78. — The Whole and Its Parts, 79. — Beyond Causation, 82. — (I) The Element of Chance, 83. — (II) Predictability, Probability, and Critical Common Sense, 85. — (III) The Ontological Fact, 90. — (IV) Transition to the Modern Point of View, 92. — (V) The Predictable and the Unpredictable Nevertheless Join Hands, 95. — (VI) Two Theories of Creation, 99. — (VII) Creation Contrasted with Both Chance and Cause, 104. — (VIII) Creation and the Dilemma Inherent in all Existence, 107. — (IX) The Total Unity of Being—God or Nature, 108. — (X) Does Creation Predetermine or Predestine the Fate of Its Creatures, 110. —

CHAPTER IV

IS THERE A MORAL WORLD ORDER 114

The General Problem, 114. — Nature the Only Possible Scene of the Moral Life, 115. — Man—The Center of Significance, 116. — Nature as Process—The Emerging Human Spirit, 117. — The Moral Life as a Factor Making for Happiness and Survival, 121. — The Moral Factor in Organized Society, 125. — Between Doom and Salvation — The Present Crisis, 128. — God and the Reality of Evil, 130. — Evasive Solutions, 130. — The Necessary Basis for Moral Values, 132. — The Involvement of God in the Moral Life of Man. 137. —

CHAPTER V

RETRIBUTION AND THE FAITH IN IMMORTALITY 145

Introductory Remarks, 145. — Theories of Divine Retribution in Biblical Literature, 147. — (I) Justice in General, 147. — (II) The Sins of the Fathers, 148. — (III) Collective Guilt, 149. — (IV) The Rhetorical Questions, 151. — (V) The Primacy of the Individual, 152. — (VI) Tentative Doubts, 154. — (VII) The Skeptical Classics, 159. — (VIII) The Ethical Function of Suffering and Martyrdom, 166. — Theories of Divine Retribution in Rabbinic Literature, 172. — (I) Complexity of the Problem, 172. — (II) The Paradox of Human Mercy as it Clashes with God's Justice, 177. — (III) Immortality and the World to Come, 179. — (IV) Above the Desire for Reward or Fear of Punishment, 182. — (V) Beloved is Suffering, 184. — (VI) Suffering and Natural Necessity, 187. — Immortality, 189. — (I) Statement of the Problem, 189. — (II) The Mythology of Death, 189. (III) The Reification of Death, 193. — (IV) Time as Possibility and Time as Actuality, 197. — (V) The Nature of the Here—Now, 198. — (VI) The Future as Actual, 199. — (VII) Time and Eternity, 201. — (VIII) Immortality as an Actual Experience, 208. — (IX) Moral Consequences, 209. —

CHAPTER VI

MORALITY AND RELIGION 218

Must Man Believe in God to be Moral, 218. — Must There be a God if Goodness is To Be, 219. — Revelation and the Moral Imperative, 220. — The Abnormal not to be Equated with the Untrue, 222. — Revelation and the Eternal Verities, 225. — The Relation of Religious Faith to the Moral Life, 226. — Nature No Longer Regarded as Mechanical, 229. — Theism and Humanism, 231. —

INDEX 241

CHAPTER ONE

OBLIGATION

The Two Categories

The moral life of man operates under two categories—the 'ought' and the 'good.' These can be defined in terms of one another but they are not identical. To do the 'good' may be a man's duty, and doing one's duty under all circumstances of life may be man's highest good. The 'good' is often discerned as the ideational content of the dutiful act—that which the latter is meant to achieve. The imperative may find expression in the words 'turn from evil and do the good.' This command is given content by the Prophetic teaching *"It hath been told thee, O man, what is good,* And what the Lord doth require of thee; Only to do justly, and to love mercy, and to walk humbly with thy God." (Micah 6:8)

It is questionable whether the idea of the 'good' could of itself have given rise to the feeling of obligation towards its achievement despite the speculative optimism of Socrates who felt that to know the good is to do the good. It is apparent that the very terms good and evil apply to realms often irrelevant to the moral life. A 'good' dinner is no less good because the judgment pronouncing it good has no reference to a moral situation, nor can its connection with a voluntary act make it a category of the moral life as such. A 'good' business contract, though the result of long deliberation and final voluntary determination, may or may not have any moral quality. The word has moral significance only as the goal sought or demanded by some voluntary act already pregnant with the reality of the 'ought.' When a court says that a criminal is insane because he does not know the difference between right and wrong or good and evil, it merely means that

1

he is incapable of perceiving the distinction between things that 'ought' or ought not be done. The court does not intend to say that the accused is incapable of distinguishing between what pleases him or not, or what may or may not benefit him. The court presupposes that the term 'good' has moral significance. The insane person is thought to be irresponsible because he is unaware of the relevance of moral obligation to the act in question.

The Category of Obligation or Duty

At the root of all moral decision between good and evil lies the conviction that each act may have a variety of qualities. An act may be such as we *can* do, or *must* do, or *wish* to do, or 'ought' to do whether we wish it done or not. That a man often desires to do what he ought to do, or is compelled to do what he ought to do, does not rob the category of the 'ought' of its uniqueness. It is not the wish or the compulsion that constitutes the 'ought.' It is an imperative addressed to him or imposed upon him by a whole skein of relationships to which he has not previously consented, but in which he finds himself enmeshed from the very beginning.

Morality, therefore, is as old as humanity, or rather as old as the human spirit, if we mean to assert, as we do here, that *man is an animal who feels that his deeds may be agents not only for the satisfaction of desire but for the discharge of obligations.* Insofar as he does what he desires or is compelled to do, he acts like any other animal. The moment he pauses to ask ought I to do what now I desire, he affirms his humanity.

We employ the term obligation, rather than duty, because duty is the more generalized form of obligation, whereas the concrete facts of which the moral life is composed precede man's generalization concerning them, as we shall presently see. Besides, it is a term fruitfully employed by Bergson, and though we shall permit ourselves to differ somewhat, both from his analysis of the concept, and from his ideas concerning the development of the moral life on its highest level, it can serve as a point of departure. Obligation, according to Bergson, is inherent in even the most primitive society—deriving not from choice, but from status.

The individual with no social connections is a pure abstraction, as is the physical entity without the field of force which relates it to others of its kind. Such abstractions both in the logical and the literal sense—something abstracted for purposes of observations from the larger whole in which it finds itself and out of which its individuality emerges—is useful for purposes of analysis but must not be confused with the concrete reality prior to its abstraction.

No mere aggregate of human individuals constitutes a society. The gregarious instinct in man is *only* an instinct, a compulsive force, and at best could organize men into flocks or herds or packs or hives or ant hills but not into societies. Such an instinct, inherited from our subhuman past, may give support to, or may constitute a problem for that type of solidarity which is characteristic of man—it is certainly not identical with it. Nor, at the other extreme, can we picture the units of this aggregate resolving suddenly to exchange certain duties for certain rights and thus by "social contract" creating forms of social living. Such contract, receiving the sanction of reason, may indeed be implicit in all types of social obligations, but becomes explicit only in legislation, oral or written, in comparatively advanced societies and could not have constituted the explicit motivation for transforming the human aggregate into a social unit.

The fact is that man is born into the society which he helps constitute and finds himself from the beginning involved in a skein of obligations as real as any other set of relationships, binding him to all other constituents of the one world in which he must live out his life. The awareness of such obligations to one another and to the society which defines the status of the individual constituent, is the force which transforms the aggregate, the gregarious multitude, into a society of human beings.

The Importance of Status in Defining Obligation

There is no escape from such obligation or duty, as

defined by status. As child, as man or woman, as parent or elder, a human being that lives in society and does not merely run with a pack, becomes aware that only the discharge of his obligations gives him the right to expect certain benefits from the society in which he dwells. In the most primitive Indian tribes, it is expected that the squaw will nurse the papoose, gather wood, keep the home fires burning, and cultivate the small area where the wild maize grows. It is expected that the elders shall sit at council and decide matters dealing with the hunt or the wars and it is expected of the young men that they be the hunters and the warriors. Squaw and elder and young brave know that they are under obligation though they have no written constitution and no 'Tables of the Law.' It is the awareness of such social relations and the feeling that though he cannot refuse the obligation attendant upon any specific status save at his peril (the tribe will be avenged), nevertheless, that, *at his peril* he can repudiate it, he can conform or rebel if he so chooses—this experience constitutes the essential beginnings of social morality in its personal aspects. Let me repeat again, this sense of obligation is not instinctive save as gregariousness may be instinctive. It must not be confused with the tropisms and reflexes which through innumerable generations organize the hive or ant hill. These are all in their innumerable variety only the instinctive preludes to the human conception of duty dependent upon status.

When an aging wolf fails in leading the pack to the kill, he is set upon and slain by the pack itself. The wolves and the insects dispose of failures, they do not punish offenders. There are no social rebels or outlaws where obedience is instinctive and the law consists of the repeated uniformities of compulsive behavior. Some vestigial survivals of this attitude towards failures can be found in the practice of exposing unwanted female children or the helpless aged so that they be quickly eliminated. There is no guilt involved in such acts. (Those of us who are not well acquainted with biology or zoology must beware lest we take our knowledge of animal behavior from the classic masters of fable, beginning with Aesop and on to Kipling and Walt Disney. The elder Roosevelt, who knew wild life and who turned in wrath against what he called "nature fakers" uttered, I think, a very useful warning. The amiable fablists whom we have mentioned make no pretense at objectivity. Their animal characters are only darts which they aim at human weakness.)

Bergson is at pains to distinguish the elements of freedom, instinct and natural necessity in human conduct.

"In a hive or an ant-hill the individual is riveted to his task by his structure, and the organization is relatively invariable, whereas the human community is variable in form, open to every kind of progress. The result is that in the former each rule is laid down by nature, and is necessary: whereas in the latter only one thing is natural, the necessity of a rule. Thus the more in human society we delve down to the root of the various obligations to reach obligation in general, the more obligation will tend to become necessity, the nearer it will draw, in its peremptory aspect, to instinct. And yet we should make a great mistake if we tried to ascribe any particular obligation, whatever it might be, to instinct. What we must perpetually recall is that, no one obligation being instinctive, obligation as a whole *would have been* instinctive if human societies were not, so to speak, ballasted with variability and intelligence.

It is just this necessity that we perceive, not actual but virtual, at the foundations of moral obligation, as through a more or less transparent veil. A human being feels an obligation only if he is free, and each obligation, considered separately implies liberty. But it is necessary that there should be obligations; and the deeper we go, away from those particular obligations which are at the top, towards obligation in general, or, as we have said, towards obligation as a whole, which is at the bottom, the more obligation appears as the very form assumed by necessity in the realm of life, when it demands, for the accomplishment of certain ends, intelligence, choice, and therefore liberty."[1]

We shall attempt to prove that natural necessity enters into conduct and emerges as moral freedom on a much wider basis, when we reach our analysis of morality under the category of the 'good.'

Limitation Upon Free Will Imposed By Obligation

Let it be noted here, though we shall discuss the whole question more fully later on, that the moral freedom which expresses the essential character of every decision having moral value must not be construed as freedom, on the part of man, to be or not to be moral. Neither the freedom with which he chooses between alternatives, nor the alternatives confronting his choice are of his own making or determined by his will. He discovers both, within his own self and in the circumstances in which he finds himself. Similarly, man does not first demonstrate the cogency of reason before embarking upon a logical inference, for, in order to make such a demonstration he would have to employ the very laws of logic, the cogency of which, is now in question. The rational nature of man and the logical order in reality lead to the distinction between truth and error, and the moral nature of man entails the fact of obligation and the distinction between good and evil. If he is free to choose between them, he is also *under necessity* to make such a choice. Freedom to choose freely is mere tautology.

This is important because of a prevalent sophistry which seeks to deny obligation on the ground that man must first choose freely what his obligation is to be, in order to be morally responsible. In its most infantile form, it expresses itself in the wearisome plaint of adolescent rebelliousness, "did I ask to be born" or more specifically, was I consulted concerning my parents or my people or even my inclusion in that species, half beast half god, that is never at peace with itself because it is forever burdened by reason and haunted by conscience —man.

There is, therefore, a certain bitter-sweet realism, despite its rather naive eschatology, in a statement of faith such as the following: "Let not thy evil imagination persuade thee that Sheol is thy final refuge, for without thy consent wast thou formed, without thy consent wast thou born, without thy consent art thou now living and without thy consent wilt thou die and without thy consent wilt thou in the future give account before the supreme King of Kings, the Holy One, Blessed be He." [2]

People sometimes persuade themselves that they are not immoral but that they have a code of their own creation. In their intellectual confusion they sometimes advance this as an excuse for some imputed sin. As a matter of fact, there is no such thing as an individual code of ethics. Obligation always springs from status, real or imagined. We speak of 'honor among thieves' in circles where the greatest sin imaginable would be the betrayal of one member by another. This simply means that the society which outlaws them confers upon them a special social status. They form a robber band or an outlaw 'society.'

Fiction, especially when dealing with the Old West, is prone to romanticize the honest gambler and his code. He, too, views himself as having a special status. He has no hesitation about taking in the unwary and unskilled though he knows the chances of their winning are almost nil, but he will not mark or manipulate the cards. His status is that of a gambler and not that of a thief. When biographers seek to condone the moral vagaries of genius, when they try to excuse some Glorious Apollo for his cruelty to the women who loved him, or some well known artist for his drunkenness, they will usually tell you that one must not judge genius by the common code. What they really mean is that people of genius must be viewed as having an exceptional status in the society to which they belong and their deeds must be judged by their status as geniuses. That emotional intensity which enters into their art may also entail a certain emotional instability. A glamorous young screen star who was accused by her husband of desertion because she had remained absent for three years to achieve artistic triumphs on many continents, justified herself by declaring she owed this to her public. In all these cases it is presupposed that exceptional conduct may perhaps be excused

7

where you admit exceptional status, but not otherwise. "There seem to be always moral protestants" remarks the late Morris Raphael Cohen, "who think that by merely breaking the traditional moral rules they will attain freedom and happiness. Alas for the irony of fate! In order to stand strong in each other's esteem and to make up for the disapproval of the multitude, these moral non-conformists must develop a code of their own. The Bohemians of the Quartier Latin or Greenwich Village have their own taboos no less rigid than those of the Philistines." [3]

So long as Nietzsche wrote romantic poetry glorifying 'superman' and condemning the 'slave morality' which he scorned, little harm was done, but when thousands of young people began to regard themselves as members of a Herrenvolk and therefore in duty bound to obey the voice of the Volksfuhrer, the horror of Hitlerism was in process of incubation. They sought to justify their deeds on the ground that the German people and the German leader had special status. They were, together, the destined rulers of the world and nothing must be permitted to stand in their way.

Why I have gone to great length to cite these examples is only to point out that no man can claim a moral code of his own if he simply does as he pleases. He then has no code at all. If he claims to live by such a code it is only because he also claims to have a special status which is as yet unrecognized by the world at large. Insofar as status and obligation have a necessary and inevitable connection, we may say that morality has its roots in nature and natural necessity as has every phase of human life.

The Growing Burden and Complexity of Human Obligation

Paradoxical as it may sound, it is nevertheless true that there is nothing static about status. Man's status both expands and develops in human society. A man is born with the status of a child but when he marries, though his status as child has not altogether been abandoned, he assumes the status of husband and finally may have the status of son, husband, and father. In the expanding horizon of civilized society, the tribesman often becomes a member of the nation, a citizen of the state, and feels himself finally a human being bound to all mankind. He goes even a step further if he harbors the religious conviction that he is also a creature or a child of God, made in his image. He imputes to himself a spiritual status which binds him in obligation to God even above all his fellow men. All his obligations to his fellow men are also obligations to God and all his sins against his fellow men are sins against God. Yet, the true rebel like the true prophet often challenges in the name of a higher obligation the very structure of society in which obligations arise. In the course of history, he has questioned the status of slave and master, of king and subject, and all the obligations flowing therefrom. The true rebel like the true saint is never at ease in the society in which he lives. They are always numbered among the unadjusted. God save us if some psychologists have their way with them for then civilization would be robbed of its richest promise.

Rebellion As Instinctive

It is gratifying to observe that there are today certain psychotherapists who are quite ready to surrender the concept of adjustment, or peace of mind, as their principal goal of achievement. One of them has stated the case very emphatically, when he makes room for rebellion among the instincts characteristic of human life:

"Among these instincts is the natural urge to rebellion, the restless and powerful disposition to master, the unconquerable impulse to revolt and change which is basic to the nature of the human animal. Among animals inferior to man, this instinct is either not present or of a rudimentary character. This is revealed by the fact that animals other than men change their own natures according to the demands of the environment and generally fit themselves to live only under a single set of conditions. Such 'autoplastic' adaptation results in specialization, which is an evolutionary cul-de-sac and certain doom to a species. But with man, the presence in him of the instinct to rebellion gives him the ability to change his world, to manipulate and control and master his environment, and to avoid that extinction testified by the bleached skeletons of species that aimed only to conform to what was thrust upon them by a capricious Nature. It is this instinct which compensates so radically and so successfully for man's biological weakness, for the fact of his helplessness at birth. Out of it, product of its subtle processes, have come the triumphs he has won and continues to win over his environment, the separate identity he has acquired from all other forms of life and individually from the members of his own species, the functions of remembering, anticipating, symbolizing, imagining, and reasoning." [4]

The only weakness in this presentation lies in the last sentence. If memory, imagination, symbolization and reason (which includes judgment and decision between alternatives) are all equally instinctive with man, they cannot properly be lumped under the instinct of rebellion. They are employed by man, in the course of history, to justify both loyalty and rebellion. They are simply phases of the movement of the animal man, in the direction of his humanization. Man adapted himself to his environment both by adjusting himself to the latter and by transforming the environment to his own ends. Primitive man both found shelter in a cave and learned to build a fire. Rebellion against any established order—physical, social or spiritual is always undertaken by self-conscious rational man in the name of some higher order, which he has already imagined or anticipated, and which his judgment has approved. It is in loyalty to the ideal that he attacks the actual—not otherwise. Now, the ideal which can never be completely actualized, in any one context of experience, is God. With Him is the eternal alternative to any actuality, and therefore, loyalty to the divine order as imagined or anticipated, in contrast to the actual order in which man lives, and to which he is sometimes compelled to submit, is the source of all rebellion. The epistemological idealist, always in danger of solipsism, is here likely to interpose an objection. When we serve an ideal, we are really loyal to an idea of ours, and since the idea exists in our minds there is no need to invoke the transcendent. The realist can only answer with another question—what is the idea of a new order the idea of? Surely not of an actual society or state. If the idea is not only a subjective state of consciousness, if it reflects or expresses an objective fact, the object to which it refers must be sought in some realm of possibility. For this, there is no other word than God, who is the reservoir of all possibility and through whose creativity there is established a relevance of the possible for the actual.

What is not now in existence can have present reality, if any, only in God. Through God it becomes a possibility or goal for existence. Mr. Wieman has expressed a very similar position in the following words:

> "Now the best possible, like any other possibility, can be a possibility only because of something going on in existence which makes it a possibility. This something going on, especially in respect to what exceeds the conscious control and projects of man, is God." [5]

And later, in the same discussion, he touches on a question of which we shall have more to say in some future chapter, but which, likewise approaches the idea of God that is here advanced.

> "Now the only intelligent way of finding the trail which leads the farthest and highest, is to hold all our projects, desires and ideals subject to correction and improvement in the light of all we may discover concerning the Highest. But this we cannot do unless we are always seeking the Highest, always

devoted to it, always ready to discard our present specific objectives whenever we discover some further objective which is better. We cannot thus readily relinquish our hold on our present cherished objectives, no matter how mean they are (we will not think them mean), unless we have this higher loyalty for the transcendent God, on beyond our present specified goals. This highest goal, which is God and God's way, must be left undefined in those areas which exceed the scope of our present understanding, and such areas are very extensive indeed. But we must have this highest devotion to God if we are to be responsive to new insights, and capable of changing the error of our ways, when these new insights reveal the error." [6]

The true prophet always speaks in the name of God whether he mentions the name or not and whatever may be the psychological nature of his compulsion. The finest example of this challenge to mankind for the sake of mankind but in the name of God is found in the words of Jeremiah:

"Behold, I have put my words in thy mouth;
See, I have this day set thee over the nations
and over the kingdoms,
To root out and pull down,
And to destroy and to overthrow;
To build, and to plant." (Jer. 1:9-10)

and again, more specifically:

"For, behold, I have made thee this day a fortified city, and an iron pillar, and brazen walls, against the whole land, against the kings of Judah, against the princes thereof, against the priests thereof, and against the people of the land. And they shall fight against thee; but they shall not prevail against thee. For I am with thee, saith the Lord, to deliver thee." (Jer. 1:18-19)

Dr. Lindner is then quite right, even in the theological terminology which he employs, when he insists:

> "My point here is that the resources of human salvation can be found more abundantly among that very group whom we have been instructed latterly by every possible means to despise and dismiss as lost than among the thronging shadows of the so-called 'adjusted.'" [7]

The Assumption That Religion is Always the Opiate and Soporific

It is a pity, therefore, that Dr. Lindner should himself be so irrevocably 'adjusted,' or one might even say subjugated, to the Marxian-Freudian cliché, that religion in general, and especially the Judaeo-Christian version of it in the Western world, is an opiate and soporific concocted to quiet or dispel the rebellious instinct. Viewed from this standpoint, history itself suffers distortion. Thus he tells us,

> "It was Paul, more than any other single individual, who perverted the creed of rebellion for which his Master died and perpetrated upon our culture the initial development of the idea that salvation and happiness can be found in acceptance, in abject and humiliating submission. Until recently—until, that is, adjustment was taken up by Science and spread abroad with its trademark and approval—the Christianity imposed on the West by the man of Tarsus has been the major force in what amounts to the sellout of mankind. The brew he distilled and spoon-fed to the world through his church, the soporific that left its chief arteries at the time of the Reformation and flowed through the veins and capillaries of that church's numerous offshoots, was the most potent of the many opiates administered humankind in the course of the past two thousand years. Its effect has been to soften the muscles of resistance to exploita-

13

tion and make pulp of the bones of determination. Blending Hebraic tribalism with an Eastern mysticism and an Oriental passivity that had, even by his time, already decayed and left debilitated more than half of the then-known world. Paul ignored the last great Prophet's clear call to revolt. Bridled by this inspired and ecstatic man, the Avenger became a lamb and in the name of this meekest of animals—a fitting totem, by the way—humanity has been slaughtered whenever it has dared to raise its head." [8]

The Lesson From History

I find it difficult to justify Paul. His teaching, from the Jewish point of view, was undoubtedly a deviation from the doctrine of Jewish messianism and his relaxation of certain aspects of the discipline of the law, in favor of gentile converts seemed to the Jews, an unwarranted concession to the urgencies of propaganda whereas his doctrine of salvation was other-worldly in a sense not quite in harmony with authentic Judaism. Nevertheless, against the background of Imperial Rome, Paul and the Christian propaganda which he initiated was a revolutionary movement subversive of pagan society and among the factors which led to the fall of the Empire. Pauline Christianity certainly was not a mere "blend of Hebraic tribalism with an Oriental passivity."

The effect of the impact of Christianity upon Roman government and society is especially corroborated, not by the theological historians of the church, nor even by the rather mystical and religious philosophers of history such as Toynbee, but by such men as John Stuart Mill and W. E. H. Lecky, who had no particular sympathy for revealed religion and gave only grudging credit to the high claims of the church.

In apology for Marcus Aurelius, one of the truly noble minds of antiquity, who, nevertheless, despite his high ethical sentiments, did not attempt to abolish the gladiatorial games but asked only that the gladiators blunt the points of their swords somewhat, and who ended his brilliant reign with a persecution of the Christians, John Stuart Mill has this to say:

"Existing society he knew to be in a deplorable state. But such as it was, he saw, or thought he saw, that it was held together and prevented from being worse by belief and reverence of the received divinities. As a ruler of mankind, he deemed it his duty not to suffer society to fall in pieces, and saw not how, if its existing ties were removed, any others could be formed which would knit it together. *The new religion aimed openly at dissolving these ties;* unless, therefore, it was his duty to adopt that religion, it seemed to be his duty to put it down. Inasmuch, then, as the theology of Christianity did not appear to him true, or of divine origin; inasmuch as this strange history of a crucified God was not credible to him, and a system which purported to rest entirely upon a foundation to him so wholly unbelievable, could not be foreseen by him to *be that renovating agency which, after all abatements, it has in fact proved to be;* the gentlest and most amiable of philosophers and rulers, under a solemn sense of duty, authorized the persecution of Christianity."[9]

That the new religion aimed to dissolve the ties that made Roman society possible—with its deification of the emperor, the degradation of the immense slave population, the abasement of the people through the bloody spectacle of the gladiatorial games—seemed quite evident to this noble stoic. It is certainly proof that he did not regard the rise of Christianity as anything but a threat and a menace to the pagan world. (It is not without historical significance that Titus, who destroyed the Temple at Jerusalem, dedicated the Coliseum at Rome in which many a victim of his conquests suffered death. One misreads history completely, if one cannot see that the triumph of Christianity is symbolized, not by the glories of the Vatican, but in the ruins of the Coliseum.)

What Christianity brought to the Roman world, under the symbol of the crucified messiah of the Jews and his redeeming passion, was not Hebraic tribalism, but Jewish universalism, through which national boundaries would be transcended by a common faith. It made no difference whether the messiah had come or had not come (on which, of course, Paul and the Jews differed). It regarded the crucified redeemer and his imminent second advent, as the fulfillment of all the universalistic prophecies concerning the messianic age, found in the biblical books. It brought, in his name, to all communicants the Ten Commandments and the Sermon on the Mount (almost every sentence of which finds varied expression in parallel rabbinic texts).[10]

Christianity did borrow from Judaism, in its revolutionary fervor, something unique and damaging to the whole structure upon which the Roman Empire was founded. Lecky shows how the great moralists of the Empire, with their critical freedom of thought concerning the ancient gods and their standards of behavior, nevertheless, felt themselves obliged, out of loyalty to the state, to show formal submission to them. Whence this remarkable statement:

"No one did more to scatter the ancient superstitions than Cicero, who was himself an augur, and who strongly asserted the duty of complying with the national rites. Seneca, having recounted in the most derisive terms the absurdities of the popular worship, concludes his enumeration by declaring that 'the sage will observe all these things, not as pleasing the Divinities, but as commanded by the law,' and that he should remember 'that his worship is due to custom, not to belief.' Epictetus, whose austere creed rises to the purest monotheism, teaches as a fundamental religious maxim that every man in his devotions should 'conform to the customs of his country.' The Jews and Christians, who alone refused to do so, were the representatives of *a moral principle that was unknown to the Pagan world.*"[11]

The bestowing of divine honors upon the emperor, though it was largely a formal recognition of the loyalty due to the state, Lecky observes, was refused by Christians as it had been by the Jews. Because of this attitude, which the noblest of pagans, it seems, could not understand, Marcus Aurelius dismisses the whole spirit of Christian martyrdom—incurred at times by their denial of imperial divinity, by their refusal even to enter the arena except as victims, by their denunciation of the pagan gods—as mere stubbornness:

> "'What mind,' said Marcus Aurelius, 'is prepared, if need be, to go forth from the body, whether it be to be extinguished, or to be dispersed, or to endure? —prepared by deliberate reflection, and not by pure obstinacy, as is the custom of the Christians.'"[12]

Lecky, despite his admiration of the noblest of the pagan moralists—with their true belief in humanity and tolerance—is well aware that this was all made a prop and support of the *status quo*.

> "The Romans were prepared to tolerate almost any form of religion that would tolerate others. The Jews, though quite as obstinate as the Christians in refusing to sacrifice to the emperor, were rarely molested, except in the periods immediately following their insurrections, because Judaism, however exclusive and unsocial, was still an unaggressive national faith."[13]

He is evidently not aware, despite his admission that there were many individual converts to Judaism that in all probability the missionary ardor of the Pharisees which even Jesus rebukes[14] was taken over by Paul and his followers in establishing the gentile church. There was nothing passive about the process.

> "Proselytising with an untiring energy, pouring a fierce stream of invective and ridicule upon the gods on whose favour the multitude believed all na-

17

tional prosperity to depend, not unfrequently insulting the worshipers, and defacing the idols, they soon stung the Pagan devotees to madness, and convinced them that every calamity that fell upon the empire was the righteous vengeance of the gods."[15]

It is true that Paul himself preached submission to established authority but only insofar as it did not involve worship of pagan gods and the denial of the supreme messianic king whose kingdom, it is true, was now in heaven but was soon to be revealed. To Paul, emperor and empire, government and social structure, were only an interim arrangement which the faithful could afford, for the present, to ignore. "God chose what is weak in the world to shame the strong, God chose what is low and despised in the world, even things that are not, to bring to nothing things that are" (I Cor. 1:27-28) or again "For the form of this world is passing away" (I Cor. 7:31) and finally "Then comes the end when he delivers the kingdom to God the Father after destroying every rule and every authority and power" (I Cor. 15:24).

This attitude in the minds of increasing multitudes of men, citizens and soldiers, slaves and masters, was not calculated to evoke reverence or awe for the reigning emperor or pride in the majesty and glory that was Rome. That transvaluation of values which emphasized above stoic pride and courage, meekness, love and faith, certainly did not tend to strengthen the sinews of empire. The faithful obeyed it but mocked it as already bearing the imprint of doom upon its brow.

Jesus himself was not, so far as I know, a rebel—though he engaged, if the gospel account be true, in many a rancorous controversy with contemporary priests and Pharisees. Otherwise, he was a conforming Jew, and by no means untouched by what has often sneeringly been called Jewish particularism. It was he who was reluctant to "cast pearls before swine," (Mat. 7:6-7) and who desired that his message be directed only to "the lost sheep of the house of Israel" (Mat. 10:5-6) and who gave it as his opinion that "It is not fair to take the children's bread and throw it to the dogs" (Mat. 15:26). It is simply not true that 'the avenger became a lamb' at the hands of St. Paul and through the propaganda of the church. The reverse is the fact. The *lamb*—the crucified messiah who atoned for sin—in time, became the avenger, and the brood of the *she-wolf* was no match for him and the influences of which, according to St. Paul, he was the source and the symbol.

Let not the poets deceive us by their metaphors. In Pauline theology the crucified messiah was the lamb of God. According to Isaiah, Israel is called "thou worm, Jacob," and yet, while calling him "worm" the prophet adds,

"Behold, I make thee a new threshing sledge
Having sharp teeth;
Thou shalt thresh the mountains, and beat them small,
And shalt make the hills as chaff.
Thou shalt fan them, and the wind shall carry them away,
And the whirlwind shall scatter them." (Is. 41:15-16)

Can a worm thresh a mountain small? Why not? The worm of God can gnaw patiently at the roots of monstrous evils until they collapse. Even the kingdom of God may, for long eras, be driven underground.

What it seems that Dr. Lindner has forgotten, is the difference between the explosive power of new ideas and the inertia of institutions. We need not overlook the crimes of the Christian emperors or the sins of the church against dissenters, once its authority was established. There is no need to condone either the horrors of the inquisition or the narrowness of the Synagogue that excommunicated Spinoza. Religious ideas, however, are never tame and their dynamic force has never been better described than by the prophet whom I have quoted as an example of the 'unadjusted.'

"Is not My word like as fire?
Saith the Lord;
And like a hammer that breaketh the rock in pieces?" (Jer. 23:29)

The impact of Christianity upon the pagan world was just such a shattering force. Even in its many transmutations, the Judaeo-Christian tradition never altogether lost its destructive and regenerative power. Luther was not exactly a lamb, and surely Cromwell and his psalm-singing regicides had no resemblance to the gentle lamblike domesticity at which Dr. Lindner sneers.

Institutions of all kinds, religious, artistic, educational, scientific and social, oppose change by their inertia. They tend to weed out heresies in order to attain conformity. I do not know of any unconventional artist who has ever spoken of art museums as anything but 'the tombs of art.' There are some who suspect the American Medical Association, a scientific institution, with its constant cry against socialization, of being one of the reactionary forces in this country, upholding the *status quo* at all costs to guard its vested interests. The Declaration of Independence was a revolutionary document proclaiming human liberty—the Constitution of the United States was a blue print for an actual government. The United States Constitution never was, and is not now, a perfect instrument of liberty. It permitted Negro slavery for almost three quarters of a century. And yet, considering the provision it contains for amendment, would anyone with an understanding of history have preferred that the Declaration of Independence should never have entered into institutional life through government? Whatever may be its shortcomings, the area of freedom has been enlarged, not diminished, by the existence of the United States of America.

Two things should be clear to the critical mind of today, and Dr. Lindner is not unaware of these; that the atheist-materialist philosophers, whose propaganda is so rampant in the world, have supplied opiates aplenty to the people to whom they appealed. The revolution to end all revolutions, the classless society to be established under the dictatorship of the proletariat, has lured innumerable individuals to barter freedom for the beatific vision of an earthbound paradise and in no area did heresy hunting so flourish as among those who made dialectic materialism their revelation. One has only to turn the pages of Jackson's *Dialectics*[16] to be aware with what bitterness he denounces and pours ridicule upon the British socialists and all so-called Marxists who differ from Lenin's interpretation. That the prophet may, himself, have been mistaken is never seriously considered. Much blood has already been spilled by the established church of atheism throughout the world in its struggle for survival and dominance. It should be noted that National Socialism in Germany was bound to extirpate the Jewish and the Christian tradition, insofar at least as its gentleness contrasted with the Teutonic gods of war and thunder. In this, it was abetted by numerous scientists in German universities and even a representative of the latest of the sciences, Jung, added his enthusiastic amen.[17] The only opposition came from either the competing atheistic church—communism—or from an occasional Christian churchman, here and there. All this, however, is not an argument against the virtues of a socialized economy as such, established in a milieu of democratic opinion.

If one were to point to the greatest single revolutionary force of our generation, I think it would have to be Mahatma Gandhi. His "oriental passivity," his non-violent resistance to British aggression—very much akin to the opposition led by Jewish scholars during the Hadrianic persecutions—was a tremendous force. There was more rebellious momentum in his fasting, than in all the bombs and tanks of colonial military establishments. He succeeded in liberating India, and what is more, in transforming, with the help of British political wisdom, the British empire into the Commonwealth of Nations. All this teaches us that we cannot undervalue the lamb or the worm as factors in the transformation of human society.

Obligations in Conflict

We return now to the main stream of our discussion. We have found man enmeshed in an infinite skein of obligations including all his fellow men and God Himself. Some of these obligations are superimposed upon one another on different levels of society, like one's duty as a son and as a citizen. They reach through the family, the tribe, the nation, the state, the human family to God Himself. They may be in conflict with one another. Such difficulties can only be partially resolved if we regard these obligations or loyalties as forming a hierarchy, of which loyalty to God constitutes the ultimate obligation.

But there are also conflicts on the same level. Man is not merely one thing—father, son, citizen, or the like. He assumes status and obligation as member of a profession, of a labor union, of a church, and these may conflict with one another or with his family obligations. Examples such as these can be multiplied indefinitely. If man had to keep a ledger of his innumerable obligations to all his fellow men under every perspective of status, he would never find time to act either morally or immorally.

Transference of Obligation to Moral Principles and Generalizations

Our presentation of the subject thus far, though essentially true, is somewhat artificial. Man carries no such ledger of his debits and credits about with him and it would be impossible for a civilized man even to compute the sum of his obligations on any one day of his life. But he need not, for here reason becomes an ally of conscience and there occurs very early, even in the pre-historic ages of human development, that which modern psychologists call 'transference.' We use the term loosely in the sense of transference of the feeling of obligation to those significant generalizations which we call moral principles or precepts.

Most of us fail to appreciate the triumphs of reason on the humbler plane, not only before the days of Archimedes or Euclid but even before the period of written history. They were not so much speculative triumphs as they were triumphs of observation and generalization. The history of these achievements will never be known. They are hidden from us in folklore and legend. They are among the myths concerning the origins of the arts and industries in which the poets have always revelled. They are sometimes the free gifts of the gods or snatched from the gods by the heroes that defied them, as is the case with Prometheus. The kindling of fire, the discovery of the wheel, the origin of script, will never claim its pioneers and inventors, whether in the form of an individual genius or an efflorescence of the folk mind. We are astounded by the miracle performed by our baby when he utters a common noun but it is hard to imagine what feelings first flooded the mind of man when he discovered that this tree designated by the pointed finger or the demonstrative ejaculation was also *a* tree; one of a type which he could describe. Plato only rediscovered what man had known for millennia—that there were not only things but kinds of things.

Thornton Wilder in his great play "The Skin of Our Teeth" with its mixture of stark realism and high fantasy in which man is always the clown and always the hero, always frustrated and always achieving, conveys in the modern spirit some appreciation of those remarkable attainments of man before even the first calamity of which we have knowledge overtook him. You remember, the wheel and the fire are already in the room when the story opens. We shall forever remain ignorant when, or what, man first learned that things are more easily rolled than dragged, or so simple a thing that water always runs downhill instead of up and that the higher ground may at times save him from disaster. He may not have constantly worked at the achievement of these ideas, they may have dawned upon him suddenly but they were the consequences of observation and the power of generalization. Think for a moment of the wonder of man when he learned to find his way on the wide plain or the open sea, not by scanning landmarks that lay beneath his feet or on the visible shore, but by directing his eyes away from earth and raising his gaze to the heavens, to some fixed point of light like the North Star. He learned that whenever he made progress in its direction or deviated from that direction to the extent of some definite angle, he would, as the case might be, reach his desired haven. He discovered that there were usually so many moons from seed time to harvest, from heat to cold, and he established and regulated his economic life—the hunt or agriculture or the breeding of cattle—in accordance with such observations and the generalizations he had arrived at through them. No society, so far as I know, long endured before it possessed some kind of calendar, written or oral, and often of rather remarkable complexity.

Similarly, in discharging his obligations, man observed ever recurring patterns of feeling and volition. He called them 'mercy' or 'justice' not necessarily with any high implication. He felt sorry for his hurt child, he helped the wounded warrior at his side. Justice may have consisted largely in the fair division of the spoils of war, but certainly in the earliest literature of mankind, we find a certain acceptance, first of all of such precepts as make up the Ten Commandments, secondly of such virtues as kindness, justice, truth, and finally the Golden Rule. That Hillel, Jesus, and Confucius who lived five hundred years earlier, should all have included it among their ethical maxim shows how old such generalizations may have been. They were the recurrent patterns of action and emotion which man discovered in the regular discharge of his obligations towards all his fellow men. They were, to be more precise, types of response leading to the fulfillment of obligation. There are evident, of course, between various ethnic groups and on various planes of moral advance, differences of emphasis, differences in the area of their application. To savage man the duty not to kill applied largely to his tribe alone. It was only later that man recognized his duty to all his fellowmen.

What is significant is, that in the history of morals, and we are not now primarily interested in tracing the steps of this history, there was a transference of the sense of obligation to principles such as these. No great literature is barren of them, and it is this fact which delivered man from the confusion of his innumerable obligations and their conflicting claims.

We do not as a rule in our moral judgments, say that

this man, to be good, must discharge his obligations to a, b, c, because of his status as a, b¹, c¹; we simply say, the good man ought love mercy, be honest, not steal, not kill, not covet what is not his, not do to his fellow man what he would not have his fellow man do unto him. Duty is now envisaged not as a mere series of acts towards individual persons in a particular situation, but as the realization of principles such as these in all the relations of life enabling him, if they are kept in mind to discharge his various and manifold obligations more completely and spontaneously.

Indeed, as society becomes more complex and the system of obligations more tortuous, the attempt to find the widest possible generalization, not only for a certain group of specific obligations, but the widest generalization that will express the essence of the whole system as such, becomes increasingly urgent.

Examples from Rabbinic Literature

In the rabbinic tradition of post-biblical Judaism, this is particularly manifest in the centuries immediately preceding and following the Christian era. The Torah, which the scribes and Pharisees expounded, supplemented and enlarged through innumerable discussions and decisions in the field of morals, or criminal and civil law, not to speak of ritual and liturgy, involved so complicated a system of obligations, or *mitzvot,* that one might suspect that this prolific legalism would be in danger of obscuring the pre-eminence of the moral principles it held in solution. This turned out not to be the case. It seems to have kept alive the urge to search for such principles, and hence the rabbinic literature gave expression to some of the boldest generalizations to be found anywhere in the literature of law and morals.

I—The Shema and the Commandments.

It was, of course, the scribes and Pharisees, though the latter seldom speak of themselves as Pharisees, who laid the foundations of the synagogue as an institution and the ritual by which it is governed. The function of the synagogue was largely to bring the religious classics of Israel to all the people. The prayers encircled the readings from the Torah and the Prophets. There were special selections on Sabbath and festivals—either read in sequence or chosen for their relevance to the special occasion. But in the early years of the synagogue, it seems that there were two lessons which were scheduled for reading on every day. One was the 'Shema,' with its declaration of the unity of God and its command to love God with all one's heart and soul and might and to teach these things to future generations (Deut. 6:4). The second was the Ten Commandments (Ex. 20). They are called commandments only in the Christian tradition. In the Jewish tradition they remain the 'ten words.' The first of these according to the Jewish counting is not a commandment at all. It is the assertion that the Giver of the Law is also the Redeemer and Liberator. Thus, the doctrine of the unity of God and the Ten Commandments were given a prominence accorded to no other portion of Torah and this emphasized their centrality to the whole scheme of Jewish teaching in a manner which not even the most eloquent homily could equal.[18] Later on, because certain sectaries were under the impression that the 'ten words' could be substituted for the whole revelation, their reading was discontinued, and only the Shema kept its honored position as the daily lesson.

II—*The Golden Rule in its Positive and Negative Aspects.*

Hillel was an earlier contemporary of Jesus, and stood at the threshold of the period dominated by the Tannaim. There is the familiar tale of the heathen, seeking conversion, who in his zeal and his ardor asked that he be taught Torah while he stood upon one foot. Rejected by Hillel's contemporary, Shammai, he at last seeks out the great sage who has become known for his gentleness, his humility and his patience. Hillel does not hesitate to accept the challenge.

"Whatever is hateful to thyself, do thou not to thy fellow man. This is the essence of the whole Torah. The rest is interpretation. Now, go thou, and learn." [19]

We have already observed that this negative form of the Golden Rule is likewise found among the sayings of Confucius. Hillel, however, gives us also a positive statement of what he meant by his instruction to the intended proselyte. He says to his fellow Jews,

"Be thou a disciple of Aaron;
Loving peace and pursuing peace,
Loving all mankind,
Drawing them to Torah."[20]

Here we have a statement with profound humanitarian implications. It is not merely an ethical maxim. It is, in a sense, a missionary platform. The *love of mankind* which to Hillel was the essence of Torah, should be made the means by which mankind would be won to its acceptance.

It is almost certain that Hillel's attitude is more than an evidence of pedagogic skill and patience. From the fact that there is a whole series of such legends which show Shammai's indifference and Hillel's eagerness to welcome the proselyte, from the previously mentioned statement in the New Testament in which Jesus chides the Pharisees for seeking converts throughout the world, it is evident that high hopes for the conversion of the world were stirring in certain rabbinic circles at this time, and that the voice of Hillel gave them most eloquent expression.

III—Thou shalt love thy neighbor as thyself (Lev. 19:18).

"This," says Akiba, "is the principle of widest generality in the Torah." Ben Azzai says, "There is a greater than this, to wit:
'This is the book of the generations of man.

On the day when God created man, in the likeness of God made He him.' (Gen. 5:1)"[21]

This corrective of Akiba's statement answers the questions raised in the Gospel as to 'who is thy neighbor.' The statement that the biblical story is concerned not only with Israel, but with all the 'generations of man,' and that the image of God is possessed by every human individual, explains both the spirit and the rationale of the statement to which Akiba alludes.

These generalizations are not only significant as showing how rabbinic thought evaluated the spirit of Torah, but mark a milestone in the history of human morals, Professor Wolfson, after showing that Philo not only makes help to the needy 'a virtue,' as do also the Stoics; and that he uses the term 'philanthropia,' which means, of course, love of mankind, as the underlying motive for such charity, adds:

> "But the term 'philanthropia,' for which we have been using the English, 'humanity,' judging from a passage in which it is discussed, does not seem to rank in Greek philosophy among the virtues, though in later Latin philosophy the term 'humanitas' does occur as a virtue under the virtue of justice."[22]

If this be true, then the *love of mankind*, as such, takes its place among the virtues, even in Greek literature, through a Jew who was also practically a contemporary of both Hillel and Jesus. It would thus appear that the great Jewish Pharisee, the Jewish founder of Christianity and the Jewish Hellenist were in agreement in regarding this humanistic generalization as the basic principle underlying their systems of social morality.

IV—The Individual.

We have seen how Ben Azzai stresses the worth and spiritual value of man, created in God's image, as indicating the spirit of the moral law. The definition of the human individual, the intrinsic value of human personality, however, has nowhere been more boldly stated than in the following homily which, according to the Mishna, was addressed to witnesses in cases where human life was at stake:

> "God created man an individual person, not *en masse*,
> That we may realize that he who destroys one human life has, as it were, destroyed a whole world. And he who saves one human life is as though he had saved a whole world.
>
> Also, that no man may say to his fellow man, 'My ancestry is nobler than thine.' Furthermore, to demonstrate the greatness of The Holy One, Blessed Be He, for though any king of flesh and blood may stamp many coins from the same die, yet they are sure to be exactly alike, but the Supreme King, The Holy One, Blessed Be He, creates every man with the imprint of Adam, and yet no human being quite resembles another.
>
> Finally, that every human being may have the right to say,
> 'For my sake was the world created.' " [23]

Here is contained not only a declaration of the equality of men, but of the sacredness of the human personality. Every man is indispensable since, despite our common humanity, each is unique of his type. The final statement, combined with a declaration of human equality, is the spiritual basis of all democracy. The individual, however insignificant, must not be regarded as only a means to an end, a cog on the wheel of the world machine. He is a goal in the travail of creation, an end toward which nature strains. Therefore, neither nature nor the state can obliterate his significance.

V—The Six hundred and thirteen commandments.

Rabbi Simlai, a Palestinian Amora who lived in the third century, once preached this sermon:

"Six hundred and thirteen commandments were revealed to Moses. Three hundred and sixty-five of these negative, and corresponding to the number of days in the year; and two hundred and forty-eight of these positive, corresponding to the members of the human body (according to antique anatomy).

Then came David, and declared them based upon eleven, as it is said:
'Lord, who shall sojourn in Thy tabernacle?
Who shall dwell upon Thy holy mountain?
He that walketh uprightly, and worketh righteousness,
And speaketh truth in his heart;
That hath no slander upon his tongue,
Nor doeth evil to his fellow,
Nor taketh up a reproach against his neighbour;

In whose eyes a vile person is despised,
But he honoureth them that fear the Lord;
He that sweareth to his own hurt, and changeth not;
He that putteth not out his money on interest,
Nor taketh a bribe against the innocent.' (Ps. XV)

Then came Isaiah and declared them based upon six, as it is said:
'He that walketh righteously, and speaketh uprightly;
He that despiseth the gain of oppressions,
That shaketh his hands from holding of bribes,
That stoppeth his ears from hearing of bloodshed,
And shutteth his eyes from looking upon evil;'
(Is. 33:15)
Then came Micah and declared them based upon three, as it is said:
'It hath been told thee, O man, what is good,
And what the Lord doth require of thee:
Only to do justly, and to love mercy, and to walk humbly with thy God.' (Micah 6:8)

Then came Habakkuk and declared them all based on one, as it is said:
'But the righteous shall live by his faith,' "[24] (Hab. 2:4)

The word *emunah* can be translated both by faith and faithfulness or integrity, so that the verse might mean, either, the righteous lives by his *faith,* or by his *dutifulness.* The homiletic basis for the enumeration of the commandments is evident. Each day brings its temptations, which man must overcome: and each member of the body is to be enlisted in the service of God. All man's time and all man's strength is involved in the moralization of life.

It should also be clear to anyone acquainted with rabbinic literature, that Simlai did not mean to say that any of the commandments which have been declared foundation stones for the whole structure, should serve as a substitute for the structure itself. What he did mean to say was that such generalized principles as Psalmist and Prophet define are meant to pervade the whole life, since they give character to the whole system of obligation in which they are contained.

VI—Which a man shall do, and by which he shall live (Lev. 18:5)

Rabbi Meir used to say:

"Whence do we know that even a non-Jew who studies the Torah is as a High-Priest?
From the verse,
'Ye shall therefore keep My statutes, and Mine ordinances, which if a man shall do, he shall live by them; I am the Lord.' (Lev. 18:5)
It is not said, 'Which a Priest, a Levite or an Israelite shall do, but which a man shall do. Hence thou mayest learn that even a non-Jew who studies the Torah is equal to the High-Priest.

And thus it is said,
'This is the gate of the Lord:
The righteous shall enter into it.' (Ps. 118:20)

It does not mention Priest, Levite or Israelite but the righteous whoever he may be, shall enter into it.

And it is said

> 'Do good, O Lord, unto the good,
> And to them that are upright in their hearts.'
>
> (Ps. 125:4)

Not, to the Priest, the Levite or the Israelite, but to all the good, whoever they may be. Hence we know that even the non-Jew, who occupies himself with Torah, is the equal of the High-Priest in Israel."[25]

There is a variant to Rabbi Meir in certain texts. The above is in accordance with San. 59a. Besides, we know that R. Meir was intimate with and had social intercourse with the Greek philosopher, most probably the cynic Oenomaus of Gadara. He is rebuked in Julian's *Orations* (VII-209) for having destroyed reverence for the gods. He is lauded by the rabbis in the following words:

> "There arose no philosophers in the world like Balaam Ben Beor or like Oenomaus of Gadara."[26]

The Midrash further related that when the rulers of the world sought his advice as to how to overcome the Jews, he answered,

> "Visit their synagogues and their schools, and if you hear voices of children lisping their lessons, you may be sure that you will never be able to overcome them."

The intimacy between Meir and Oenomaus is attested by the fact that he visited him, once on the occasion of the death of the latter's father, and again when his mother died. On the latter occasion, the philosopher justified the elaborate mourning for the mother by quoting a verse from the book of Ruth:

> "And Naomi said unto her two daughters-in-law: 'Go, return each of you to her mother's house; the

Lord deal kindly with you, as ye have dealt with the dead, and with me.'" (Ruth 1:8) He seems likewise to have been aware of Rabbi Meir's continued contact with his heretical master Elisha. It is very likely, then, that Rabbi Meir should have had his friend in mind when he ranked the non-Jew who studies Torah as equal to the High-Priest.

The authorities are not all as generous as Rabbi Meir. Some believe that a heathen who studies Torah without any intention of committing himself to its precepts, incurs mortal guilt, for he intentionally trespasses upon the "Inheritance of the Congregation of Jacob" (Deut. 33:4). Only if a man studies Torah from a sense of moral obligation, not by eclectic preference, does he acquire merit. They are all agreed, however, that he who studies Torah to learn the duties incumbent upon all men, or in the idiom of the rabbis, the precepts included in the covenant with the sons of Noah, is equal in stature to the High-Priest in Israel.

VII—Goodness and the Holy Spirit.

In the *Seder Eliahu*, a compilation, in its present form of the late rabbinical period but containing much older material recast and rewritten in a style often fervid and deeply moving, we find this striking affirmation, as eloquent as it is sweeping in scope.

> "I call heaven and earth to witness
> That whether it be Jew or Gentile
> Man or Woman
> Bondman or bondwoman
> According to his deeds
> So shall the Holy Spirit rest upon him."[27]

The above is not inferior in its unlimited universalism to any of the statements of Paul. It goes further, however. The Holy Spirit, in Jewish thought, is sometimes equated with the spirit of prophecy. The words undoubtedly echo the sentiment found in Joel:

"And it shall come to pass afterward,
That I will pour out My spirit upon all flesh;
And your sons and your daughters shall prophesy,
Your old men shall dream dreams,
Your young men shall see visions;" (Joel 3:1)

In the Bible, however, the hope is eschatological and the Jew and non-Jew are not specifically contrasted and equated. The Midrash also utilized the term Holy Spirit in a wider sense than Spirit of Prophecy. There is some difference of opinion as to whether the gift of prophecy was not bestowed by election on Israel alone. In this instance, the observation, though following upon praise of Deborah and her good deeds, nevertheless cannot concern the gift of prophecy as such.

If this were the case, then every good man would display prophetic inspiration for the Spirit of Prophecy would rest upon him according to the degree of his goodness. Just the opposite is intended here. The Holy Spirit possesses a man to the extent that his conduct is good. Not what he sees (in prophetic vision) or what he says (in prophetic eloquence) but what he does is witness of the Holy Spirit resting upon him. It is elsewhere also remarked that the Holy Spirit is the fruit of saintliness. The Holy Spirit can here be understood as the Spirit of the Holy or the spirit of God which should animate the moral life of every human being.

Ethical Ideals—What is and What Ought to Be

There is still another step in the development of the moral life under the category of obligation. Not only does man transfer the sense of obligation to certain principles, precepts, and standards of conduct which he recognizes as having moral authority because they are involved in innumerable instances of obligation, but he also frames moral ideals and recognizes obligation towards their fulfillment. Man will persistently ask not only what ought I to *do*, how ought I to *act*, what principles should I *follow* in voluntary response to a particular situation, but what ought I to *be*, and what ought human society *become* which now it is not.

The moral life at its highest and at its best is a striving towards a realization of such personal and social ideals. Its function is to transform the self and the world as now they are and give them the character they ought to have.

If anything in finite existence can be said to reflect the creative restlessness of God, it is this quest of the human spirit. Here it is that the being of God presses against the frontiers of life. Man thus transcends nature since he sits in judgment on the world as he finds it, or if we include man in nature, then in the human spirit nature shows itself self-transcendent and hence divine.

For reasons such as these, Jewish tradition can speak of the just judge as being a 'partner with God in the work of creation.' Here the creative immanence of God in all existence finds illustration in the self-conscious aspirations of man.

We cannot here attempt to describe in full the moral phenomena we have just mentioned because we are interested in theory rather than in complete exposition. Instances, however, of what is meant can be found in such demands as "Holy shall ye be for I the Lord am Holy," (Lev. 19:1) or the statement in Psalm 24 that he who is worthy to ascend the Mountain of the Lord must be "clean of hands and pure of heart." Every cry out of the depths such as 'create in me a new heart' reflects this moral conviction that what now is can be transformed into what ought to be.

In non-Jewish literature of a rather early date, we can cite Aristotle's description of the virtuous man, or certain phases of the "Lord's Song" in the Indian epic Mahabharata. The virtues cited here would appear to most of us, brought up in the biblical tradition, rather passive and unrelated to social change but they all illustrate our main point. The man who aspires to live a moral life is not only troubled with the question of what to do but *what kind of a character to be* in order to satisfy this aspiration.

The conscience is never really satisfied with any state

of goodness. It looks askance at the human heart and at human society, convinced that what *is* is never wholly what ought to be. One cannot but be impressed with the fact that the saint above all never feels that he has done his whole duty by man and God. He always protests his failures. His fear of God is largely the fear that he may fail God, and therefore he is always praying for guidance, strength, and renewal.

In the biblical tradition, the ideal of the prophets is in the main a social ideal and whatever is vivid and virile in the social idealism of Western civilization derives from this fact. *As in the hierarchy of loyalties, obedience to God becomes the ultimate obligation, so the Kingdom of God becomes the highest ideal.* The prophet wishes man not only to fulfill his final duty to God but to transform the society of men into the Kingdom of God upon earth. In such effort of transforming whatever is or may be into what ought to be. whether on the personal or social level, man becomes the instrument of God's own creativity.

---

1. Henri Bergson, *Morality and Religion* (New York: Henry Holt and Company, 1935), pp. 19-21.
2. Abot (IV, 29).
3. Morris Raphael Cohen, *Reason and Nature* (New York: Harcourt Brace and Company, 1931), pp. 346-347.
4. Robert Lindner, *Prescription for Rebellion* (New York: Rinehart and Company, Inc., 1952), pp. 35-36.
5. Henry Nelson Wieman, *Is There a God—A Conversation* (Wieman, Macintosh & Otto), p. 123.
6. *Ibid.*, p. 240.
7. Lindner, *op. cit.*, p. 107.
8. *Ibid.*, p. 18.
9. John Stuart Mill, "Essay on Liberty" *Harvard Classics* (Collier and Son). Italics are the writer's.
10. cf. Strack-Billerbeck, *Kommentar zum Neuen Testament aus Talmud und Midrasch - Das Evangellum Nach Matthaus,* Munchen, 1922.
11. W. E. H. Lecky, *History of European Morals,* (New York: George Braziller, 1955), p. 405. (Italics are the writer's.)
12. *Ibid.*, p. 392.
13. *Ibid.*, p. 422.
14. Matthew 23:15—"You traverse sea and land to make one proselyte."
15. Lecky, *op. cit.*, p. 423.
16. T. A. Jackson, *Dialectics—The Logic of Marxism and Its Critics* (New York: International Publishers, 1936), p. 12 and elsewhere.
17. cf. Lindner, *op. cit.*, note on p. 39.
18. This is substantiated in the Nash Papyrus, cf. William F. Albright, *Journal of Biblical Literature,* Vol. 56, 1937, p. 175.

19. Shab. 31a.
20. Abot. 1.
21. Sifra to Lev. 19:18.
22. Harry Austryn Wolfson, *Philo* (Cambridge, Mass.: Harvard University Press, 1948), Vol. II, pp. 219-220, cf. authorities there referred to.
23. Mishna, San. 4:5.
24. Mak. 23b, 24a; San. 2a. There are some slight variants to the text quoted above but the general impression left is the same.
25. Sifra to Lev. 18:5.
26. Ber. R. 65:16.
27. Friedman, *Seder Eliahu* (Vienna: 1902), p. 48.

CHAPTER TWO

THE GOOD

Good and Evil

We have thus far described the moral life under the category of obligation, or duty, or the 'ought' in contrast to the 'is' and we have seen that both will and reason play their part in the definition of obligation especially as the sense of obligation transfers to moral principles or moral ideals. We may now ask, how do the concepts of good and evil, as such, enter into and direct the moral life. Our answer is they enter through the doorway of desire.

Where shall we look for the source of evil? All living things desire what is good and there are many 'goods' which they desire. Indeed, biologically speaking, the satisfaction of every desire, of every craving of the flesh, of every type of hunger, is on its own level good. The hunter deems it good to trap the quarry. The quarry certainly deems it good to escape if it can. It is good for the bird to lay its egg and for the serpent to suck its substance. To eat, to drink, to mate, are 'goods' which all life pursues because they are necessary to life's continuance. In human society these goods are greatly multiplied. Riches, power, position, fame, are all among the objectives of desire and many there are who call their attainment good. They are usually the source of satisfaction, they are often the wellspring of happiness.

Man, however, finds himself as always in a dilemma. As a human being in the world of natural existence, he cannot as man accept himself unquestioningly. He soon becomes suspicious of his own impulses. He learns from experience that the satisfaction of every desire may be good *but that it is far from good for him to satisfy every desire.*

And so he is of necessity launched upon a quest of which the lower orders of life seeking their momentary and periodic and compulsive goods seem entirely unaware. Among the welter of possible goods which life offers, he seeks what he calls 'the good.' He means by this, more simply expressed, a system of goods compatible with one another and insuring a more pervasive and permanent state of happiness than he could otherwise attain. We are not now speaking of higher and lower desires, or satisfactions, we are speaking only of such desires as will bring the greatest amount of satisfaction and happiness throughout life and will not be in conflict with one another, bringing dissatisfaction and pain and perhaps disease and death.

Out of the idea of 'the good' which man must achieve is born the reality of evil. For what is in conflict with the good, no matter how desirous in itself, must now be rejected and denied as evil. Every animal in the satisfaction of its desire has felt and known some good, but only man knows evil because he has glimpsed 'the good.' He alone has lost the purity of animal instinct, he alone has eaten of the tree of knowledge of good and evil that stands at the center of Paradise. As a result, shame has cast its shadow over the naked symbols of desire.

The Sensuality of Man

Let it never be imagined because man is possessed by what we shall presently call spirituality that therefore his sensual nature is diminished. Indeed, the truth may be that no animal in all the world is possessed of the abundant and exquisite sensuality of man. Endowed with memory and imagination, desires and their satisfaction are not easily discarded. Man's mouth may water even today at the thought of the dinner yesterday enjoyed and evoke desire all over again. The adolescent may in imagination lust for a thousand women though he may not have touched even one. In memory and anticipation, in fancy and imagination, we indulge, even the best of us, in a thousand forbidden joys to which we neither could nor would grant *entrée* into the world of our actual conduct. If it is true that the coward dies a thousand deaths before he actually perishes, so it is true that in imagination man may indulge in a thousand sins before committing himself to the performance of even one actual deed involving a decision between good and evil.

Our wishes, which are only desires craving fulfillment, pose the problem for our wills. We say that one cannot have one's cake and eat it too, but lives there a man who would not desire just that if it were possible. Perhaps the sin of Adam consisted precisely in this, that he believed the serpent when the creature said that one could eat of the tree of desire, of good and evil, and yet live forever. How nice to have both gifts—the sweets of carnal desire and immortality too. The prudent may indeed assert that you cannot burn the candle at both ends—you cannot dissipate all night and labor efficiently all day—and yet how many of us only get to believe this when it is too late. What man is there who would not desire to be a saint and experience the sweet serenity of the holy, if he would not have to relinquish some of the carnal joys for which his flesh yearns. No creature ever lived as desirous as man, compelled to find 'the good' lest he be strangled by the innumerable tentacles of desire which seek to fasten themselves upon him and drain his strength.

Civilized society does not allay desire or still the conflict; it makes it more acute. Added to the desires inherited from our animal ancestry or our savage past, the fires of which are never wholly extinguished beneath the thin crust of civilization, there are now added, as we have already learned, ambitions for wealth, position, and power. The desire for health may necessitate that we abandon the pursuit of wealth. The stress of social ambition may require the denial of love. Unless we submit to the discipline of 'the good' we shall forever be lost in the encroaching and prolific jungles of desire though we dwell in paved and sterile cities of stone and steel.

On The Spiritual Level

The refinements of the spirit do not save man the necessity for decision. The number of desires as they clash with one another remains quite the same though they break out on a higher level of human experience. Such conflicts of desire as only the truly good and deeply religious can know are met with again and again in the literature of religious experience. Is it good for a man to interrupt prayer for study or study for prayer? For one to entertain such a problem, both prayer and study are "goods" which his heart desires and yet he may under certain circumstances have to choose one or another as 'the good' though he will be constantly aware of the lure and temptation of the other which he may continue to desire. The question when is martyrdom good and when is it a sin is an example of this sort of conflict. The question to be decided really is, when is martyrdom a witness to a high faith and when is it merely a sublimated form of the death wish. In the former case it is a conflict between love for life and love for something dearer than life which only a great soul can know. These are all experiences of clashing desires subtle in their nature and taking place in a high and rarefied atmosphere of idealism.

Even the average man, however, who has developed love for what we are wont to call the "finer things in life" is often tormented with the question whether it is right for him to devote the resources at his command to music or the arts or to his library when his family may have need of them for the satisfaction of simpler but more fundamental needs. We could go on indefinitely.

What is important is the recognition that the higher we climb the wider becomes the vista in which moral conflict and the moral decision must play their dramatic role. Though the spiritual nature of man, while it never permits him to sever connection with those inherited cravings which make him a creature of flesh and blood, continuously gives rise to new longings and hence the need to find a proper place for the old and familiar in the new and higher good which his eyes have glimpsed.

The Human Spirit—A Definition of Spirituality

We had previously alluded to man's sensuality but we have also frequently paid tribute to his spirituality and employed the term, the Human Spirit. It is high time, therefore, that we sought a more exact definition of these concepts especially as they apply to the problems of the moral life.

The contrast which most often presents itself to the average mind when discussing the quality of spirituality is that involved in the distinction between the spiritual and the sensual. Physical realities, we are apt to say, are attested to by sense perception and have measurable dimension. Spiritual reality is reflected in reason and such intuitions and emotions as are not directly involved in the functioning of the sense organisms. The spiritual life, loosely speaking, would be one in which the cravings, the joys, the satisfaction of the senses play a less important part than do the passions and ecstasies involved in the higher and more remote ranges of human experiences that flow from the reservoir of man's inner life.

Yet this contrast between the physical and the spiritual will not carry us very far. First because it involves a tautology. We are asking what the spiritual life is, and we answer that it is the life of the spirit in contrast to the senses. Furthermore, this glib definition conveys the impression that spirituality necessarily involves a turning from, or repudiation of, the physical life. This, however, need not be the case. Spirituality is not to be identified with asceticism. It is not so identified in normative Judaism and Christianity. The latter may, under certain circumstances, assume spiritual value when it takes the form of personal or organized protest against the urgencies and necessities of physical lusts and desires which threaten to overwhelm the normal balance of life. A man sometimes feels the need of convincing himself that he is not to be numbered among those who are utterly carried away by their lust and therefore he may choose asceticism as the means of such self-demonstration. Maimonides who accepts the classical ideal of the Golden Mean only finds justification for the extravagances of the ascetic life in the fact that its adherents serve to restore balance to a society otherwise inclined to self-indulgence, so that the individual saint, though we may consider him spiritually unbalanced, nevertheless helps to restore a lost balance and thus enables society as a whole to live by the Golden Mean.

It is of the essence of spirituality, quite apart from asceticism, not to accept with equal relish all the emotional needs and satisfactions of life. We might say, first of all, that it is characteristic of the human spirit to pronounce qualitative judgments upon the whole gamut of life's joys and needs. It ranges them not primarily according to their intensity or their endurance, but according to their place on a scale of values intuitively designated as higher or lower. The goods compatible with one another which constitute 'the good' are discovered to abide on different levels of experience, to have different worth for human personality. Their compatibility must demonstrate itself vertically as well as horizontally. Nor does this designation of higher and lower pleasures or functions or faculties follow the biological scale of being as nature presents it to us. Indeed, it is a sign of man's incurable spirituality, egocentric though it may be, by virtue of which the forms and functions and needs of the life which he calls human are not only distinguished from but placed above those of other types of animal life. Because man's brain is on a vertical line above his stomach does not give the upright animal the right to regard himself as the measuring stick for the forms of life which pursue their being horizontally. Nature on its physical level knows no such preferences. It spawns and slays its creatures with shocking impartiality. A stroke of lightning will slay a mouse or a man with equal indifference. The upright posture with the double curvature of the spine is biologically connected with what we call man's higher life. It enables the front paws to become skillful hands, the mouth and jaw to become implements not only for catching and rending prey, but for the development of speech. It permits the eyes to look forward rather than downward and lures the imagination to paint on the canvas of empty space not only the object of sense perception which his eyes are accustomed to behold but also the strange images of his creative fancy. It makes possible the comparatively huge chamber of the skull poised upon the upright column to contain the developed brain. The judgment, however, that this compli-

43

cated apparatus gives the life it sustains higher value is the judgment of the upright creature alone—the worm goes about its business wholly unembarrassed by the lowly station assigned to it by man.

But the division of types of life into higher and lower is not the cause but the result of the distinction which the human spirit makes in the whole range of its own experiences. Because it rates the animality within itself as something lower than the distinctively human, it dares speak of creatures other than man as lower forms of life. The spiritual life may therefore fully recognize the desires and claims of the flesh insofar as they have value for human life and survival, yet it also discovers in human experience values according to which the very worth of life and survival themselves are ultimately to be judged.

Therefore, even though the physical cannot be sundered from the spiritual, the human spirit cannot accept as final the classical ideal of "a sound mind in a healthy body" or the insistence of an enlightened philistinism that the physical and the spiritual must be equally cultivated in the interest of harmonious personality. I fear such a happy delineation of spheres of influence will not quite satisfy our spiritual nature whatever value it may have for youthful discipline and education. In the earlier ages of Greek paganism, the athletic games, such as the Olympics, were festivals to the gods. The naked young men displayed their skills to delight the deities. How striking in contrast is the biblical sentiment "He is not pleased with the strength of the horse, He taketh no delight in the thighs of a man. God is pleased with those who fear him, with those who hope in His love." (Ps. 147:10) On the higher levels of biblical thought only man's knowledge of love and justice and mercy are spoken of as the things in which God delights. Maurice Samuels, however extravagant his language, is quite right; the 'Jew' and the 'Gentleman' are not always in agreement. Judaism did not scorn the health and beauty of the body, but sport, from the Jewish standpoint, could only be encouraged as healthful play, not as a major form of divine service. All cruel sports were forbidden. Hunting for pleasure, bear baiting or bull fighting, or any of the vicarious delights which men find in watching animals or their fellow men tear one another to pieces, would of course be condemned by Judaism.

The spirit would maintain that, though the physical and the spiritual elements may be equally necessary to human life, they do not constitute lateral halves. The perfect functioning of the human organism may demand feet as well as brain. The physical elements essential though they may be—feet planted upon earth—are nevertheless the lower side of life necessary to bring to birth and sustain the higher, but not of equal value with it. The human spirit envisages a world of experience divided transversely—the lower levels necessary for the development of the higher ranges of experiences but the higher ranges giving value to the lower levels as rungs on the ladder of reality by means of which man may reach the heights. When, therefore, we customarily speak of the passion for truth, the love of God, the will to self-sacrifice, as among the signs of spirituality, whereas the craving for life, the desires of sex, the delights of table, are numbered among the physical aspects of life, we are not merely making a classification, we are engaging in an evaluation. The spiritual life is always thus engaged seeking not merely the good rather than the evil, but the better rather than the good, and some supreme good above all.

Egoism and Altruism.

Before proceeding with our main discussion, it is well to call attention to the fact that some moralists propose a simpler distinction between good and evil than the one we have proposed. In our theory, evil is a kind of degraded good. A good that has fallen from grace like Lucifer the angel of Light, who is cast down from heaven because he has rebelled against God. These others would identify the evil always with the egotistic or egocentric desires of man, and the good with the altruistic nature. Such a division does have something to recommend it because in the mature person the lapse into the egocentricity of childhood is always a moral danger.

Yet it is not true to the facts of the moral life to place

the ego and the alter in permanent and essential opposition. To the normal mature self-consciousness of man, I and my fellow are two poles of one social experience—the social experience which is always my own. The pure egotist and the pure altruist are fictions of sociological theory; they are analytical abstractions from the concrete social situation. No normal person was ever born with no craving for loving others besides himself, if for no other reason than that the love and passion or union out of which he was born weaves its skein of feeling and obligation about father, mother, and child, and implants psychological attitudes other than those of mere self love. And surely no normal person is so pure an altruist that he accepts obligation to others without the hope that others will acknowledge theirs toward him, or finds joy in giving of his love without the desire that he too may know the joy of being loved. As touch always implies being touched, so love always implies the thought of being loved. Impersonal objects we like and only in extravagant speech do we claim to love them. Love, in the romantic and the ethical sense, always implies, if only potentially, a reciprocal relation.

In a developed society and in a mature individual, it is not always possible to distinguish between egocentric and altruistic emotions. A man may do the most unselfish acts because the suffering of others hurts him too keenly. A man need not be a saint to say that he cannot be happy unless those about him are happy and that he finds the cruelty and suffering, of which he is cognizant anywhere in the world, saddening and depressing. He thus serves his fellow man that he himself may be happy. Surely there is no evil in such egocentric altruism. Indeed, one of the great mystics has interpreted very literally the command "And thou shalt love thy neighbour as thyself" in the sense that thou shalt love thy neighbour as though he were a limb of thine own body so that if you love yourself, he too is a recipient of that love and in loving him you are actually bestowing love upon yourself—his hurt becomes your hurt, with a certain organic immediacy, and his happiness similarly becomes your joy.[1]

It also becomes evident that the objects of man's altruistic emotions are themselves centers of egocentric desires, possessed by a variety of ambitions, tastes and longing. To identify egotism with evil and altruism with the good fails to explain the moral problem in all its complexity for it is apparent that we must select among the egotistic as well as among our altruistic impulses, if life for all is to attain the largest and most lasting good.

All this is quite apart from distinctions between desires as essentially higher or lower. It suffices here to know that man may have discovered that the sum of all the goods and satisfactions which individuals may enjoy who seek such satisfaction in harmony and adjustment to one another so that the desires of each may be congruent with the well being of all, is greater than the sum of the goods and satisfactions which they can enjoy when sought at the expense of one another. All social obligation seeks to achieve the good involved in such perception. The antisocial impulses are evil because they prevent the achievement of such good and the enjoyment of this good. The satisfaction of desires which prevent the emergence of this larger good are evil. Here then the category of the ought and the good are blended in human experience. To do good becomes a duty and by doing one's duty one seeks to achieve the good.

The Second Transference

We now come to the same impasse which we had previously experienced when discussing the growing complexity of man's obligations. Just as no human being ever lived who before each deed, and in the presence of a concrete situation, could consult the ledger in which all his possible obligations to every individual fellow man in every possible status could be recorded, so the brain never existed which could solve the intricate problems of the hedonistic calculus by virtue of which the evil was to be distinguished from the good. The same powers of generalization which enabled man to transfer the sense of obligation to moral principles, precepts, and ideals, enable him and force him to discover the general pattern of feelings and volitions which enter into the acts and attitudes which he identifies as good. These now become aspects or types of the good and their opposite or antagonistic element is evil. They turn out to be the same set of principles which govern the 'ought.' The same acts find definitions under both categories. A good example is the famous statement from Micah "He has told thee, O man, what is good" followed by the latter's definition under the category of obligation "to do justice, to love mercy, and walk humbly with thy God."

There is a further blending of the two categories insofar as there is a hierarchy of goods as well as of obligations and the ultimate obligation may also be termed the supreme good—the goal of all striving and longing. Beyond the goods which nature or society may offer, man seeks 'The Supreme Good.' He means by this something which is not merely desirable for himself, for this man or that, but that which is good for all men in all surroundings and without which all other goods will ultimately turn to dust and ashes. In the attainment of this supreme good, many minor and individual goods find their place. Health, sustenance and length of days can all add to the happiness of man where love, justice, and peace prevail, but without this supreme good the other goals of desire are endangered and insecure. The supreme good finds room within itself for lesser goods that are congruent with it but all the lesser desires that are hostile to its achievement are the evils which life must cast out. Classical philosophy had set itself the task of finding the *Summum Bonum* in some relatively static order of truth and beauty. In certain types of Oriental thought, the highest good is the way of escape from the revolving wheel of desire and repletion and desire, of birth and death, upon the framework of which all the relative goods make their experience and are locked in mutual conflict and frustration. The high-minded Chinese sage Lao Tse discovers the Tao through which alone the good life is found. In the Jewish-Christian tradition this finds expression in a social and ethical ideal.

The Highest Obligation And The Perfect Good.

We have already seen that in depicting the highest obligation, the human spirit, in the great religious tradition of the Western world, seeks to transform the society of men into the Kingdom of God. The Kingdom of God, however, is always, and at what ever level of existence, society as it ought and might become but never society as it now is. So the spirit of man is in the end never satisfied with *any* state of goodness. *He seeks beyond every good the better and the best.* He envisages perfection. Once possessed of the human spirit, man is a creature possessed. He is haunted by a dream and a vision. He seeks it ever beyond the horizon of his present perspective and the vision lures him to horizons which he has never yet scanned. The absolute truth in religion and science always eludes man and yet the history of science and philosophy would long ago have come to an end were it not for the thought of the truth which thus far has eluded his grasp. Nearly three thousand years ago the Prophets of Israel, in a world torn by war and strewn with the wreck of empire, beheld a world in which nations as well as individuals would be united in an international order emanating from God wherein "nation would not lift up sword against nation and war would become a lost art," and their eyes dwelt upon a time when the wolf and the lamb—that is, the proud and the meek—would vie with one another in gentleness and none would hurt or destroy for "the earth would be full of the knowledge of the Lord as the waters cover the sea." Within this perfect society wherein peace and knowledge would be universal, they see each individual "beneath his vine and his fig tree with nothing to fear and none to make him afraid." Prophecies such as this contemplating a transformed and redeemed society must not be confused with Utopias, either ancient or modern. In Plato's Republic which is offered as an ideal plan for government, the classes of society, including the military class, are distinctly present. In the great Indian poem Mahabharata the caste system though somewhat rationalized, is by no means abolished. The Hebrew prophets present no constitution for an ideal state.

In God's name they make repeated demands upon society to purge itself of all evil and envisage a society so purged of all injustice and cruelty and ignorance, as the state in which history will find fulfillment.

Through countless centuries, visions such as these have pursued man down the bloodstained corridors of history. He has never realized them in life and perhaps never will or can in their completeness. Most men while paying tribute to their grandeur have never seriously set about their realization. But the saints of the world have cherished them and died for them and man amid his sin and suffering, his irrational violence, and conflicting lusts, has never succeeded in shaking himself free. These have become for man, not the measure of his success, but the measure of his failure and guilt. Can we ever allay these ghosts or give them substantial form? If we can do neither, how shall we deal with them?

Can We Experience Perfection?

Can we allow ourselves to dwell upon visions of social perfection or use such terms as *ultimate truth*? Are we making sense when we take for granted that these refer to some form of reality of which man is cognizant? No man has ever experienced perfection and no scientist or philosopher has ever believed that he was in possession of the ultimate and perfect truth. Indeed, modern realism is quite convinced that in the natural world of actual existence, the perfect and the ultimate are never within our experiences.

This must needs be so because complete knowledge of anything would mean not only objective knowledge from the outside but subjective knowledge from the inside. I can live with my friend a thousand years and I may know more and more *about* him but actually I will never completely know him. When the Bible asks concerning the human heart "Who can know it?" the answer can only be "I the Lord search the heart." It is only the infinite whole or that being which we call God who is both beyond and within every entity who can have perfect knowledge. All our knowledge is only knowledge in the perspective of our own position in the world of existence. Things may possess qualities which our senses will never be able to discover, just as we know that there are frequencies of sound and light waves to which other animals are sensitive but to which our sense organs do not respond.

It is so with goodness. Human sympathy as a virtue, is forever limited in the world of existence because I can only know my neighbor's suffering through my imagination; I can never truly suffer with him, as I ought, if I am to understand him. If we speak of God as being perfect love, do we not mean that the Infinite suffers with us? He is in the human heart as well as outside the human heart. Existence always implies the externality of one thing or another. So no experience, individual or social, can contain all of goodness. Something always perishes that something else may take its place. The sweetness of childhood disappears as we attain the responsibilities of adulthood. The romantic virtues of chivalry vanish in the presence of a new order of democratic equality and cooperation. This being the case, how then dare we speak of perfect goodness and perfect knowledge and take for granted that somehow they are real. Even if there is a realm of reality beyond existence, we can know of it only through existence and through our experience in the existent world, and if it is real its reality must manifest itself by throwing some light upon existence as such.

Let us try to answer our query as to the reality of perfection by reversing the question and inquiring what can man mean when he protests his own imperfection or the limitation of his own wisdom. How can man know that he is imperfect or that he does not know everything? Einstein has beautifully expressed his wonder that man is permitted to know even a fragment of infinite wisdom and order, "To know that what is impenetrable to us really exists, manifesting itself as the highest wisdom and the most radiant beauty which our dull faculties can comprehend only in their most primitive forms—this knowledge, this feeling is at the center of true religiousness." But how in any particular situation, moral or epistemological, can man know that he or the world can be better than now they are or that the sum of knowledge is greater than that which is now in his possession. Maybe there is no more. Maybe tomorrow the scientists instead of saying, as one did recently, that it will take another hundred years to know anything about the nucleus of the atom, will say knowledge is just a finite enterprise easily contained within the world of existence. We have just finished all there is, burn your laboratories, throw aside your test tubes and do something else.

The point that I wish to make is simply this—when a man says I am not perfect, he only makes sense if he means "I know I am not perfect for that which I am seeking is." When a man seeks truth he knows that every fragment of truth which he achieves is a facet of the ultimate and perfect truth for which he is groping, otherwise it is not truth at all. Every affirmation we make intending to express the truth may be only partially true, but it is never intended to represent complete and perfect knowledge of a partial truth (there is no such thing) but rather the imperfect and partial knowledge of the whole truth which may have being beyond our ken.

The statement that we have neither empirical knowledge of perfection nor of imperfection but that we live in the assurance of both, will, I know, be challenged. Such apparent commonplaces as the biblical statement "There is no man upon earth who doeth good and sinneth never" or the more colloquial cliché "There's always room for improvement" illustrate my meaning. They envisage the continuity of the moral life and its insatiable demands upon the human spirit. They imply there is somehow endless goodness to which every finite level of the good is an approximation but to which it is never a limit. The moral will, no matter how feeble be its effect or how circumscribed its scope, always aims at this perfect goodness.

A man who says to his conscience "I will go with you part of the way, I shall seek to do justice but shall be content with partial justice, I believe in compassion but I shall choose the extent of my compassion" will not take one step forward on the path of goodness or duty. If a man can in advance limit the justice, right, mercy, and truth he aims to establish to suit himself and to salve his own ego, he has joined hands with the forces of evil and becomes a danger to the society which harbors him. The truly good know that in their weakness, in their ignorance, under the pressure of actual physical circumstances as these happen at any moment to condition a man, he may advance but a short way on the path of perfection but that it is only on that path that he advances at all. For no matter to what moral heights he or society have climbed, there will be no end to his quest, for Infinite Goodness will both lure him on and thrust him forward. The reality of perfection is therefore not merely the reality of the ideal. *God is not merely the idea of perfection but the dynamics within the world of existence by virtue of which the human spirit cannot accept any limit to goodness and truth.* We have already spoken of this as the creative restlessness of God immanent in actual life.

It will be said that the above is all very beautiful but it is an idealistic description of the moral will straining towards perfection. As a matter of fact, the average good man wants to do what he can and no more. The perfect and the infinite do not enter into his calculation. I cannot too emphatically deny that this is so. The good man wants to do *at least* what he can in the service of the truly good. He never limits the truly good to what he can do.

The Perfect Truth

In a similar sense, we may say that the search for the complete, the absolute, the infinite truth is at the basis of all scientific research and investigation. No scientist, no matter how fragmentary and inadequate he may confess the present result of his studies—say of Mars, or thermodynamics, or biochemistry—to be, has set out to discover the partial truth of anything. He desired always the full and absolute truth, the truth which he himself knows only an infinity of observations in an infinity of relational perspectives could yield. In the pursuit of this elusive goal, he may pass one after another the many milestones which mark the actual progress of his science. Of this he seems to be assured, that the road to truth comes to no dead end.

Again, one may point out that the above is a deliberate romanticising of the empirical situation. The scientist, one may remind us, is much more matter of fact. If he seems never to let up, it is not because the siren song of perfection gives him no rest. He may be quite skeptical about the reality of perfection or absolute truth. What he is really after is to learn *more and more* about his subject and this he knows is always possible with persistent and intelligent application.

The foregoing analysis seemingly so realistic since it dispels all the golden mist of metaphysics with which we have glorified the situation, nevertheless misses the main point. We speak so glibly of the 'more and more' as though the naive faith that no matter how much one knows there remains *more* to be known were not laden with the profoundest metaphysical implications. What particular experience has taught man that no matter how much truth he may have mastered or how much knowledge he may have acquired or be destined to acquire, there remains the inexhaustible 'more' still to be achieved?

Because man is always confronted and surrounded by the unknown, because the "Infinitude of Nescience" always challenges him no matter how industriously he may have enlarged the area of his science, we might be driven erroneously to embrace the myth of the 'unknowable'— of some realm of being eternally and essentially impervious to thought and reason, an infinite irrationality. The unknown is only truth waiting to be revealed to the mind of man or perhaps already revealed to some superior mind. It is myth-making to equate the unknown with the unknowable, to give independent and distinctive reality to the ignorance our knowledge has been unable to conquer or dispel, as men have invented the devil to explain the evil they have been unwilling or unable to deny or overcome. We must always be careful lest we invoke the *black* magic of metaphysics in our haste to avoid its *white* magic.

If, as a matter of fact, man ever felt himself confronted with what he thought to be the unknowable, something essentially and eternally irrational and opaque, when the veil of outer darkness obscured his vision, he would not have evolved a more powerful telescope, actual or metaphysical, as he has repeatedly done. He would simply have called an end to the wearisome enterprise of knowledge and despaired of further inquiry. He has never done so and, I believe, never will because in every finite advance of knowledge in repeatedly and laboriously correcting old errors in the light of new truths he knows, as we have already observed, that he is serving with every fragment and facet of his truth that perfect truth of which it is a fragment and facet, the whole of which can never be reflected in any state of human knowledge but abides eternally with God—for God is, according to our definition, the infinite whole of all being which involves and transcends all perspectives actual and possible from which reality can be envisaged by any of the creatures held within its unifying embrace. The whole wisdom of God can be known only to God, but it is an ineffable wisdom, not a realm of unreason. It is unknowable because it is divine not because it is demonic. In every flash of illumination man senses perfection.

Messianic Vision and Perfect Goodness

We can now go back to the question we have asked (on page 50) can we ever allay these ghosts or ever give them substantial form?' We reiterate that if we read carefully the major biblical passages to which we have alluded, we discover at once that they are no mere Utopias, they propound no plan of government; they envisage human society redeemed and transformed. There is perfect peace, perfect international understanding. The world is full of the knowledge of God. No fear grips any human heart. The Messianic King is neither the head of a state nor of a priestly hierarchy. He is like a prophet in that the spirit of God rests upon him. In later tradition, he is *the* Messiah, that is, *the* 'anointed one.' All the other anointed ones, though approved by the prophets in their time, now become mere pretenders.

It is at once evident that all this cannot find realization in any state of actual existence no matter in how remote a future if we interpret "the end of days" as signifying this indefinite future. Perfection of character or of society cannot be a finite state of being. The idea of perfection or the infinite or the absolute has this as its essential characteristic, that it cannot have realization on any finite level or rather that no degree of goodness which may have been attained can exhaust the infinite possibilities of the good. All evils now evident to the sensitive conscience sitting in judgment upon itself or on human society as we now observe it may be overcome, but in overcoming them, the cleavage between good and evil will break out on a higher level and as a result of the good already achieved.

Nor can we interpret the term "the end of days" in an other-worldly sense as an event belonging to a realm of being different from that of the actual world. Jewish folklore oscillated always between such views of the Messianic Age as saw nature miraculously transformed and glorified or which regarded it as an earthly prelude to the World to Come. Occasional rationalists like Maimonides deprived it of its essential element of transcendent perfection to keep it on this side of the veil which separates existence from the World to Come. There is no doubt that these visions were never meant to be mere promises of miraculous salvation beyond history. Their reference is always to man upon earth. It is only as we translate them from eschatological ends in a particular time, to *eternal* ends for *all* time, that they remain significant and bear testimony to that perfection which is exemplified in every social advance and finds its source and fulfillment only in God. When so grasped, they become not only ideals of perfection which give direction to human history in all stages of man's progress, but historical forces which can mold and transform society not once and for all but world without end.

The Reality of Progress and the Primacy of Evil

How evil is both older than the good and yet derives reality from the nature of goodness, as nature embraces higher levels of being, can only be demonstrated if we realize that the creative advance is never wholly smooth and unimpeded but that there is always something essentially catastrophic involved in the achievement of new levels of being. The gulf between good and evil yawns anew, each time some primitive good is left behind. There is always a certain rupture of older harmonies involved in the appearance of a new moral order.

In the life of the individual, this is illustrated with striking vividness. Prenatal existence within the womb entails a state of being the peace and harmony of which is destroyed by the eruption of the embryo. In the uterus, the foetus has all its wants satisfied while enfolded by the maternal life. The process of parturition necessitates the severance of the umbilical cord. The placenta, through which the unborn child is fed, becomes so much waste material which must be discarded. Life fulfills itself by a rupture of all the old ties between embryo and mother during which the unborn babe drew to itself all that was good for its growth and vigor. That a higher and more complex order may come into being, life rejects the more primitive perfection, and presents mother and child as separate individuals to take their place as units in the family, where obligation instead of mere physical need, eventually becomes the bond between them. Let it be clear that we are here using the term perfection not in its absolute sense but perfection within the framework and context of a finite experience.

In view of the new and larger order with its greater range of possible desires and satisfactions, the old perfection remembered organically and subconsciously, becomes an evil—the wish to shake off responsibility and return to the womb. We are not here concerned with the morbid aspects of these cravings as it might express itself in various neuroses. The longing of the individual to find security in the primitive, the flight from reason and duty to inarticulate instinct which overcomes all scruples, the search for God not within and beyond and above but down below, in the deep caverns of the unconscious, are all symptoms of the same disorder. They point the way back to the womb where the human spirit may lose itself in the warm darkness. They are forces of evil because they are in conflict with the good sought on the higher reaches of life and being.

Every human being is born twice, not only in the

57

sense in which James speaks of the 'twice born' in his *Varieties of Religious Experience,* or as we are familiar with it in the description both biblical and rabbinic of that spiritual rebirth which by the grace of God a man may experience through repentance and contrition, but in a simpler and more literal sense. He is born out of the womb of his mother, and again, if he is ever to become a ripe and mature individual, out of the womb of the family. The stream of life, rushing onward through the embryo, destroying the foetal self-sufficiency of the unborn to produce the child, reaches flood tide when, in the physical and spiritual sweep of puberty and adolescence, it shatters the sheltering shell of infancy and childhood and leaves the individual to confront the adult world.

We always look back wistfully to the lost paradise of our childhood and our youth before we had eaten of the Tree of Knowledge and learned of love and pain and death as we stood naked before God. The innocence of childhood, the sweet dependence of the child upon its parents for food, shelter, guidance, and education, the fostering love of father and mother and the loving response of the child even in its most demanding moods —the poets of the world have sung of all of this. These constitute the lovely but ephemeral "Clouds of Glory" of which Wordsworth speaks, and yet it is precisely the rupture of this type of complete dependence which becomes necessary if a healthy individual is to emerge. Childhood indeed is good and beautiful but we know today that infantilism is evil. The latter means the inability or disinclination to make attachments of love and loyalty beyond the family circle. In the psychological sense this time, there must again be a cutting of the umbilical cord—"Therefore a man leaveth his father and mother and cleaveth to his wife." We are all too familiar from literature, if not through science, of the various complexes induced by the father and mother image, cherished in childhood, but becoming a fixation, preventing the formation in maturity of normal ties between the sexes. Eugene O'Neill made a literary reputation through his skill in the dramatic treatment of these symptoms.

Much of the cruelty in the world is due to the fact that the torturers and inquisitors are people who have never outgrown the self-confident egotism of the child by virtue of which his own sufferings are very real and cry for amelioration whereas the anguish of others, because of emotional and imaginative immaturity, are completely unreal and give him no pain. We impute no fault to the child. In our defensive love we are likely to say, "Leave him his childish innocence—he will soon enough learn of the 'suffering of all living things.'"

To harden one's heart to human suffering is not always a sign of callousness induced by use; it is often the voluntary refusal to shed one's infancy, to permit the sorrows of others to play their part in our own life. Because in infancy our vital needs are generally supplied by others, the tyrants of the world, from Nero to Hitler, with their passionate reiteration of their own desires, with their hysterical tantrums under frustration, with their assumption that the world is best organized when it serves them or goals which they have chosen, can best be viewed as souls which have never matured. They are the 'enfants terrible' of the world, not in any whimsical or facetious sense, but in the dark and sinister reality of the term.

What all this leads up to is merely that what, on a certain level of life in the history of the individual is 'good' and can be accepted and cherished as altogether desirable, must be discarded and regarded as evil if life is to advance into maturity. In the light of the newer and higher obligation which confronts the adult, in the light of the deeper understanding of human suffering, in the light of the larger love of which he is capable, the infantile reaction enters into the very definition of evil when carried over into adulthood. What we must remember if we are to be saved both from undue pessimism and undue optimism is that we cannot *grow up* without *outgrowing* even the good which once we cherished.

As with the foetal life within the womb of the mother, or the parent and child relationship in the protective shell of the family, so nothing is quite so perfect as the organized life of certain animal societies on their own level of existence. The rhythmic and patterned migration of birds wheeling in the skies, the complex solidarity of the societies of ant and bee, illustrate a perfection of order never attained by man. The fierce efficiency of nest and den and lair for the young, whose identity is utterly lost, once the periodic seasonal urges of mating and procreation have worked their magic spell, are the case in point. Beasts may prey one upon another for food, or rend one another in mating when the rutting season bears them in its grip, but no beast ever rose in revolution against the cyclic order of its existence or threatened to change the pattern of the life in which it was spawned. This excess of perfection is precisely that which permits of no learning, and provides for no voluntary deviation. The shortness of animal memory and imagination, though animal societies may endure for eons of time, makes that society one without history. The history of life is a human experience, not an animal one. In animal societies there are parents and young but never, so far as I am aware, ancestors and descendants. Every act tends to preserve the species but no act is undertaken for the sake of *posterity*.

Then, in some apelike creature, the light of reason and conscience begins to burn amid the murk of animal urges and cravings, and all is confusion. The creative light has broken through. The old relationship is shattered, and only fragments of the old life can be integrated into a pattern of obligation and a quest for the good which involves judgment upon the past and aspiration towards a future yet unborn, and calls upon reason and will to assist in its realization.

It is useless to tell man to rely on his instincts even for mere survival. He cannot grow a thick fur in the winter as does the fox, he must learn to make a coat, yes, and to build a fire and lay the foundation of industry. To maintain himself against the jungle he had to devise weapons longer and sharper than the tiger's fangs—the club, the sword, the sling, and the arrow. He could learn by the use of his hands to adapt the environment to his own needs rather than remain in complete subjection to its decree. If he had to rely more and more upon intelligence and imagination—on those peculiar properties which enter into personality—human society had to become a society of persons and not an aggregate of animal units. The former were bound together, as we have seen, by a skein of relationships other than those involved in the gregarious instincts of the herd. The conflict between good and evil therefore is not merely a conflict born of the quest of the good on the human level, born of the clash of will and purpose arising within human nature and the structure of human society, but also born of the incompatibility of the primeval order in its *perfection* with the new order about to come into being. The dictates of primitive instincts surviving in the life of the animal man must be made to pass the censorship of will and reason and thus be integrated into an order of obligation and good envisaged by the human spirit. To shake off the new responsibility, to allow ourselves to sink to the animal level, to silence conscience and reason that animal instinct and urges may meet with no obstacles, becomes one of the chief sources of evil. Man must deny the wish to become the *perfect animal*—beautiful in strength and innocence—that he may become *even imperfect* and *guilt-ridden* man, seeking the fulfillment of his spiritual nature in infinite and eternal goodness, in a perfection that is absolute.

When we speak of the formal perfection of animal life on its own level, we are not romanticizing nature; quite the contrary, I believe that we are viewing it realistically. There is a tendency on the one hand to ascribe to nature (animal nature of course) all the sentimentalities of the human heart. The bees and the birds and the beasts not only mate, they have their romantic love life. So for the sentimentalists. On the other hand, the hardheaded, especially those who are anxious to show that nature displays no trace of divine goodness, are apt to din into our ears the cruelties of nature's creatures, life preying upon life, the tragic cooperative living of host and parasite in all forms of living tissue, the black widow spider devouring its mate, and so on ad infinitum. What they fail to see is that they are really unloading the burden of human guilt upon the animal kingdom. Man who kills his fellow man is cruel, not the tiger stalking his prey. The human parasite who sucks the lifeblood of others that he may live is the voracious fiend, and not his animal counterpart.

All living things may suffer pain, and the evil of pain endured is a fact of life and a challenge to philosophy which we hope to deal with in another connection. We are now dealing with *moral* good and evil, not with the function of pain in the history of life. There is no moral evil in animal life or society. Its instinctive innocence, and the order founded upon it, is precisely what tempts man to repudiate the human spirit within him in favor of animal instinct. When he acts the animal he becomes the sinful man, not the guiltless beast. It is only the emergence of the human spirit, the birth of will and conscience which brands the surrender to animal instinct as evil. The good which should have been outgrown as life advances becomes now a residue from the past which must be subordinated to the needs of the spirit lest it lead man backward and downward instead of forward and upward.

The catastrophic character of social advance is revealed in the less tragic features of human history as well as in its punctuation by bloody war and revolution. It is doubtful whether there has ever been an increase in the sum of human virtue, or if the total amount of human suffering or human happiness has changed one iota in all the centuries. There are no fewer moral problems pressing for solution today than confronted our ancestors of old. Indeed we will be persuaded, we children of the Atomic Age, that the issues pressing for decision today are so pregnant with good and evil that they may involve the survival of civilization itself. All these considerations need not shatter our faith in the reality of progress for we shall see that progress has no relation to the quantitative determination of virtue or happiness. It is not a pageant viewed from without whose sweep we are called upon to applaud. Progress is being made as the moral issues arising in any age or in any type of social order are on a higher level and require more wisdom and sensitivity for their solution than those of the preceding era. Yet I think one will find that the obstacle to further advance is not in the explicit will to evil, or not alone in such a will. The selfish, the cruel, the greedy, the lustful, will of course seek as ever to advance themselves at the expense of their fellow men. The difficulty always lies in something more fundamental.

The appearance of free labor, for instance, meant not merely the destruction of certain practices that were evil and inhuman, but also much that appeared tender and idyllic. The responsible and affectionate paternalism that marked the behavior of the good master towards the ignorant and perpetual children of his household gave the slave a certain freedom from care and an economic security that the free worker has forever lost. Freedom means standing on one's own feet, for better or worse, supported only by the sense of right and justice of other free men. There were slave holders in the South who, even after the Emancipation, shared with their impoverished freed men what food they had left after their own economic ruin. The right of a worker to demand a higher wage and better conditions of labor and to organize in order to obtain these was, and still is, opposed by men who insist that they wish only the privilege of taking proper care of their own workers. They want their business to be their own but they are always ready, they say, to raise salaries voluntarily, when profits or the cost of living warrant such a raise, and they deeply resent the imputation that it should require pressure even of union men sometimes in other plants to achieve this result. That workers should owe what they are earning to the generosity of their individual employers rather than to the strength and importance of labor in the whole industrial process determined by collective bargaining and tested by the strike, seems to them the ideal condition.

This sentiment was appropriate on occasion to the slave state and reflected credit on the masters who voluntarily exercised such generosity and kindliness and thus took care of their dependents. It is inappropriate to the free state. It is a form of nostalgic morality which is to be repudiated if a free society is to have continuance and assurance of further development. The American Abolitionists had to fight the argument that the slave was happier than the free worker, for as a matter of fact he often was. He had greater security and little responsibility as compared with his free brothers in the mills of Manchester and Worcester, before organized labor came upon the scene. That any human being should absolutely depend upon the generosity of another for the work he does and the bread he eats is precisely the evil which the Emancipation sought to eradicate. It had to discourage the older harmonies which permitted slavery to endure so long. These now became the bulwark of the evil with which the world of free labor is still struggling.

It is not only the employer however who is under the spell of the idyllic element appropriate to slavery and a paternalistic morality. Labor too can be and has been tempted to yield freedom, initiative, and responsibility, for what it imagines to be a security once enjoyed. That such decision is usually born out of a crisis of want and despair does not mitigate the evil it entails. The anachronisms of national socialism in Germany and totalitarianism in Soviet Russia with the impulse to adore the leader and dictator and accept a discipline which negates all individual criticism—all these are examples of mass reversion, of collective longing for a security once remembered to have existed and now seeming to have vanished. Biblical literature with its insight into human motivation makes it quite clear that what threatened to wreck the enterprise of freedom and frustrate the purposes of the prophetic emancipator and God Himself, was the constant lusting after the 'fleshpots of Egypt.' The taskmaster's lash was soon forgotten. The fleshpots contrasted with the austere fare of the free men of the desert became the lure and temptation that threatened to undermine the work of prophet, lawgiver, and liberator. The slave felt himself secure in the master's need for his service and therefore the need to supply him with sustenance. Freedom, the path of which usually leads through the wilderness before it attains the promised land, is a risky undertaking.

Another instance of a former good becoming a present evil and an obstacle to social progress on a higher plane, is evidenced in our groping for a core of international authority which will curb the aggressive and bellicose spirit of rival states and therefore prevent the periodic recurrence of such global conflicts as twice in the life of one generation have drenched our world in blood. International law, from Grotius to the present day, had as its foundation the equal sovereignty of all states great and small. This idea of equal sovereignty made possible the system of international usage aimed at safeguarding every state from aggression and from dictation from without in regard to its internal affairs. It helped to define neutrality and belligerency. The experience of the last few years, especially the futility of the League of Nations and the occasional frustration suffered by the United Nations through the exercise of the veto, has demonstrated that unqualified national sovereignty may not be the last word in international organization. The slaughter in Nazi Germany of Jews and political dissenters as a result of a racial chauvinism become a national aberration, and ultimately bursting national boundaries to menace the world, is a case in point. The spectacle of the Soviet Union and the United States deadlocked on many great issues because by agreement each can negate, in the Security Council, the decision of the General Assembly of the United Nations—has shocked mankind by its essential unreason. Somewhere and some way the principle of national sovereignty must be limited and subordinated to international decision. I am not prepared to say just where this point may be found. It is doubtless involved with the problem of disarmament and other such perplexing questions. What is important to our discussion is the fact that a principle central to international law must be repudiated, modified, or at least re-interpreted no matter how well it may have served humanity in the past, if global peace and amity is to be attained.

Such a transformation will have far reaching effects

for the individual. It will mean discarding certain sentimentalities and loyalties involved in the glorification and maintenance of national sovereignty. "God and King" or "God and the flag" will have to be abandoned for such other slogans and sentiments as will support within state and nation loyalty to something higher and more inclusive than is represented by the individual state. If the insistence on national sovereignty is now suspected of being a possible evil, it is only because the need for something better has appeared upon the horizon of human history and is beckoning us on though the prophetic goal remains still unsatisfied.

A Definition of Progress

Is faith in progress justified if we never come nearer the actual and final extermination of evil? If the truth never stands completely revealed whatever knowledge we have acquired, but if the solution of one problem in any field of knowledge only reveals new and unsuspected mysteries which clamor for understanding? As we look back, we may have come a long way and overcome many evils and won many a victory for righteousness' sake. We may be able to trace the lengthening way as we go from strength to strength. We know, however, that we shall be far as ever from our journey's end. There is no last term in the dialectic of good and evil. There is no final word of truth in the realm of actual existence. Plenitude of value and of truth are only in that unity of all being which includes and transcends every finite series of events in space and time. Indeed, it may be doubtful that in all the history of civilization there has been any increase in the sum of human virtue or that the total amount of human happiness and misery has changed one iota in all the travail of the centuries. We may already suspect that progress perhaps has no relation to the quantitative determination of either virtue or happiness.

Let us then state more clearly what is involved in faith in progress. Progress may be discerned as one social order and its institutions yielding to another, make possible the emergence of newer and higher needs and satisfactions than were possible under the older order and present to the moral judgment problems of good and evil rising out of the relation of these needs to one another and to the more elemental desires and cravings satisfied by the more primitive order which in part it inherited, transformed, and replaced.

When we speak of the catastrophic nature of the social advance, let it not be thought that we are referring to the need of war and revolution in the history of human society. These latter, indeed the employment of violence in general to promote social change, though they may from time to time have served the ends of progress are themselves, as in the view of the Prophets, survivals of a passing order which in the course of progress will have to disappear entirely.

Progress, Peace, and Democracy

Democracy is in the long run the political instrument which will make them passé. The moral hope of democracy is to arrive at social decisions within the state or within human society through free discussion and the free expression of the will of all units concerned. Democracy is a clumsy and slow affair, regulating life by trial and error, but the only cure for its defects is more democracy. If the channels of democratic action are not obstructed so that the right of the individual, as a nation or a person, to free expression and free negotiation is not abridged, then in the long run it is our hope that national and international decisions can be made and enforced without the shedding of blood. There can be no war if decision made by a parliament of nations is adhered to. There need be no revolution where social change can be submitted to the vote of all who are interested and where men will abide by this decision. Error there will still be, and suffering and injustice perhaps, because of such error, but the errors made can always be corrected by the ballots that made them. Democracy is a political tradition and therefore a moral demands, as yet on the part of only a small portion of the human race. Our hope for peace depends however upon its triumph and its extension.

Tradition and Progress

Faith in the continuity of progress uninterrupted by the wastelands of war and revolution presents another question. Are faith in progress and reverence for tradition contradictory elements in social morality? Does reverence for tradition really mean adoration of the past and is it therefore likely to be always on the side of reaction and in defense of the more primitive? Must progress in order to be real deny the reverence for tradition since its goal lies always in the future? It is a fallacy, I believe, to identify the reverence for tradition with the adoration of the past. Tradition as a living force in any human society, a nation or a church or an educational institution, has a two-fold function. It both accepts from the past and transmits to the future. If it accepted everything out of the past there would be continuity without progress. If it transmitted nothing out of the past there would be neither progress nor continuity. It would mean that creation began anew at every instant of every individual life or of the life of society. We could never become conscious of progress since progress means a carrying on. We would never recognize anything new since we would never experience anything old. Tradition must select out of the past something to transmit to the future and transmute the heritage from the past so that it can be so absorbed and transmitted.

The selective and dynamic character of tradition is well illustrated by a fact such as the following. Lincoln and William Everett both delivered addresses on the occasion of the dedication of the battlefield of Gettysburg to the uses of a cemetery. At the time, it seems that Lincoln's address made little impression. Sandburg shows that the newspaper reports, with a few notable exceptions, merely stated in effect that 'the President also spoke.' The New York Tribune reports "Dedicatory remarks were delivered by the President." The reporter of the London Times stated "The ceremony was rendered ludicrous by the sallies of that poor President Lincoln." Nevertheless, the Gettysburg address has become an integral part of the American tradition. It belongs to what Van Doren calls the American Scripture. Every schoolboy can quote its deathless lines, whereas the official speech of dedication has been gratefully dismissed into oblivion.[2]

Traditional Judaism as we know it, does not reflect the whole scope of the Jewish religious past or imply reverence for it. Judaism is comparatively a thin trickle from the vast domain of Israelitish or Judaic thought and life. It has reached us from the Prophets whose books were preserved and canonized by the Scribes and were saved from obsolescence by the Pharisees. Judaism is colored mainly by Pharisaic thought rather than contemporary Saduceeism. It reached us through the House of Hillel (though the School of Shammai is remembered with respect), through the Tannaitic literature climaxed by the Mishna in contrast to Apocryphal and New Testament Hellenism ("He who reads from the non-canonical literature as though it were an authoritative text has no share in the world to come,") and so on. Traditional Judaism never therefore imposes upon its adherents a reverence for the whole of the past but only for those portions of the past which successively were deemed worthy and capable of reception by the future. It must not be identified with any dogma which ascribed infallibility to any one age or any one period in history.

Professor Gilbert Murray, the great classical scholar, in his fine collection of essays entitled *Tradition and Progress* and especially in the essay on "The Religion of the Man of Letters" points out that there is such a thing as provincialism in time as well as in space, from which only a study of the past can liberate us.

"But the thing that enslaves us most, narrows the range of our thought, cramps our capacities and lowers our standards, is the mere Present—the present that is all round us, accepted and taken for granted, as we in London accept the grit in the air and the dirt on our hands and faces. The material present, the thing that is omnipotent over us, not because it is either good or evil, but just because it happens to be here, is the great Jailer and Imprisoner of man's mind; and the only true method of escape from him is the contemplation of things that are not present. Of the future? Yes; but you cannot study the future. You can only make conjectures about it, and the conjectures will not be much good unless you have in some way studied other places and other ages. There has been hardly any great forward movement of humanity which did not draw inspiration from the knowledge, or the idealization, of the past."[3]

A society that lives only within the present is like one which lives only in a geographically isolated spot though its provincialism is temporal and not spacial. Nothing is so quickly outdated as what is merely up to date. Human culture, intellectual, moral, and spiritual has for its arena the whole extent of human history, the past as well as the future. Much in the present may be destined to replace the past but much of it, however startling, may prove ephemeral. How much of today's morality and philosophy will form the structure of the future no one can yet tell. As we have already observed, there can be no continuity if science or morals began anew each day. There can be no progress unless something of the past is assimilated by the present and passed on to the future enriched and transformed.

We must not, therefore, define the purpose of education in the pragmatic spirit alone, as something which should teach the young person how to make a living, for education deals largely with the things for which a person should live, not the things by which he might live. Reaction has always clamored against an expanding educational program which instead of teaching young people to be efficient in office or in factory also excites the imaginations and may feed the discontent of genius. Nor do I believe that the purpose of education is to teach a person how to think. I am not quite sure whether it is possible to teach a person how to think without perverting the attempt itself into mere propaganda rather than education. The essence of all orthodoxy, religious or materialistic, is the assumption that if you reach certain conclusions held by the educator you are engaged in right thinking and if you reach opposite conclusions, your thought has been vitiated by some hidden fallacy. One can only teach a person how to think by stimulating his thinking and giving him something worth thinking about—putting the young person in touch with the great thought and thinkers of the present and the past and forcing him to face these not in abject submission but as a challenge to his own mind.

We might say briefly that the purpose of education, moral and intellectual, is to redeem man from spiritual and social provincialism. The educated man ought to be familiar with some language beside his own. He may begin the enterprise of education with the traditions of his own family or his own people or his own nation or the scientific achievements of his own age, but no American is a cultured person intellectually or morally who does not know the Jordan as well as the Mississippi and their connotation for human history, who does not realize that great minds like Euclid or Aristotle or Confucius or Buddha rose in societies other than his own, and that the stream of human progress wells from many sources and flows continually, sometimes churning up foam in shallow rapids and sometimes almost quiescent in its stillness but advancing continually, though no man knows today through what channels it may force itself tomorrow.

We must live in the hope that through the development of the democratic process and the extension of true education, the time may come when man will be able to avoid the wastelands of war and violent revolution and understand that the catastrophic nature of the social advance, through which old perfections are shattered as a new order emerges, is only an instance of the need of outgrowing involved in all growth. We must sometimes abandon or transform what was good in the past because something better has become possible.

The experience of the human spirit in its pilgrimage

on earth is very much like that which one of the Hasidim is said to have communicated to his disciple in a dream concerning his journeys through the celestial world. The dead man said:

> "Know, that from the moment I died, I have been wandering from world to world. And the world which yesterday was spread over my head as Heaven, is today the earth under my feet, and the Heaven of today is the earth of tomorrow."[4]

---

1. Martin Buber, *Tales of the Hasidim, The Early Masters* (New York: Schocken Books, 1947) p. 190.
2. Carl Sandburg, *Abraham Lincoln—The War Years* (New York: Harcourt Brace and Company, 1939), Vol. II, p. 472.
   It should be noted, however, that Everett himself wrote to Lincoln as follows: "I should be glad if I could flatter myself that I came as near to the central occasion in two hours as you did in two minutes."
3. Gilbert Murray, *Tradition and Progress* (Boston & New York: Houghton Mifflin Company, 1922), p. 19.
4. Martin Buber, *Tales of the Hasidim, The Early Masters* (New York: Schocken Books, 1947), p. 157.

CHAPTER THREE

MORAL FREEDOM

The Problem of the Freedom of the Will

The problem of free will or, to liberate it from its psychological involvement, of free moral decision from which derives moral responsibility, is at the heart of every discussion concerning ethics. We have already stated that such freedom must not be construed in an absolute sense. Only God can be absolutely free insofar as He is unconditioned by anything outside of His being. Man is not free to be or not to be moral; "neither the freedom with which he chooses between alternatives, nor the alternatives confronting his choice are of his own making or determined by his own will."[1] To this extent we may concede the Spinozistic thesis that all man's deeds flow from the inner necessity of his being. Yet if man is to hold himself morally responsible, he must impute to himself some degree of free decision by virtue of which his self is not only determined but his very nature is self-determined. There are, however, other limits to freedom.

All normal men may be equally free and yet the areas of their freedom may not be equal. Every circle has 360 degrees and if we consider a revolving needle within the circle it will be capable of passing through each one of the 360 degrees—yet the needle that passes through a circle of a smaller radius does not cover the same area as the needle that traverses the degrees of the circle with the larger radius. The radii of freedom may vary, but whatever may be the magnitude of the radius, the degrees of freedom remain the same. It is a common experience that some men are wise and some foolish, some easily tempted to certain vices, some to others, some in complete control of themselves in specific areas of behavior and without control in other areas. Extreme examples of the latter are the drug addicts or the organic alcoholics or the sex perverts who cannot be left at large, not because they have no moral life, but because the index of their freedom does not register against certain areas of human experience. Only God knows exactly the area in which a human being is free and for that reason Judaism which insists on legal justice to protect society also contains such warnings as "Judge no man until thou art come into his place" and "Judge every man in the scale of merit." "No one man may judge another save The One alone."

Therefore all that can be meant by freedom is that every human being who experiences any moral responsibility whatever, who can say to himself 'this I should *like* to do, and this I am *compelled* to do, but this is what I *ought* to do'—is in some sense and some area free. The denial of moral freedom issues from several sources. One of these is the commonsense reliance upon character.

Character as a Determining Factor in Human Behavior

There are some men who simply cannot tell a lie or be guilty of an act of deliberate cruelty. We would trust them with our lives and our substance because we build our hopes upon the firm rock of their character. Of others we say 'that person has a character which cannot be trusted.' Our observation of the general direction of his life and the quality of his deeds convinces us that he is undependable and irresponsible. If we are in a charitable mood, we might concede that he is helpless in the grip of his character and that nothing good should be expected of him. If we are inclined to be cynical, we will say that no man is worthy of either praise or blame. Each can only do what his character permits. In other words, we assert that a man's character is always the determining factor in his moral behavior.

Plausible as the statement appears, it involves a logical fallacy against which we must guard ourselves. The fallacy consists in regarding character as something apart from the deeds which illustrate a man's character and therefore exercising a compulsory influence upon them whereas it is only a qualitative generalization arrived at from observing the deeds themselves. We might as well say that the blue of the sky is caused by the character of blueness possessed by the sky as to say that the character of goodness qualifying any man's deeds is caused by the goodness of his character. The deeds define his character, not the reverse. A man's character is never fully developed until his last act has been counted and weighed. We may think of a certain individual if we had had an unpleasant experience with him, that he is wholly evil; yet before his death, by some act of repentance, he may have shown himself possessed of the character of a penitent rather than that of a sinner. The Talmud tells us that when the hardened executioner and torturer of Hannina Ben Teradion hastened the latter's death because he could no longer endure the saint's suffering, and consigned himself to the flames knowing that his act would forfeit him his life, a voice from Heaven cried out that he had won immortal life because "some there are who acquire claim to Heaven through years of effort and some achieve immortality in one fateful hour." The executioner as well as the rabbi proved that they carried within them the capacity for heroic self-sacrifice. None of us knows at what point our moral resistance may break. No one can tell what sublime heroism some common and commonplace individual may be capable of displaying when his hour strikes. I was told by an intimate friend of mine, an officer during the first World War, of a young man who, when ordered to advance, endangered the lives of all the men in his platoon because he was suddenly frozen stiff with fright and could not advance another step. My friend, the officer in charge, drew his gun and threatened to fire unless the lad obeyed orders. He finally moved on, and he kept moving, and throughout the remainder of the war proved himself a man of courage and devoted to duty. At which moment did his real character express itself? Who knows concerning himself or another when the temptation to evil will overcome resistance and what great deed he may not be capable of for those whom he truly loves or for a cause which enlists his service? What I wish to emphasize over again is that a man's character cannot wholly determine his deeds because his character has not been determined before the last deed has been enacted. Character, therefore, must not be regarded as some shadowy substance existent before the moral life begins and compelling it in one or another direction.

Yet we cannot dismiss too lightly the factor of character as one of the determinants in our moral life. Character is largely the essence either of genetic predisposition or our acquired moral habits. Our deeds, our social habits build our character as truly as our character builds them. A man who has accustomed himself to doing good will manifest, in time, a good character—he will find it difficult to do evil. And a man who has debased himself by doing evil will find it increasingly difficult to do good. It will require a greater putting forth of will to alter the path of his life. Therefore, at any one point in a man's career, it is true that organic habits such as those to which we have already alluded and which he may have acquired through heredity, or patterns of behavior and habit which he had traced within himself through past deeds and attitudes, will help condition his future deeds. It should never be forgotten that the areas of freedom are not equal for all men. One of the factors restricting the area of freedom at any one time is the pattern of reaction which we have built up as habits by our own deeds. The interpretation in Rabbinic literature of the phrase that God hardened the heart of Pharaoh illustrates what we have in mind, as does also the dictum that certain habitual sins which man commits are punished by the fact that they deprive him of the power of repentance. The familiar saying that a good deed brings in its wake other good deeds and that a sin brings in its wake other sins, that the reward of an obligation fulfilled is another obligation, and the consequence of transgression is another transgression—all these illustrate what we have been trying to explain. A man's character at any one period of decision is one of the conditioning facts which the moral will must take into consideration. It is not, however, a determining cause. Determinism implies that something in existence, prior to the event contemplated, compels the said event to be what it is. Man's character has no existence prior to the sum of his deeds nor can he be judged until the record of his deeds is full. What all his deeds have been and what his character has been, we shall know only after he and his deeds are no more. This is the psychological truth behind the statement "repent one day before your death" and the query arising from it "how does man know the day of his death" and the response to the query "repent therefore every day." Man's character and his acts define one another reciprocally. Character is not a pre-existent determinant nor are his deeds subsequent effects. They come together into the world of existence. If man can be said to be creative in any sphere of life, it is precisely as he creates through his deeds his own moral habits and therefore and thereby those predispositions which help to define his character in any particular moral situation.

God's Omniscience and Man's Freedom

Another obstacle to freedom is thought to lie in the theological doctrine of God's omniscience, that is, the divine foreknowledge which God is said to possess of all that is yet to be. His knowledge of the future, many observe, makes it impossible that man shall choose his way. He is bound to act in a certain manner since God knows in any present instant of time just what his future conduct is to be.

The fallacy in this contention is the thought that because God knows all things in all time that God's knowledge of today includes His foreknowledge of tomorrow. This we shall discover, when we treat more fully of time, eternity and immortality, is simply not so. What we really mean by God's omniscience is that God knows eternally both today and tomorrow but not that His knowledge of today includes that of tomorrow. They remain two items in His eternal wisdom. God's knowledge of all time is due to the fact that all time is in God, not God in time. If then we cannot truly say that God knows what is going to happen tomorrow, the element of determinism does not enter. Let me repeat again that all we mean is that God knows both today and tomorrow in an eternal knowledge the form of which transcends our own. Theological theories of predestination are largely based upon the fallacy we have been discussing. Since God knows from the beginning of time who will be saved their salvation must depend upon previous election.

Spinoza's Denial of Freedom

Such scientific and metaphysical monisms as that of Spinoza are often cited in opposition to freedom of the will. According to Spinoza, God is the necessarily existent or substance. Existent entities are all modes of this substance in its various attributes. They are what they necessarily must be as phases of substance. From this point of view, freedom of will is an illusion due to our ignorance of the cause that compels our decisions. It has no reality of its own. It has often been pointed out that when Spinoza calls the acknowledgement of this necessary relation between things, and its free acceptance, the intellectual love of God and elevates it to the sole condition for blessedness, he implies that the mind at least can exert power by choosing its way. In other words, a man can make up his mind. At least this is the understanding of the situation expressed by Joseph Ratner in his introduction to *The Philosophy of Spinoza*, "But man's salvation, just as much as his damnation, is within his own control. Salvation or blessedness is something man can achieve by his own efforts; it is not something he can achieve only by Divine Grace." [2] If this be so, then Spinoza has gotten over the difficulty by shifting the center of gravity, as regards man's freedom of decision, from will to thought. Furthermore, the writer whom we have just quoted interprets Spinoza's attitude as follows,

"But if the ends are the ends of our natures,—that is, if teleological determinism is not perverse and arbitrary but rational and scientific—we are, as Spinoza constantly points out, free. Only when we are subject to alien ends or the ends of alien natures are we enslaved. For freedom is not opposed to necessity or determinism; it is only opposed to an alien determinism. Freedom consists not in absolute indetermination, but in absolute self-determination. And self-determination is the very last thing that can be called fatalistic."[3]

Whether this be the correct interpretation of Spinoza's point of view, I am not here prepared to say, but if not, then Spinoza himself is guilty of the popular fallacy which regards the whole as determining the character of each one of its parts or phases and assuming that part and whole stand in some causal and compulsive relation to one another.

The Whole and Its Parts

This is not true even of a constructive unity. Two semi-circles do not make a circle unless they are situated on opposite sides of a diameter of the circle which already stands in relation to them as whole does to its parts. Three lines and three angles do not constitute a triangle unless the three sides enclose the angles within the triangle of which they are parts.

We may speak of a five-room house, but five rooms do not constitute a house. They may be five rooms in five separate hotels. Five rooms cannot constitute a house unless they are under the one roof of the house which they already constitute. In other words, in all such cases the whole and its parts are mutually determinative. They have a reciprocal relation to one another. The parts are never the cause for the existence of the whole, nor is the whole a cause for the existence of the parts. The whole does not exist prior to its parts nor the parts prior to the whole and, therefore, neither can be said to exert causal compulsion upon the other. They are related only by logical implication.

This is more clearly the case with organic unities. It

is a fact that the cells in any organism or in any organ of any organism are what they are because of the whole in which they function. But it is likewise true that the animal organism is what it is because of the cells which constitute its being. They define one another. They are mutually constructive of one another. Their relation is a reciprocal one. There never was a living animal that existed prior to its cells and compelled its cells to enter into relation with one another. There never were separate cells which, in a manner of speaking, held a biological conference to constitute a living animal. The animal is what it is by virtue of the cells which constitute its living tissue. The cells are what they are because they are elements in the whole organism within which they function. Causation, on the other hand, always implies a temporal series of events one of which is prior to the other.

Now the infinite whole of reality which includes both the universe of actual existence and of possibility cannot be said to stand in causal relation with any one of its aspects. Nothing can exist without it being previously possible (in the logical not the physical sense) and no mere possibility can of its own accord become actual. Where everything is equally possible, nothing can *possibly* have actual existence. All actuality involves the decision between possibilities as Whitehead so often observes. From our point of view, God as supreme and infinite being provides every possibility exemplified in existence and calls into actual existence the possibilities which they exemplify. The actual can never account for the possible nor the possible for the actual. A thousand possible trees will never produce one actual tree. Nor can a thousand actual trees make any tree possible. The possibility of there being a tree must have been real prior to the thousand actual trees for otherwise none of them could have entered into existence. We know that trees are really possible because we have experienced their actuality. Our knowledge of what is possible emerges from the world of nature, of actual existence, but only our *knowledge* of possibility, not possibility itself. Knowledge is an epistemologicsl fact. Possibility and creativity (as we shall explain presently at greater length) are ontological facts. The primal miracle is that some possibility must have become actual before any other actuality could have become possible.

What we have said about actual and possible trees simply means that no number of universals (which are forms of possibility) can add up to a concrete actual fact. And no concrete individual thing can exhaust the number of universals. From this it follows that the universe is creative in the sense that it provides possibilities, and such decision among possibilities that certain possibilities may become actual.

No causal relation, as no spacial or temporal relation, can therefore be thought of as between the creature and the creator. Time, space, and causality are relations which establish themselves between actual entities and events within nature, within the world of actual existence. Time, space, and cause came to be with the creatures that interact with one another in spacial, temporal, and causal processes. They are not prior as a cause precedes its effect. There was never a time when there was no time. There was never a space unoccupied by entities possessing dimension and standing in spacial relations to one another. There was never a cause which did not have a prior cause of which it was the effect. The creative source of all things therefore cannot be a determining cause, since it is not an effect, and it is not an effect because it has no temporally prior cause.

Nothing is the effect of creation but everything is an instance of creation or creativity—star, man, or worm. And since the creative and Infinite One stands in no causal relations with any part and concrete thing, creation does not exert a causal compulsion upon its creatures. You and I are not effects of God's creativity, We are instances and exemplifications of what is creative. The creation of anything is not a process before its existence as it does not come after its existence. It is not temporal in any sense for time itself is only a form of existence. We can logically speak of creation only as eternal. God's creativity is immanent in all things. Light was not the effect of God's word, it was an exemplification and embodiment of his creative word.

If this be so, then the selective freedom of man may in some way be coherent or congruent with the creative freedom present in nature as a whole including, of course, human nature. Creation has no date; it is never at one time (say some five thousand years ago) because it is in all time. When we say "In the beginning God created the heaven and earth" we can rationally mean only that the logical beginning and source of anything is God's creativity. He who believes in the creative spirit pervading all the evolution of matter and life has room, I contend, in his experience for both natural causation and moral decision. Whatever be the nature of free voluntary decision, you may be sure that the physical conditions will in retrospect have been complied with. The scientist will see to that. No miracle need have intervened.[4]

We have so far allowed ourselves rather broad and generalized statements concerning the relation of part to whole, creature to creator, and in doing so have employed terms which we have not yet adequately defined. It will be worth while, then, to examine the terms cause, chance, freedom, and creation as they make their appearance in the vocabulary of modern science and in the interpretation of scientific phenomena on the part of scientists with a speculative bent. This will lead to the conclusion, I believe, that the scientific weltanschaung of today does not preclude faith in moral freedom and the reality of moral decision. We will call the subject under consideration, which for purposes of clarity we shall consider under various headings,

BEYOND CAUSATION

What, to the layman, cannot be other than interesting in the climate of present-day scientific philosophizing—especially in the realm of physics and cosmology—is the search for something often referred to as 'beyond causation,' or 'beyond causality' not only because it must furnish the ground for cosmic existence including causality, but also because it must especially account for the emergence of causal law itself out of the apparently uncaused vagaries of quanta phenomena. It must answer the question 'how does the indeterminate become determinate and to what extent?'

I—The Element of Chance

Let me call attention to an article by Professor Paul Epstein of the California Institute of Technology, printed as long ago as July 1937 in the *Scientific Monthly*. It is entitled "Physics and Metaphysics." The author evidences a wide and sympathetic interest in metaphysical and theological doctrines of predestination. He chides the theologians for having illegitimately applied the scientific doctrine of determinism to realms other than scientific. His main contention is, "The views of modern physical science are incompatible with the doctrine of predestination and determinism which are not longer tenable. This statement should not be construed as an attack upon religion and metaphysics (God's Omniscience, I presume. J. K.). In fact, it should be a boon to them. It will be well to repeat here that the metaphysicians were those who invaded the fields of science by postulating as truth the religious equivalent of the law of causality. In doing this, they quite unnecessarily created for themselves difficulties which they could not resolve. Science is showing them the way out." Speaking of those atomic phenomena which are by their very nature unpredictable, he raises the question of how the principle of indeterminism effects the laws of causality. His answer is "We may say that it lies *beyond causality.*"

The latter is an alluring phrase and those of us anxious to find some trace of the spiritual values that we cherish, even in the structure of the physical universe, are all too ready to define that which lies beyond causation as something akin to design or at least to creative freedom. In this attempt, Professor Epstein gives us little encouragement. The unforeseeable points to nothing so exalted. Of certain of these elementary phenomena he has only this to say, "These events are unpredictable and subject only to chance." Physical laws are determined, by statistical methods, on the basis of these chance phenomena at the foundation of all physical reality. Beyond causality only chance holds sway and physical laws can only be formulated where large numbers of these elementary entities are involved. Then the behavior of the mass can be foreseen with a high degree of probability and predictions may be ventured which, while not absolutely certain, approximate to certainty for all practical purposes.

In at least two regards, I believe, the speculative thinker must accept the findings of the expert physicist at their face value: first, that the uncaused need not necessarily spell freedom—it may imply only chance at the root of all nature; furthermore, that the phenomena in question must be viewed as though they *were mere chance,* whatever we may believe them ultimately to be, by the statistician seeking to predict their behavior in mass. When the safety engineer seeks to forecast the average number of automobile fatalities likely to occur in a city during the next year or two, he must regard it as mere chance that it should have been (a) rather than (b) who helped justify his predictions, and all this despite the fact that (a)'s death may have been due to a deliberate determination and design to commit suicide.

Here however we might interpose a word of caution. Because the uncaused does not necessarily spell freedom, it need not of necessity be identified with chance. Are we not being as dogmatic, when we assert that all that is unpredictable is governed by chance alone, as were those who asserted that scientific predictability implied *pre*determination? James K. Feibleman in his recent work on *Ontology*[5] also occasionally dubs that which is beyond cause as chance. "Whatever happens" he says, "without cause happens by chance," but he also avers "Chance is the positive nature in the sheer self-determination and randomness of things and events. Everything is what it is in existence, and every event happens as it happens, at least in part, by chance. Nothing in existence is absolutely determined; therefore, everything admits the chance element to some extent." He presses the point still further however: "Chance has no cause unless to say that it is *self caused* is to specify a cause. It belongs to the category of absolute singularity, the element of sheer individuality in all existing things." Now, apart from the fact that neither cause nor chance, as we shall see, can be accounted ultimate categories of explanation, the moment we stretch the term chance or the undetermined to include the *self determined* and the *self caused* or *the essence of pure individuality,* we are opening the door to new metaphysical and theological interpretations and the region 'beyond causation' involves implications hitherto unaccounted for.

II—Predictability, Probability, and Critical Common Sense

It did not require the discoveries of modern quantum physics to suggest that perfect and complete predictability was impossible through the inductive and experimental method upon which science stakes its claims, and that the most successful hypotheses were only those carrying with them the highest degree of probability. Dr. Gideon Freudenberg in an illuminating article entitled "Probability and Induction in the Light of Modern Physics"[6] sketches briefly a history of this concept beginning with an essay by Masaryk in 1882 on "David Hume's Skepticism and the Calculus of Probability in which allusion is made to an even earlier refutation of Hume attempted by Moses Mendelssohn on similar grounds, and leading up to the work on "Theory of Probability" by Jeffrys (1939), showing that probability is at the core of any adequate theory of induction. The gist of the article, for purposes of this discussion, lies in the quotation found in the English summary: "Heisenberg's uncertainty principle is of the first importance in physics but the idea that it contains any startling novelty in philosophy can be attributed only to ignorance."

At least we shall have to concede that critical common sense has always recognized unpredictability as something never to be gotten rid of no matter what progress science may be destined to make. I suspect that no true scientist ever predicted the appearance of some remote star on the basis of a carefully worked out astronomical hypothesis without saying to himself 'this will surely happen *if* my observations and inferences are correct *and if* the situation is not disturbed by some force outside the field of observation, which in the present state of our science I could not possibly have foreseen.'

The unpredictable in each separate case was ascribed to some defect in the process of human knowledge or in the limited scope of the instruments, telescopes or microscopes, by which observations were made and measured. In theory, a perfect and infinite observer exercising inerrant logic could at any one instance know all things for all time.[7] It seems seldom to have occurred to men that the persistence of the unpredictable may be due to an ontological *fact* rather than to an epistemological *defect*, that every event in nature, entity or process, invites prediction and defies prediction, is in some way both determinate and indeterminate.

Ignoring for the moment all recent speculation on the so-called principle of indeterminism as established in quantum theory, and reverting to the standpoint of classical physics, logical analysis should have detected that complete and exact prediction was forever impossible from the nature of things—the nature of the observed as well as of the observer. Setting aside also Hume's main contention and admitting that we have real experience of causation—of continuity in the redistribution of matter and energy as event succeeds event—so that we have not mere barren sequence and association but the reaction of one event to the force exerted by the previous and contiguous event or by the field of force in which they both lie, there still remains the fact that knowledge of causation is one thing and the knowledge of causality or *causal law* is quite another.

The scientist can predict an effect, not because he is certain that it is caused by something, but because he knows through observation and inference the mathematical equation which expresses the relation between certain *types* or *classes* of past events and events of the type whose coming into existence he is now predicting. There is no causal law operative between particular events but only the fact of causation. The causal laws are all between *types* of events, or better still, between events of the same type, and equations like v=gt indicate such typical elements by the symbols they employ.

The truth of this rather obvious situation is attested to by the tautologous character of all natural law. The laws of electricity govern all electrical phenomena because electrical phenomena can be defined as those which follow the laws of electricity. The laws of gravitation govern falling bodies insofar as bodies, when falling, exemplify the laws of gravitation (or constitute by their relation to one another the gravitational field). The behavior of the genes obeys the Mendelian law because the Mendelian law describes how the genes behave in the genetic process. All this does not reflect either upon the truth value of the hypotheses upon which scientific predictions are based, or upon their practical utility.

What need here be pointed out is that there can never be any exact certainty, but at most a high degree of probability that the event about which a prediction is ventured—the reaction of a patient to a drug, tomorrow's weather, or next year's eclipse—will be so typical of observations and calculations in the past, that it will satisfy the hypothesis based upon these observations. There may always be some individual deviation in the contemplated event which will exclude it from the type relevant to the hypothesis, and the prophecy, in such a case, will fail.

If we decide to call the unpredictable element in nature the chance element, then it is involved in every natural object and in every event. It is not that our powers of observation fail us and we cannot describe with full and perfect exactness the events from which unfailing natural laws may be derived which will enable us to predict the consequences flowing from all similar events in the future. The fact is that nature will give no guarantee that there will be any future event which, though it may display resemblances to the past, will be so exactly similar to the phenomena upon which our scientific hypothesis was based so as to be bound to conform to its specifications. On the contrary, though grounds for classification exist aplenty, and though all existent things, all natural objects and processes share at least the essence of existence, there are no two existential facts that are exactly alike. No two apples are identical, no two stars show complete resemblance, no two thunderstorms viewed by the meteorologists ever followed undeviatingly the same course. If the physical universe as a whole shows from moment to moment an increase of entropy as some scientists claim, then the universe itself is not objectively identical with itself from day to day. There is no causal explanation of the sheer arbitrary self-determining individuality of a certain event whether it be the rise or death of a universe, or an event within the universe, but only such aspects of the event as are typical of phenomena previously observed and classified by means of the universals that define them.

How, in the advance of science, does causal lawfulness deal with novel deviation? If a certain bright flash in the sky should indicate to the viewing astronomer that he was witnessing an exploding nova, he would feel free to predict certain definite consequences of the explosion in that portion of space which his telescope was exploring. Should the anticipated consequences not follow with that mathematical exactitude which the science of astronomy demands, the astronomer might react in a number of ways. He might recommend a revision of the hypothesis concerning novae upon which his prediction was originally based, so as to account for the noval phenomena which had baffled him. He might, on the other hand, declare that what he had mistakenly taken to be a nova was not a true nova at all but must belong to some other order of astral event. If he and his fellow investigators fail to find such an order, they might then claim the distinction of discovery. They have found a new order of astronomical phenomena. They will not deny that the event in question belongs to some order or type of event even though, for the moment, that class has only one member, and they will perhaps devise a new hypothesis expressing the causal law which determines the behavior of all members typical of the order. When such an individual again appears, he will literally have given the password and been admitted to the order.

Let us consider another sphere of investigation. A biologist searching for specimens in a hitherto unexplored region of the earth finds a little creature clinging to a sun-baked rock. He puts it into his bag and tentatively calls it a lizard. On further study, however, he discovers that it does not behave as lizards should. It does not react to its environment, to heat and cold, to sunlight and shadow, according to the biological laws, the tropisms and instincts, which determine the behavior of lizards and which he expected the little animal to verify. He may even discover certain slight structural variations from the saurians he had hitherto described. For the time being, our scientist may be disappointed but not at all nonplussed. He will remain firm in the conviction that lizards must conform to the laws that define their nature as lizards and distinguish them from other reptile species.

He will admit however that either his knowledge of lizards is defective and his theory concerning them will have to undergo revision, or that the creature under observation cannot possibly be a lizard. For the time being, the little animal is a scandalous thing, a causal outlaw—it is just itself. He will be classified in time and his actions become predictable. If he is a scientist of the old school, our explorer will remain convinced that the specimen just discovered is subject to causal determination as are all things in nature and his behavior therefore must be predictable. "If we have failed," he will explain, "it is only because he is not quite typical of the specimens, upon observation of which, the known biological laws were formulated. Nor could we possibly have foreseen the prevalence of new laws by virtue of which predictions may yet be made concerning his behavior, before encountering the unexpected specimen and finding the type of creature which he might exemplify." The same situation faces astronomer and biologist. The unpredictable fact, insofar as it presents an individual deviation from type, only becomes predictable through laws, the existence of which were unpredictable save after observation and study of the previously unpredictable fact.

I am afraid that all this has been rather naively put and greatly oversimplified, for the evident reason that the writer has only very superficial and sketchy knowledge of any of the physical sciences. Yet, I venture to say that the same situation is met with in complex systems constituting a gravitational or magnetic field. The changes within the field are predictable and predetermined insofar as they are typical of previously observed changes on the basis of which the equations were arrived at through which the general resultant is now being computed. If the changes in the field turn out not to satisfy the equation as anticipated, new equations will have to be substituted which the field will be bound to satisfy, or the unpredictable events within the field will be attributed to forces not originating in the field as mathematically determined but due to influences from without which the field equations could not have foreseen. These new phenomena may then be brought within the field by a more inclusive hypothesis as to the latter's constitution, or new causal laws will be proposed by virtue of which the relation of the field to these foreign fields of force may be formulated and future disturbances in the field thus made predictable.

III—The Ontological Fact

When we say that the unpredictable is everywhere present in macroscopic as well as in microscopic events, we are affirming an ontological fact which expresses itself in the very structure of language. The book I happen to be examining is never merely *a* book but always and forever *this* book—individual and unique never to be duplicated, never to be repeated when once it wears itself out, and *this* book is never merely this book but always *a* book among books, one of a type or class or set of objects with a certain pattern of universals (possibilities of quality and structure) repeating themselves again and again in experience. A fact of nature is always subject to causal laws and therefore predictable.

This fact need not necessarily be predictable, because I must first determine the *kind* of a fact it is. It may prove the kind of thing to which the known causal laws are not relevant. I will then cast about for some hitherto unanticipated law which will govern this kind of fact.

I may meet the same *kind* of thing in nature again and again and thus become familiar with its modes of behavior, but never would I meet the same thing twice. All the quivering leaves of the aspen differ from one another though the poet may describe them as dancing leaves. No two crystals, no two stars, no two rivers exactly resemble one another. Each thing, as each kind of thing, is a novel emergent, an irreducible individual, and must not only run true to type but must be permitted to go its own ineffable way. In fact, no two observations of the same thing exactly resemble one another so that, as I return to it again and again, I can say 'at least one natural fact I shall fully and completely know.' The chemistry within the leaf changes the leaf's texture even as I gaze upon it. My friend is not quite as I observed him yesterday. The sunset of this evening is not even the setting of the same sun which yesterday glorified the heavens. In the meanwhile the heat that it has radiated into outer space has altered its inner structure. Always the ontological fact remains.

Processes of change have also their kind, their dimension, their momentum, and can therefore be foreseen, but always there remains the fact that the time and character of the next transformation is predicated upon equations derived from the observation of past transformations. Should the process and rate of change remain the same as it was in the past, our prediction will be fulfilled. Should they not be fulfilled, we will be convinced that either we had misreckoned or something had transformed the process. The lengthening of the average life span might play interesting pranks with statistical predictions. Five hundred years ago a man would have been justified in saying that the average person born in the year 1900 will have died at a certain date before the middle of the century. His prediction will have failed because he will have miscalculated the life process. Prediction and the unpredictable again walk hand in hand. Nature cannot purge itself of either. The postulate of the uniformity of nature simply means that—to use Dr. Epstein's definition of causality—"A given set of earlier observations will always follow a uniquely determined set of later observations" all other conditions remaining the same, as when the previous observations were made. Such promises nature cannot undertake. The controlled experiment is a tribute to nature's deviousness and of her independence when left to her own devices. The critical common sense of both scientist and layman will suggest that so long as we have no reason to suspect some relevant variation or deviation in the subject under consideration, we will proceed on the assumption that it will conform to those types of behavior it had previously exemplified. Such assumptions, the more frequently they are justified, will lead to predictions of such high probability as to approximate certainty. The result remains an approximation however. Exact and complete predictability remains forever beyond our reach.

IV—Transition to the Modern Point of View

Why then should the principle of indeterminism and the calculus of probability, as they figure in modern quantum physics, have made so great a stir in the world so that the average intelligent man is not quite sure whether he should exult as at the triumph of a liberating revolution in human thought, or weep at this betrayal of man's hopes by nature, as she brazenly confesses that all his wooing is in vain, that she will pursue her wanton ways and that she prefers chance to order, chaos to law?

Hitherto any failure to make exact predictions of the future concerning the course of any particular entity or event or series of events could always be attributed, not to the ontological fact, but to the observational failure. Our knowledge was fragmentary. We could not view the object under investigation in every possible perspective. Our instruments, including of course our sense organs, were crude and lacking in precision. Our inferences were often fallacious even when our information was exact. We lacked wisdom and that divine trifle called omniscience. We therefore, of necessity, had to content ourselves with what we know to be only approximations to natural law.

Classical physics, however, assumed that every physical object was compounded of material elements or points called atoms. Each atom at any instant of time was possessed of definite location in empty space, and endowed with velocity (a measurable amount of the energy of motion). The physical elements or points were thought to be exactly typical of one another. Every event in the life history of these elements was typical of any other. An observer could exactly predict the necessary stages in the progress of a material point moving from location (a) to location (b) with a certain velocity. A mind therefore infinitely penetrating and analytical and at the same time omnipresent, observing the whole universe at a particular instant of time and noting every atom constituting every physical entity—its location and its velocity—could then calculate the future position of each, the force with which they would impinge on one another, and the resultant changes which would ensue in the whole system to the end of time. The natural history of the universe would unfold itself before him. All that we now call novelty could be discounted in advance. Everything was predetermined and the unpredictable was not something inherent in existence but only in the feeble mind of man. God in any particular moment could know everything that was to be as it was destined to be.

The shocking discovery of modern physics lay in the fact that precisely the elemental constituents of the universe turn out to be largely unpredictable and possessed of incurable individuality. The classical laws of nature by which we were wont to predict the sequence of macroscopic events were only, after all, approximations to reality where large numbers of the atomic units were involved.

Though Einstein himself, we are told, does not hold the present stage of quantum theory to be the final word in the development of physics,[8] yet even he acknowledges that

> "There is something ineffable about the real, something occasionally described as mysterious and awe-inspiring; the property alluded to is no doubt its ultimacy, its spontaneity, its failure to present itself as the perfect and articulate consequence of rational thought. On the other hand mathematics, and especially geometry, have exactly those attributes of internal order, the elements of predictability, which reality seems to lack. How do these incongruous counterparts of our experience get together? 'As far as the laws of mathematics refer to reality, they are not certain; and as far as they are certain, they do not refer to reality.' "[9]

Where, in the lines above, the author uses the term reality I would prefer to substitute the term existence or actuality. At any rate, here is a beautiful and significant statement of the element in nature, spontaneous, unpredictable, lawless, versus the conceptual lawfulness and perfection of mathematics. To illustrate the truth of the last two lines in the foregoing quotation, one need not have recourse to complex equations. Take so simple a geometric figure as the circle. Given any point as the center and a radius of definite magnitude, we can determine the periphery of the circle with perfect exactness. It happens, however, that there is no reason to suppose that any natural object illustrates a true circle. Among all the round apples there is no perfect sphere. Of the stars and their orbits we can only say that they are spherical or that we can measure the mean radius of their orbits. Circularity is a universal, not an individual thing. The circle belongs to the universe of essence, not to that of existence. It is an 'eternal object,' not an actual entity. Nature seems always ready to barter the sterile perfection of essence for the spontaneous and variable particularity of existence.

V—The Predictable and the Unpredictable Nevertheless Join Hands

But even here in the final analysis of matter, the dual aspect of all physical existence again comes to the fore. The electron may be a particle of matter or energy, the position and velocity of which cannot both be determined with exactness and the future position of which is unpredictable, but matter has also a wave function which indicates the area in which the material particle will most probably be found.

The relation between wave and particle is almost inconceivable to one who, like the present writer, cannot follow the mathematical verifications of the terms used by the physicist. We can only gather that the situation points to the following. Whereas in the macroscopic phenomena, causal determinism still does not imply absolute and unfailing predictability, so in quanta phenomena the vagaries of the unpredictable are somewhat limited by what at least resembles the haunting presence of the causal. Walter Heitler seeks to explain matters in these words,

> "We have stated above that the wave function of an electron develops in space and time much in the same way as a classical field does, i.e. its future course is predictable when it is given at a time, say $t=0$. But its very nature and its physical interpretation (as a probability distribution) makes it clear that it is not itself the physical object we investigate (in contrast to the electromagnetic field of the classical theory, which is a physical object which we may consider, observe, and measure), although it is inseparable from the object under consideration (the electron, for instance)."[10]

Heitler does not leave us with this bewildering introduction to something 'that is not itself a physical object but is inseparable from the object' and which, though it is not physical yet 'develops in space and time much in the causal way of a classical field,' without further philosophical clarification

"It appears that we are dealing with different aspects of the object: One is the world of observations in space and time, in which the objects under consideration have measurable positions, velocities, etc. Only one of these quantities has a sharply defined value at a time. The future values of these quantities are not precisely or entirely predictable. The other aspect from which we can consider the object is the one of the wave function. It escapes our immediate observation by apparatus or (ultimately) sense perception entirely. It can be grasped by us only through our thinking, our spirit, not through our senses. It is in this world where the development is causal (in the sense used above). It casts its projection into the world of happenings in space and time, allowing us to predict probabilities for the results of any observations we choose to make (in some cases also their exact results). It is futile to argue which of the two aspects is the 'real' one. Both are. For both are but two *different projections of one and the same reality,* both are inseparable from each other, and both together only give the complete description of the object we consider."[11]

Born calls the relation between the causal development of the wave function and the observation 'complementary.' We have seen above that Einstein is not ready to substitute chance for causality as an ultimate principle of explanation. Born quotes a letter to this effect which he received from Einstein on November 7, 1944.

" 'In our scientific expectation we have grown antipodes. You believe in God playing dice and I in perfect laws in the world of things existing as real objects, which I try to grasp in a wildly speculative way.' These speculations distinguish indeed his present work from his earlier writing. But if any man has the right to speculate it is he whose fundamental results stand like rock. What he is aiming at is a general field theory which preserves the rigid causality of classical physics and restricts probability to masking our ignorance of the initial conditions or, if you prefer, of the pre-history, of all details of the system considered. This is not the place to argue about the possibility of achieving this. Yet I wish to make one remark, using Einstein's own picturesque language: If God has made the world a perfect mechanism, he has at least conceded so much to our imperfect intellect that, in order to predict little parts of it, we need not solve innumerable differential equations but can use dice with fair success. That this is so I have learned with many of my contemporaries, from Einstein himself. I think this situation has not changed much by the introduction of quantum statistics; it is still we mortals who are playing dice for our little purposes of prognosis—God's actions are as mysterious in classical Brownian motion as in radio-activity and quantum radiation, or in life at large."[12]

Significant, it appears to me, is the expression 'pre-history.' In this connection it evokes metaphysical reverberations. A pre-history of matter, even if it becomes observable to us as wave and particle, is precisely the quest of modern cosmology. Out of this 'pre-history' (that is, prior to any natural history of any kind), if there be such a reality, must emerge both wave and particle, causality and spontaneity.

In the light of these more recent discussions, is it not somewhat arbitrary and dogmatic to maintain that there can be no possible connection between the unpredictable behavior in the atom and that freedom which man imputes to himself? No one is so rash as to ascribe volition to the spontaneous and random movements of the electron, but may not the voluntary movements of a human being, the choice which he feels himself making between this and that alternative with its consequent sense of personal responsibility, not become intelligible through the fact that in every atom of every cell of every tissue that makes up his physical being, matter exercises its unpredictable and self-determining prerogative, which may finally find integrated and organic expression in self-conscious volition. This does not imply that man is ever perfectly free, but only as we have already had occasion to stress, that his acts are not completely determined in advance. Man's selective freedom is conditioned and determined by many factors within and without the structure of his own being. But if there is in human conduct ever so slight an area of freedom where will is effective, may it not be because the unpredictable element inherent in all matter comes on the human level to self-conscious realization. Indeed the connection just alluded to has been stated in reverse order,

> "We make the (causal) presupposition in order to carry on science and to make predictions; but we may, of course, reach limits; and the presupposition is (only) an hypothesis, whereas the consciousness of freedom is obvious in experience. If, however, existence at the human level demands freedom, or at least possibly demands it, does not then an aspect of freedom enter into all strata of existence, even into those of the vital and material: Any reality which would be nothing but driven, pushed, pulled, and kicked would be a purely passive being, and such a world would be a world of marionettes which is (merely) being played. Determinateness does not in any case belong as ideational necessity to the concept of being. To the contrary, real active being includes within itself a degree of determination of the indeterminate." [13]

Attention should likewise be called to a statement some time ago by the late Professor Boodin (*Cosmic Evolution*) in reference to an opinion by Weyl. "Weyl thinks that all the properties of matter are due to the field. This means, in the language of Schroedinger, that they are due to an inherent 'gestalt' or pattern which is not a sum of individual impulses or waves of energy but superimposed upon them and immanent in nature. This does not mean that matter can be reduced entirely to the field. We cannot do without the individual corpuscle of matter. Matter in action is both wave-like and corpuscular. But the guidance is furnished by the field." If I understand this correctly, it presupposes a pattern superimposed and immanent in nature which weaves together the individual unpredictable and the causal so as to insure cosmos instead of chaos in the whole realm of physical existence. Wenzl, whom we have already quoted in a statement much more recent than Boodin's, comes to a similar conclusion,

> "Here we confront a bifurcation of the roads which try to interpret the world meaningfully; Is there a divided principle at the foundation of the world? Or is the arbitrary element, the aspect of chance, included in the self-willedness of finite beings who nevertheless are under meaningful direction."[14]

From all that has been said, it should be apparent that causality has never shaken off the exuberant spontaneousness and unpredictability of experience no matter how far science has advanced or what the magnitude of the masses under consideration; nor can the chance and unpredictable constituents of reality ever exorcise the haunting shadow of causality (or that which so nearly resembles it that no statistical computation could possibly be made save on the determining ground of probability furnished by what can only be described as a wave). In other words, that which is beyond cause must also be beyond chance, as we shall presently see, and I believe it is for this reason that the terms creation and creativity are again being evoked by the cosmologists as well as the ontologists of today.

VI—Two Theories of Creation

In discussing the cosmology of P. Jordan, the becoming of the material world from a minimum number of particles, say two neutrons, which move away from each other and in so doing make space for the appearance of new particles, Wenzl observes,

> "Jordan rejects the question concerning any 'before' as meaningless; for time arises precisely as does space with matter. What, however, can not be rejected is the question concerning the 'before' in the causal sense: What causes the first particles to form themselves? No man can disregard the *'ex nihilo fit nihil.'* Even for religious faith the world is a creation out of nothing only insofar as matter itself had a beginning; but not insofar as its appearance came out of nothing; rather in the sense of the story of creation it is the will and idea of God—to whom himself is ascribed timeless eternity—which constitute the ground for the genesis of space, time, and matter."[15]

He then follows through

> "Consequently one would still have to imagine preposited a potential state without any materialization of corpuscles before the cosmogony of Jordan; a potential state whose transition to the empirical form of being introduced at the same time a temporal becoming. Once again, therefore, potentiality would precede actuality. But, in the final analysis, this means: Every physical cosmogony comes necessarily to the boundary of transcendence and must end with an unsolved problem."[16]

The important affirmation in the foregoing is this: "The potential state without any materialization of corpuscles," to which materialization there can be nothing chronologically prior, since time appears with matter and causation with both, brings us at last to the 'boundary of transcendence.' There must be being which contains the possibilities of existence, which is logically not *temporally* prior to space and time, corpuscle and wave, cause and chance, physical determinism and unpredictable individuality—which, transcending all these, is the ground for all, and hence is immanent in them all.

Religious thinkers like Wenzl do not hesitate to push the above considerations to their logical conclusions,

"If we raise the question at all concerning the essence, concerning the 'inner nature' of matter, concerning the bearer of the orderly relations, we must recognize the fact that we shall either have to waive any claim to any answer—which would still be no reason for saying that the question has become meaningless; for questions are meaningless only if they already contain within themselves a contradiction or a lack of relation between subject and predicate—or else we shall have to weigh the possibility of placing the 'inner nature,' the 'essence' of the being of matter in analogy with the only being with which we can connect any meaning at all, namely with the becoming effective, which is grounded upon a 'will.' This appears to be pure speculation. In fact, however greatly differing *Weltanschauungen* has been able to get around the necessity—nor will any such ever be able to get around it—of taking into account a volitional element which expresses itself in actuality."[17]

The volitional element which expresses itself in actuality is in a way tantamount to Whitehead's 'decision' in each concrescence, and the latter's objection to equating creation with the act of volition is valid only if we try to impute to God, or the creative process, the psychological faculty of volition as experienced by man. What we really mean, however, is that the selective freedom of human volition, in the world of actual existence, is the symbol of the creative decision involved in the actualization of mere possibility in its transition from essence to existence. Since it lies beyond that 'border of transcendence' on the hither side of which are to be found both cause and volition, it can be identified with neither the one nor the other. Nevertheless the term volition points the direction in which our thoughts wander as we speculate upon the relation between that which lies beyond time and the temporal world including our wills to which it gives rise. God's creation, we say to ourselves, cannot be less free and self-determining than the will of man. Creation may be supra-volitional but it can scarcely be infra-volitional.

Wenzl here supplies a footnote to the effect that questions only become meaningless if they contain an inner contradiction. "Questions today are all too readily cut off by the dictum that they are meaningless. The question is meaningless whether a primary number is red but a question is not meaningless because it is empirically unanswerable." These words are a protest against that school of logical positivism which would strangle philosophical speculation by denying logical relevance to any proposition not dealing with a fact capable of empirical verification. Every true realist, who believes that the area of being is wider than that of empirical fact, will naturally support such a protest.

So much for Wenzl with his view of creation compounded of scientific theory and mystical insight. Let us now consider a second theory.

Fred Hoyle in his intriguing little volume *The Nature of the Universe* also alludes to several cosmological or cosmogenic theories including that of P. Jordan already mentioned above, and finally states his own views as follows:

> "So we see the Universe being what it is, the creation issue simply cannot be dodged. And I think that of all the various possibilities that have been suggested, continuous creation is easily the most satisfactory."[18]

He is lucid enough to leave us no doubt that he means by creation, creatio ex nihilo, for he says

> "The most obvious question to ask about continuous creation is this: Where does the created material come from? It does not come from anywhere. Material simply appears—it is created."[19]

This theory seems to offer him first of all certain aesthetic satisfaction,

"Without continuous creation, the universe must evolve toward a dead state in which all matter is condensed into a vast number of dead stars. The details of the way this happens are different in the different theories that have been put forward. But the outcome is always the same. With continuous creation, on the other hand, THE UNIVERSE has an infinite future in which all the present large scale features will be preserved."[20]

He makes his meaning quite clear. The vast galaxies will continue to vanish from our sight at astonishing speeds as the universe expands but the skies will be as full as ever of observable galaxies to take their place. The theory of continuous creation, Hoyle believes, will in the long run satisfy not alone the logical need of the astronomer, but, he avers, "I believe that much will be learned about continuous creation especially in its connection with atomic physics."

What is astonishing about such a theory, to the average layman, is that for the first time in the history of human thought, so far as I am aware, we are asked to accept a doctrine of creation not alone *out of nothing* but *by nothing*—no creator is involved as a presupposition. The author does take pains in the chapter designated "A Personal View" to expose some of the paradoxes and contradictions of materialism but he also confesses that he can find no escape from the confusion in formal religion either as church or doctrine.

The impasse which scientific theory here has reached must be rather amusing to the logician however tolerant he may have become of the inconsistencies of human thinking. Mr. Hoyle himself, it seems, seeks to soften the shock by explaining that though, according to his hypothesis, the matter created per second, spread over the whole of space, runs into those fantastic figures we are accustomed to associate with astronomical measurement, yet the average rate of appearance of matter amounts to no more than the creation of one atom, in the course of about a year, in a volume equal to that of a moderate size skyscraper. This reminds one of the young woman who was found to be pregnant when she should not have been, but who entered the plea, in extenuation, that she was only a *little* pregnant. The fact of the matter is that the seed of miracle has been implanted in the womb of being and the physical universe has once and for all lost its scientific chastity.

It is not the writer's intention to dismiss frivolously a serious and brilliant hypothesis advanced by an eminent astronomer who has been kind enough to strip his exposition of all technical elaboration for the benefit of the non-scientific reader. All that I would add from the philosopher's point of view is that if the hypothesis of continuous creation be true, it will require certain additional postulates of a metaphysical nature to make it intelligible. It should be noted that in the ancient traditional prayer book of the synagogue, God is praised as "He who renews each day continuously the works of creation."

VII—Creation Contrasted with Both Chance and Cause

The fact of creation, it would seem to me, whether we are prepared to liken it to a cosmic will or leave it uncharacterized, must involve something other than either cause or chance. As creator, strictly speaking, even God cannot legitimately be called a first cause since cause and effect are contrasting and complementary elements characteristic of a cosmic order manifesting itself in space and time. They cannot therefore be legitimately employed as ground or logical explanation for the coming into existence of that very order. In the scientific description of nature there is no specific cause which is not the effect of previous causes and no effect which does not play its part as cause in subsequent events. If God is the cause of things, He must also be the effect of previous causation and the childish question 'who made God?' becomes perfectly legitimate. Only if God is viewed, not as a fact *within* any natural history, temporal, spacial, or causal, but as logically prior and necessary to, though subsequently perhaps immanent in all, that can he be called Creator.

Those who soon grow impatient with speculative thought are here likely to interpose that the whole argument is a matter of words. It has become fashionable in modern discussion to turn one's back on the arduous task of following the subtleties of Aristotelian or Spinozistic thought, or for that matter, any close-knit argument dealing with matters of no immediate practical interest, by throwing up one's hands and in weary sophistication declaring "It is all a matter of semantics." It is self-evident that we must always judge a word or phrase in metaphysical discussion by the philosophical context in which it appears. A philosopher has the right, if exercised with discretion, of choosing his own vocabulary much as the creative artist can choose his own pigments. What meaning he wishes to convey by each particular word becomes clear only when we discover the whole pattern of thought woven by the relation of these words to one another and to the leading idea which they have been chosen to convey. There can be no objection to the science of semantics but only to those who invoke it as a magic charm to dispel the troublesome demon of metaphysical thought.

Thus many scholastics were quite aware that when they spoke of God as a *first* cause they gave the word a special and unique meaning, that God was not a cause like any other since he was creative of nature, and in nature there is no first cause. Spinoza distinguishes between contingent and necessary substance. Only God is necessary substance—all other substance is contingent. God therefore is substance in a sense inapplicable to anything else. A man can therefore say he is a Spinozist and yet take exception to the term substance (as do both Whitehead and Alexander) or he may employ the term substance and differ radically from Spinoza. My objection to speaking of the creator or creation as the cause of anything at all lies in the fact that the terms cause and causality have had an important history during the last three hundred years not in abstract thought but especially in the applied sciences. In the course of that history they have been given rather exact definition. To transfer the terms to a field of thought where they have acquired no such definiteness, no matter with what qualifications and reservations, only makes for confusion rather than for lucidity. We had better then, if only for logical reasons, hold fast to the theological term—creation.

It is true that one may claim that we here use the term creation—despite its important position in theology—not at all in the theological sense, and without reference to God, but only as a characteristic of the universe as a whole. Hoyle's theory, someone may remind us, only affirms that the universe is constantly creative, if only of hydrogen atoms, or to be more exact, that creativity is a general characteristic of the universe. If this be so, then the universe may itself reveal a divine element. There can be no objection, from the standpoint of theology, of equating the universe as a whole with God if that wholeness is made to cover more than mere existence. Whitehead does not hesitate to speak of creativity, the introduction of novelty, as the "divine element in the world." The fact of creation may not point to God—since the God-idea answers to other needs of the human spirit than merely the logical one of establishing the ground and source of actual existence—but it does inevitably point to something 'beyond causation' in which and out of which the natural history of the cosmos emerges.

One could ask finally, may not the regular and non-causal entrance of new matter into the realm of physical existence be sheer chance, may it not just happen? We have already seen that though we accept the principle "ex nihilo nihil fit" the religionist can still insist that he means, by "ex nihilo," nothing outside of God, but that through and in God, His being, His will, His word—there is that which finds actualization in matter. There is no way however in which the principle "ex nihilo nihil fit" can be reconciled with the emergence of matter by chance out of nothing.

We can only speak rationally of the chance (under certain circumstances and with reference to a definite object or event) of something or something *else* happening, of finding the definite velocity or location of the electron, of something being here or elsewhere. We cannot inquire with equal rationality as to the chances of something or nothing happening. First, for the simple reason, that 'nothing' does not happen. I cannot see how we can speculate as to an existent electron making its location definite here or *nowhere*. We can only speculate as to the chance of its being here or elsewhere or everywhere, before its possible location is actually determined. The chance of something happening where nothing is presupposed is zero. Nothing can possibly happen save through the decision of that which would disprove the void which we had previously posited. To speak then of the fundamentally unpredictable in our concept of matter and energy as being a chance phenomenon, and to say that, if the events in nature can never be fully and completely predicted in advance, then only chance governs the physical world, is again giving to the ever-recurrent zero a sort of mythological status and life of its own, such as antique thought gave to primal chaos and the void, a tendency which even high Greek thought never quite overcame.

If matter and energy and the natural history of the cosmos can be said to have a *pre-history*, if something other than chance and cause must be postulated, beyond that border of transcendence to which modern science has led us, it must be some universal ontological necessity, something in the nature of being exemplified in the existence of every event and every process and every entity no matter how minute or how gigantic and overwhelming.

VIII—Creation and the Dilemma Inherent in all Existence

If we call this creation and search for a Creator, it is because of the dilemma which we have previously touched upon, symbolized perhaps by the wave and particle function of matter. It is something which lies at the heart of all existence. That which we experience as actual, and meet within the space-time continuum, must previously have been possible else it could never have entered into existence. All existence is the actual realization of some possibility or set of possibilities. Should we say existence itself carries the possibilities whereby the actualities of tomorrow emerge from the potentialities of today, we would still be stating a deceptive half truth for the processes of today's transformation and the sequence of today and tomorrow on to infinity, or to that end where time and space and matter collapse and existence is extinguished, is precisely the matter in question. The whole and all its parts, fact and all its processes must have been possible ere they could become actual. Yet being, conceived only as infinite and eternal possibility (Santayana's Realm of Essence, or Feibleman's Universe of Essence) cannot of itself translate mere possibility into actual existence.

IX—The Total Unity of Being—God or Nature?

If being therefore embraces both the reality of the possible and the reality of the existent, the Supreme Being or the Total Unity of all Being, of which each is a phase, cannot be identified with either, but must transcend both, since it is not merely their sum but that which makes them relevant to one another—which provides the possibilities for existence as well as the existence of certain possibilities.

We might choose to call this ultimate and all inclusive reality Nature rather than Supreme Being or God. Indeed, the author of the work on *Ontology* to which I have already made reference and with which, in its main outline, I find myself in general agreement, makes this admission, "There is a sense in which this entire work consists in a plea to have included within the concept of nature not only the universe of existence with which it has always been identified but also the universe of essence and destiny (teleology)." I cannot join in such a plea. The purposes of precision, I believe, are better served when we limit nature to the entities and processes in actual existence and use the word Supreme Being or God for that whole of being which embraces all the ontological universes and transcends them all since it provides the possibility for actualization and the actualization of possibility. This latter is the ontological fact which theology calls Creation.

Since I have already leaned on Feibleman's vast work on *Ontology*, let me quote a few of the salient propositions from that book which more clearly convey some of the main ideas towards which we have been groping.

> "The primal postulate may be stated quite simply as the proposition that there is a unity of being. This means that whatever has been, is, or will be in existence, and whatever is or could be in essence, is part of a single inclusive whole. The proposition of unity is one which involves an ontological monism. The whole which includes all parts is an independent whole upon which each of the parts depends. Thus the notion of a total unity tends to acquire theological properties and is to be named God. The primal postulate might be described also as the theological postulate."[21]
>
> "In the ontological sense there is only one whole: The whole which consists in the unity of all being."[22]
>
> "God is, of course, the central problem of theology, the hypothesis of a highest being or of a total being is inescapable just as the complete knowledge of what this could mean is unattainable. The being of God is a hypothesis difficult to escape and equally hard to prove."[23]

To the writer, it seems the height of unreason not to surrender to a conclusion that is inescapable. We can hold out if we so will, but our skepticism then is as dogmatic as is the faith of the man who believes in what is demonstrably impossible.

Now, just as God the Creator cannot with any exactness be termed a first cause, so God cannot be said merely to exist without diminishing or annulling His creative function. The creature is given existence by God. God does not *merely* exist because He is the ground for both possibility and existence. If God can be spoken of as existent and actual, it is only insofar as He is immanent in all existence as all possibility is immanent in Him.

With the above qualification and without committing

109

ourselves to all the other elements involved in the Philosophy of Organism, the following propositions from *Process and Reality* might well be found congruent with the idea of God the Creator.

"The notion of God which will be discussed later is that of an actual entity immanent in the actual world but transcending any finite epoch of being, a being at once actual, eternal, immanent, and transcendent."[24]

"Transcendent decision includes God's decision. He is the actual entity in virtue of which the entire multiplicity of eternal objects obtains its graded relevance to each stage of concrescence. Apart from God, there could be no relevant novelty."[25]

If we remember the restricted sense in which we ascribe actuality to God and the wider sense in which we speak of Him as a being, and taking the eternal objects to be forms of possibility, then the above propositions approximate very nearly to the view we are seeking to develop.

X—Does Creation Predetermine or Predestine the Fate of Its Creatures?

This total unity of being, this supreme being, God the Creator—who transcends every possibility and every actuality since both have their source in and are relevant to one another through His eternal creativity, must not be thought of as predetermining the fate of any of His creatures. This is true first because time is a general characteristic of existence and comes into existence with matter and energy and the processes they initiate. There is nothing antecedent or subsequent to time save in the sense of logical necessity. When we say "In the beginning God created" we can only mean that God's non-temporal creativity is logically prior to all existence including time itself. Predeterminism is therefore a misleading term and it is fallacious in another sense as we have previously anticipated. Creation is not causal compulsion. Causality is also only a form of order among existent things in time. We cannot speak of anything as being the *effect* of God's creativity, neither earth nor sun nor man and his works from ox-cart to jet plane—they are all *instances* of His creativity, "He commanded and they were created." They spring, in other words, from the logical imperative of His being. Cause and effect are equally exemplifications of His creativity.

The total unity of being must be self-determined in a sense which we can only grasp speculatively as Spinoza sought to grasp it. No being, outside itself, can limit its freedom of self-expression. No environment can condition its scope and history for every environment as every history exercises its function within God while God has no history. History begins on the hither side of creation. This uniquely singular being is therefore self-determined and spontaneous, and every concrete instance of its creativity inherits a fragment or phase of that freedom which, it is true, is limited and determined, but only by the freedom inherent in all others as they enter into relations with the first. Every being within certain limits is self-determined and individual. It is not wholly the plaything of outside forces but is active and resistant as well as yielding. So far as we know, man is unique only in being *conscious* of himself as a free individual, of exercising his volition in the choice of possible alternatives. In consequence, he imputes to himself moral responsibility and his acts assume a moral significance characteristic of human behavior. His freedom differs from that of all other creatures, in inner awareness as well as in range and scope since he is served by reason and imagination, by memory and hope that can range through the centuries and outrun the millennia. That does not mean that he is totally free as God is free. He too is within limits determinate. He too, as an entity within the physical universe, is both predictable and yet unpredictable. The glory and tragedy of human life consists in the fact that, paradoxical as it may seem, man is *compelled* to be free, choosing always between good and evil, between truth and error. To that extent he is under compulsion, the compulsion of his humanity, of being the *kind* of creature known as man. Insofar however as he can choose, he is a free personality reflecting God's image.

We conclude with the following propositions which summarize our findings:

A—The creative fiat in each instance brings into existence certain possibilities, and a particular kind of thing or event or process exemplifying these possibilities.

B—The particular *kind* of thing however is also and always *a particular thing of its kind*. Otherwise, the defining possibilities, or essences, or universals would still be arid possibilities and have no existence at all.

C—In its particularity, in its unrelieved concreteness, an entity or event is never wholly predictable, yet its spontaneity, its self-determination, its chance character, as the mathematicians put it, is always modified and limited by the *kind* of *thing* it is.

D—The predictable and unpredictable elements in experience are twin phenomena found everywhere in the world of actual existence.

E—They present a hopeless paradox only if we try to make one or the other ultimate and final, or when we seek to derive one from the other. Their origin is not in existence, but in that Unity of all Being which theologians call God but which includes all existence and all possibilities for existence, and transcends them both since it is by His transcendent decision that certain possibilities are made actual and certain actualities are made possible.

---

1. Cf. supra p. 7.
2. Joseph Ratner, *The Philosophy of Spinoza* (New York: Random House, 1927), p. xlix.
3. *Ibid.*, pp. xxxix-xi.
4. For confirmation of this statement, see the article by F. S. C. Northrop in *Science*, April 23, 1948, entitled "The Neurologic and Behavioristic Basis of the Ordering of Society by Means of Ideas."
5. James K. Feibleman, *Ontology* (Baltimore: John Hopkins Press, 1951), pp. 302-303.
6. *Iyyun*, a Hebrew philosophical quarterly, Philosophical Society, the Hebrew University, Vol. IV, January 1953.
7. The view of the present writer is, that if God were only the perfect observer knowing in one instance the location and velocity of every item in the universe and cognizant of all causal laws, he could still not predict with absolute certainty

now what would occur in the next instant. It is as the *eternal* and non-temporal creator, not as the perfect but temporal observer, that God is omniscient.

8. cf. p. 127.
9. H. Margenau (Sloane Physics Laboratory, Yale University), "Einstein's Conception of Reality" *Albert Einstein—Philosopher-Scientist* (Evanston, Illinois: Library of Living Philosophers, Inc., 1949), p. 250.
10. Walter Heitler (Dublin Institute of Advanced Studies) "The Departure from Classical Thought in Modern Physics" *Albert Einstein—Philosopher-Scientist* Evanston, Illinois: Library of Living Philosophers, Inc., 1949), p. 193.
11. *Ibid.*, pp. 193-194.
12. Max Born (Department of Mathematical Physics, University of Edinburgh) "Einstein's Statistical Theories" *Albert Einstein—Philosopher-Scientist* (Evanston, Illinois: Library of Living Philosophers, Inc., 1949), p. 176.
13. Aloys Wenzl (Philosophical Faculty, University of Munich) "Einstein's Theory of Relativity Viewed from the Standpoint of Critical Realism, and Its Significance for Philosophy" *Albert Einstein—Philosopher-Scientist* (Evanston, Illinois: Library of Living Philosophers, Inc., 1949), p. 600.
14. *Ibid.*, p. 605.
15. *Ibid.*, pp. 596-597.
16. *Ibid.*, p. 597.
17. *Ibid.*, p. 604.
18. Fred Hoyle, *The Nature of the Universe* (New York: Harper & Bros., 1950), p. 125.
19. *Ibid.*, p. 123.
20. *Ibid.*, pp. 131-132.
21. James K. Feibleman, *Ontology* (Baltimore: The John Hopkins Press, 1951), p. 190.
22. *Ibid.*, p. 195.
23. *Ibid.*, p. 507.
24. Alfred North Whitehead, *Process and Reality* (New York: Macmillan Co., 1930), p. 143.
25. *Ibid.*, p. 248.

CHAPTER FOUR

IS THERE A MORAL WORLD ORDER?

The General Problem

The problems constituting a philosophy of ethics arise largely through the fact that the material under discussion stems originally from two different sources. The idea of the unity of God and the unity and destiny of man is largely a contribution of Judaism to the civilization of the West. The idea of the unity of nature is on the whole a Greek contribution. There is no word for nature as such in the Bible. All things, even according to the Bible, have some relation to one another since they are all created by God. They are in their collective oneness called 'Olam' or 'Hakol' but these are not the equivalent of what later Jewish rationalism, influenced by Greek philosophy, has called 'Teba.'

By the *unity* of nature we mean that within the world of existence separate events and phenomena are all related to one another by some inner necessity so that the spontaneity and individuality inherent in each is limited and conditioned by the field created by them all. This is the field of natural law, the physical universe as science knows it, which was first systematically studied by the Greeks. Archimedes, Galileo, Darwin, and Einstein are all investigators of that field. From our point of view, God himself cannot break the chain of necessary interaction between things in time, a necessity which He himself establishes, without destroying the whole universe.

The question, therefore, of a moral world order is the question whether the physical universe tends in any way to conserve the values of the moral life and the distinction between good and evil characteristic of that life. Is there anything in nature which shows a preference for the good and to what extent if so, and in what manner.

This involves the whole question of reward and punishment, and we shall have to investigate the theories of divine justice in the world as outlined in the ethical tradition of Judaism and try to determine how far in the realm of actual experience these ethical demands are substantiated. If they are not fully substantiated, a position already voiced in Job and in Ecclesiastes, how far can reason justify some concept of immortality to compensate for the imperfections of the temporal order in which man is born, lives, and perishes?

But all this is subordinate to a larger problem arising out of our faith in God. There is that in the universe of our experience which the moral judgment of man designates as evil. Suffering and sin have their place in life and any denial of their reality is only an attempt to escape from the problem they present. Whether nature does or does not show a preference for the good, the theologian faces the question, why should there be evil at all in a world presumably created by perfect goodness, or does the reality of evil disprove the postulate of ethical monotheism that God is just and merciful as well as omnipotent.

We are now at the heart of the theological dilemma. We can either posit a principle of evil and assert that the world is partly divine and partly demonic, or we shall have to examine the fact of the involvement of God in the evil of the world and His responsibility for its sin and suffering. It resolves itself into the question, could an omnipotent being have created an actual world of moral values without providing for the contingencies of pain and evil?

Nature the Only Possible Scene of the Moral Life

We have set ourselves the question "Is there anything in nature which shows a preference for the good and to what extent and in what manner?" One thing is obvious, the physical universe, the cosmos, is the scene of man's moral life. Whatever views on immortality, on heaven and hell and the World to Come man may entertain, from the most naive to the most sophisticated, it was always taken for granted that only man's life upon earth offers him the opportunity of demonstrating his righteousness or his wickedness. Only this world is the world of moral opportunity. The World to Come, whatever be its nature, is regarded only as the world of compensation (Olam Hagemul). It is only in the natural world where a man by virtue of his nature must eat and drink, propagate his kind, suffer and rejoice, live and die, that the moral life has actual existence. We may call nature, among other things, the theater in which the impressive drama, sometimes heroic sometimes sordid, of the struggle between good and evil takes place. Considering all we know of the unimagined extent of the physical universe, of the innumerable forces that govern it and of the multitudinous creatures that inhabit it, can we with any claim to exactitude speak as though man and his problem occupy the center of the stage? I think we can, for more reasons than one.

Man—The Center of Significance

The transition from the Ptolemaic to the Copernican astronomy is often supposed to have robbed man of his privileged position. In antique thought, the earth was supposed to be central to a series of spheres that encompassed it. Man, therefore, could picture himself spacially central to all the majestic structure of the heavenly spheres and therefore feel, with some semblance of truth, that the house had been built for his occupancy.

Our present view of the cosmos, with its innumerable galaxies of various size and composition, of stars newly born and stars dying, of cosmic eras in which there was no life at all, of distances measured by light years, of immensities in which our globe is but a mote of dust, satellite to a star than which there are more majestic luminaries—this cosmic picture should make man humble, we are told, and extort from him at last a recantation of his ancient boast "For my sake was the world created."

All this, it seems to me, is due to a pardonable confusion because, though man may not occupy the physical center of the cosmic stage, wherever the mind of man faces the universe, *he is its center of significance—the spot where fact flowers into meaning.* It will help us to understand this picture if we remember that in the eyes of the audience the center of the stage, even theatrically speaking, is not always its physical center but wherever the spotlight is made to illumine the scene.

For the cow or the worm, there is no terrifying glory in the vast expanses of space. If the heavens declare the glory of God or only the glory of the astronomical mathematician, they declare it to some other mind. It is man who can feel humble because the lines that measure space radiate from his mind. The astonishing fact which modern science calls to our attention of the fast disintegrating galaxies can fill only the human spirit with the terrors of the transitory. Whatever new meaning the Copernican or Einsteinian revolution may have entailed, that meaning was discovered by the mind of man and has its repercussions, philosophical and religious, in the thought and life of man. Nature therefore remains what it always was, the scene in which man is launched upon the pursuit of truth and value and goodness.

If there are other minds equal or superior to that of man in remote regions of the physical universe, I would not hesitate to say that wherever such a mind exists there emerges a center of significance which illumines with its light, however feeble that may be, the whole cosmic scene, and which the vast unknown, the unsolved mysteries of existence, will lure to new explorations of nature and impel to new decisions. However puny may be man's penetration of the puzzle of nature, the mystery of the unknown is itself a tribute which the mind of man levies upon the cosmos for the delights and terrors of the mysterious are not in the physical universe, except as they dwell in the mind and imagination of man.

Nature as Process—The Emerging Human Spirit

Nature however is not only or chiefly a static fact, it

is primarily a process. The cosmos has a history and many histories. The history of man is a phase and chapter of this process. It is a process, we shall see, with definite and irreversible direction.

One of the great differences between modern and classical thought is that we no longer view the dominant movements of nature as mere flux or cyclical rhythm, like the coming of day and night, the passing of seasons, the courses of the stars, the succession of life and death and life again.

On the contrary, the history of nature turns out to be a history that never repeats itself. The sun with all that is beneath it and above it can never be what it was yesterday because of the history that lies behind it. Nothing is merely a diffuse movement, every infinitesimal atom in the remotest reaches of space has its reverberations everywhere so that you and I are what we are at the moment, in part at least, because some frog has croaked or some butterfly has lifted its wings.

In space-time, nothing ever returns upon its tracks. Though summer and winter may return through long, uninterrupted series, and life and death and pleasure and pain repeat themselves with bewildering variety, the summers of today are different because of all of the summers that have gone before, and the pleasures and pains of today are in part determined by the pleasures and pains suffered in the yesterdays that have gone forever.

That this process, from the dead chemistry and physics of the stars to the life and instincts of the flesh, to the mind and spirit of man, goes on to its enrichment, seems self-evident. In the vast realms of space, probed by the astronomer and his telescope, there is much matter and radiant energy that is without life, but there is no living animal whose life is not conditioned by the inorganic substance of star dust and earth dust, by the radiant energy of light and heat that comes from remote space, by the laws of gravitation, by the electric and magnetic fields manifest in the dynamo and the currents coursing through our nervous system. Life always possesses the universe of dead matter as its cosmic environment and its structural scaffolding, whereas not all inorganic matter by any means possesses life. Living tissue is richer than inorganic tissue by this inclusiveness.

So, also, there is much life that is bare of mind and spirit, but there is no mind and spirit that is not also in possession of life and conditioned by its laws and reactions. Mind is living tissue so organized that it becomes the channel through which the human spirit emerges, and life is inorganic matter so organized that it becomes organic tissue, sensitive finally to pleasure and pain. In this very real and descriptive sense, *minded being* is qualitatively richer and more inclusive than are the lower levels of existence.

In the last sentence, we have betrayed ourselves, for though nature shows a direction from dead matter through life to mind, and though it may on each succeeding level be richer in the variety of the cosmic forces and qualities that enter into it, have we any right to speak of the life of the spirit as being *higher* than that of the amoeba or the atom? Does not this represent a human prejudice, an evaluation rather than a scientific description? The answer, as we have already pointed out in our definition of the spiritual life, is yes, for the nature of mind in the human being is precisely this, that it is not merely the instrument of feeling, of will, of knowledge, but of evaluation. It is that element of nature which will not accept nature on its own terms. It is the curious paradox that asks not only what are the laws of nature and society *by* which it may continue to live, but what is there *for* which it may live. The mind of man seeks not merely means, but goals, and in seeking these goals it looks not backward, but forward. The whole travail of nature becomes worthwhile because man finds in the spirit certain things worth living and dying for. All these values which emerge in the spiritual life of man have a natural history. They would never have presented themselves to man's hope or imagination if they had not had value for life. But in the last analysis, it is only they that to the civilized man give value *to* life. It is in this sense that the descriptive terms, higher and lower, become terms of evaluation. The goals of life lie ahead and not behind, and the region wherein nature brings them to self-consciousness is the highest level of human experience.

As is the case with reason, so it is with values. Only a faith in reason justifies us in calling things true and false, and only a faith in the objectivity of value justifies us in calling some experiences higher than others.

If there is some objectivity in the value judgments of the human spirit, then the cosmic process shows not merely direction and progressive enrichment, but may be said to display in the human perspective, *purposiveness,* an enrichment not merely in form, but in value.

That ideas such as the above are not only advanced by philosophers and theologians but by biologists as well, is borne out by a series of quotations from an article by Edmund W. Sinnott, Director of the Graduate School at Yale University, and entitled "Cell and Psyche."[1]

> "The life sciences are in a strategic middle position, and if we can relate them with the lifeless universe below and the universe of man and the human spirit above, we shall have accomplished a major task. Biology is at the crossroad between the physical sciences and the humanities and social sciences, between matter and man. Our major problems all ultimately center in this remarkable living stuff that we call protoplasm. . . . ."
>
> "Vital activities seem to be goal-directed, or as a philosopher would say, teleological. It looks as if a living thing knew where it was going in its development. . . . ."
>
> "The thesis I am proposing is this: that biological organization (concerned with developmental and physiological activity) and psychical activity (concerned with behavior and thus leading ultimately to mind) *are fundamentally the same thing.* This may be looked at from without, objectively, by a biologist in the laboratory as a fact in his science, or it may be looked at from within, subjectively, as a direct experience of desire or purpose. . . . ."
>
> "Just as the form of the body is thus immanent in the egg from which it grows, so, I think, a purpose

or psychological goal yet to be realized may be said to be immanent in the cells of the brain. ......"

"Thus all the conscious life of man, full of ideas, aspirations, intellectual subtleties, and emotions is simply the manifestation of an organized, biological system raised to its very highest level. The regulatory action of protoplasm in growth and physiology merges imperceptibly into instinct, and out of this emerges the complex mental activity of the higher animals and finally the rich life of the mind and spirit of man. There is no break anywhere. The basic problem is the regulatory activity of living stuff, shown in all types of biological organizations. ...."

"Many say that science has no concern with values, but that is a mistake. Values, in the last analysis, are indications of the direction of protoplasmic goals. Protoplasm has its preferences. It is moving toward something. You have all heard of the second law of thermodynamics, which states that lifeless matter is always going toward greater and greater randomness, greater disorganization. It is a curious fact, though living things do not violate the second law, the whole history of evolution and embryonic development shows that life is moving toward greater and greater organization. It is as though there were two tendencies in the universe, one going down and one going up. Values show the direction in which this remarkable material of which we are built tends to move. Protoplasm has its own natural history and so does the human spirit. ...."

The Moral Life as a Factor Making for Happiness and Survival

Though protoplasm may have its 'preference' as Dr. Sinnott seems to believe, and though the history of life may seem to be moving toward the progressive emergence of spiritual values including those of the moral life, the question still remains, can matter itself, the cosmic process as such, satisfy the demands made upon it by that ethical conscience which it itself has brought into being?

It is obvious to every compassionate heart that there is a burden of suffering placed upon all creatures of flesh and blood that bears no direct relation to moral innocence or guilt. If nature can be said to display a moral world order in any sense which the conscience of man can recognize, it must demonstrate that there is some necessary relation in the natural order between well-being and well-doing. Evil must be shown to be *actually*, not only logically or ideally, detrimental to the life and happiness of those who perpertrate it, and it must be demonstrated that righteousness does help to foster and enhance the life of those who practice it.

We have observed that the universe of actual existence, the realm of space and time and energy and matter, is the cosmic stage on which man must play his part and enact the drama of his moral life. It is also, however, the creative processes in the course of which man's ethical value and purposes make their appearance. All these are phases of a natural history, geological, anthropological, and cultural. These various phenomena are rooted in natural necessity—even man's moral freedom is a necessity of his being as man. His loyalties toward God and the kingdom of God, man's highest faith in infinite goodness, though they point to something that is supra natural (which includes and transcends nature, not something which is supernatural and therefore other than natural) are all bound up with man's organic being and spring from his relations with his fellow creatures and with the environment in which he lives and perishes.

Now, if we regard the moral life of man as not supernaturally imposed, or just because we do not picture it as so imposed but developed in the course of life's evolution and recorded in human experience, it must at the very least have survival values in the factual sense. We do not for one moment doubt that the webbed foot of the duck, the claw of the eagle, the fleetness of the antelope, the soft pad of the jungle cat, the sting of the bee, or the instincts which hold them together as they breed or hunt in lair or pack or swarm or herd, are all instruments by which these creatures maintain themselves in the struggle for life. These multifarious variations and mutations could scarcely have perpetuated themselves save as they proved useful to the creature so endowed. The biological processes which gave the creatures birth showered upon them the peculiar gifts which define their being and enable them to cope with their environment both organic and inorganic.

We have no reason to believe that man could ever have survived in the struggle with the jungle save as the convolutions of his brain and his articulated exploring hands, his inventive reason and his sense of obligation, all of which enter into his moral life as we have observed, have made him a force which could pit itself against the oft encountered terrors of cosmic catastrophe and the hostile societies of bird and beast and insect. He could never have lived long enough upon earth to develop reason and conscience and spirituality except that in the long run, societies which are bound to one another through reason, love and duty, whose constituent individuals were capable of choosing The *Good* from the possible *goods* that offered themselves, proved tougher than the instinctive compulsive grouping of swarm and flock and pack and herd.

Hence though we reject the dogmatic optimism which asserts there is no human suffering without sin and that prosperity and honor and length of days inevitably attend the righteous—a view which we shall see already outgrown in biblical times—we may still believe that not only Scripture but Nature cries out to man 'I have set before thee life and good and death and evil,' 'therefore choose life that thou mayest live, thou and thy seed.' It may be a wisdom born out of the accumulated experience of the ages which defines itself as follows: "To fear the Lord, that is wisdom, and to depart from evil, that is understanding." Such wisdom, in poetic personification, speaks with realistic accents of empirical truth when it is made to say

> "Happy is the man that hearkeneth to Me
> Watching daily at my gates
> Waiting at the posts of my door.
> For whosoever findeth Me findeth life and
>   obtaineth favor of the Lord

But he that misseth Me does violence to himself
All they that hate Me love death." (Proverbs 8:34-36)

How in fact shall we estimate the value of forces working for good or ill with reference to any particular entity in a definite situation? It is absurd to say that if we plant a tree in a certain type of soil it will inevitably flourish and bear fruit, and if we plant it in a soil of different chemical composition it will undoubtedly grow up stunted and barren. There is no scientific value whatever in such a statement and no true scientist would ever venture it without definite reservations. You may plant a palm tree in the most fertile of soils but if you plant it at the North Pole instead of Palm Springs it may still be doomed to death. What we really mean in a statement such as the above is that temperature, light, and moisture remaining the same, the soil that we have analyzed will further the development and fruitage of the tree whereas a soil less rich will weaken and blight it. The good soil, in other words, is a factor in the tree's future and destiny. It may often be an important factor, sometimes even a decisive one. We might think of innumerable other examples in the fields of chemistry, physics, or medicine. The general state of any natural entity cannot be traced to any one of the forces playing upon it at the moment, but is the result of its complete reaction to the total environment in which it finds itself. The same criterion must be applied in evaluating morality and the moral will as factors contributing to human life and happiness. The truth may well be that self control and moral aspiration—character in its honorific sense—are among the beneficent forces providing life with its ultimate goal and making life more secure and rewarding to those who pursue that goal and to the society which they exemplify. The very emergence of the human spirit within the history of human life seems to force us to such acknowledgement.

Nevertheless, if we would not deceive ourselves, we dare not evade the necessary logical reservations. All that our thesis implies is that given two individuals starting out with similar physical and intellectual capacity and played upon by the same natural forces, the one who can control his appetite and desires stands a better chance for happiness and survival than he who dissipates them in profligate living. Our thesis does not affirm that if one is attacked by a typhoid germ which the other escapes, the one so attacked will necessarily escape the disease because he is numbered with the righteous. Nevertheless, we would feel justified in asserting that whatever perils may confront them both from without, the man who has led a well regulated life of self discipline rather than lust and dissipation has a better chance to fight the battle through.

Consider for a moment the social rather than the personal virtues. It may not follow that a man who has lived a life of integrity and has given love and kindliness to wife and child and fellow man will never experience sorrow or suffer the perils of fire, storm, or earthquake, or even will always bask in the love and deference which is his due. What can be truthfully maintained however, is that where a kindly destiny saves both from natural mishap and sudden death, the man who practices the social virtues has a better chance for life and happiness, of reaping love and tenderness because he has sown them, than the ruthless and insensitive whose reward may, at worse, be the hostility and punitive justice of men and, at best, the searing ice of their indifference and hate. Thus the good is always the ally of all the forces that make for life and hope, and evil the ally of all the forces that make for bereavement and death. They remain factors in human destiny, and often one or the other becomes the decisive factor.

The Moral Factor in Organized Society

As it is with individuals, so likewise with organized societies. In a society pervaded by the spirit of righteousness and justice, every individual has a better opportunity for life and happiness than in one dominated by cruelty and greed, and therefore every contribution made by the individual to establish freedom and justice is a possible contribution to his own happiness and that of the posterity with which his happiness is intertwined. Such contributions may entail many sacrifices, sometimes the supreme sacrifice of life itself, which the saints and martyrs and the banner-bearers of freedom in every age attest. But the sacrifice will be made with the consciousness that life, security, and well-being will increasingly become the lot of man through his death as through his life. The martyr, we should always remember, never embraces death because he is weary of life but because he loves it so fervently that every sacrifice becomes worthwhile which will enance its value in time and in eternity.

It is a surmise not too far fetched but on the contrary borne out by the general course of historical development, that societies most sensitive to the demands of justice and love, in which the individual is most free to seek and to express the truth that is in him and thus find self-fulfillment and realization—that such societies are likely to be tougher and more enduring than societies incapable of rising to these moral levels. We are not unaware that barbarous hordes have from time to time trampled over weaker and more defenseless people in which some promise of high civilization may have been germinating, or that older and prouder civilizations graced with culture and containing great monuments of art and literature have been trampled under foot now and then by vandal hordes seeking mere spoils. In the advance of civilization, no uniform rate of progress seems to be discernible on the vast field of historic change and transformation. There are always human areas that remain backward through long periods and that suddenly lead the march of progress and reveal that in their backwardness genius lay nascent, awaiting some turn of events to evoke its revelation. The Arab tribes before Mohammed are a case in point. Perhaps the modern Orient, India and China, will within the not too remote future outdistance the West in social and cultural achievement. No one can tell what potentialities lie beneath these rebellious stirrings against Western domination.

There are also evident, as we follow the course of history, tragic lapses from freedom and right where we thought progress was assured and only awaiting further fruition. In such lapses the innocent and vulnerable may suffer untold agonies. We moderns who have lived through two world wars fought in vindictive heat, and one with an icy frigidity which may at any time defrost, do not have to learn such things from books.

Yet when human life is viewed in proper perspective and we realize that the whole of recorded history is but a fertile loam resting upon depths of time unscanned, when instead of lamenting the distance man must still travel to his true humanization we look in awed wonder to how far he has come from the protoplasmic slime of life's beginning, we are not unjustified in our optimism. After all, the history of man and his culture is a phase of cosmic history. It too displays not only varying form but also definite direction. The bound societies governed by habit and taboo tend to be superseded by societies governed by decree and legislation defining status and right and obligation. All such social organization already displays intent and purpose. Law defines not what one does but what one is expected to do by the powers recognized as governing. In much later eras, the trend seems to have developed from societies defining right and authority as inherent in king (the king can do no wrong) or priest or oligarchy, aristocratic or industrial, toward a conception of right and duty which is the equal endowment and obligation of all. The governing officials become the guardians of such right. They are expected to defend them for all and to enforce the obligations owed by each to all. All this laborious and complex process means the increased moralization of society. In modern democracy, rare though it be in its pure form, power is said to be derived from the free will and conscience of the people. It clothes with authority only the expressed will of the majority and, what is more important, it imposes upon the majority the obligation to safeguard the individual and the minority group in its right of free dissent. On grounds such as these it makes its demand on the loyalty of all its citizens.

There is no perfect government and there is no society so morally perfect that it can establish one. We have already disavowed moral perfection for man in discussing the relation of Messianic vision to actual history. Nevertheless, the history of civilization justifies the hope that organized societies such as we have described will outlive and replace societies which prove themselves incapable of making the moral adjustments. Societies not held together by a sense of mutual obligation, voluntarily assumed, not devoted through government to fostering love and justice and equal opportunity for all, but whose strength rests on some form of authoritarian unreason or on dictatorial tyranny, political or economic, will in the end undergo either revolt and transformation or collapse and disintegration. *No institutional dams can forever, anywhere, stay the onward sweep of the human spirit.* They can only obstruct it till the waters rise high enough, for history, though not immediately responsive to our moral indignation, is not altogether indifferent to moral values, nor merely neutral in the struggle between good and evil.

Between Doom and Salvation—The Present Crisis

That the future of mankind will depend not so much on its mastery of the forces governing the physical universe as upon the spiritual forces shaping human conduct is forcing itself more and more upon the attention of thoughtful men, whether scientists or philosophers. We have ruthlessly ravaged the earth in search of power. We have tapped in turn the storehouses of water, iron, coal, and gas. It is a truism that, as far as our globe is concerned, we have eliminated distance. All the old devices of fairy tale and fable, the Flying Carpet, the Seven League Boots, Kefitzat Haderek, are quite outmoded. As our fliers crash through the sonic barrier they outrun even the threatening thunderbolts of the ancient gods.

We are now on the verge of blazing, through stellar space, new trails of human exploration. When I was a boy, to "reach for the moon" was a metaphor for wishful thinking, for aspiring to the impossible. Today even with sober scientists it is only a question of how long till we actually reach it. More important than all, we have unleashed the fearful violence that sleeps at the heart of the infinitesimal with the hope that we may rain death on the enemy. We may deny God and therefore give no credence to those who claim to be His chosen prophets, and yet nature and history now cry out to humanity which, with bated breath, is awaiting its fate "I call heaven and earth to witness against thee this day that I have set before thee life and death, the blessing and the curse. Therefore choose life that thou mayest live, thou and thy seed."

No suspended Damocles sword ever struck such terror to the heart of any man as the bombs which now remain suspended, by gossamer threads of fear and love, over the human race. Their fall will not only kill, but may poison the air, corrupt the earth, and pervert the very seed of life in man and beast. It can not only destroy the monuments of civilization but also possibly make uninhabitable the globe which man thought it was his destiny to 'populate and subdue.'

Little chance will remain for man's real conquest of earth and sky already looming on the horizon of scientific possibility unless the conscience of man shall make the right decision, unless the pursuit of peace and the sacrifices peace entails shall banish war forever, unless the nations permit themselves to become units in a society in which only the united will of all mankind shall be sovereign, unless a united mankind shall face together the challenge of nature's mysteries and learn to employ these strange forces, full of promise and of menace, to serve the human spirit.

Every step in this direction is a step towards the salvation of man in his cosmic environment. Every delay may spell misery as yet unimagined or, perhaps, ultimate extinction. Nature was never less indifferent to man's moral decision than at the present moment.

Let me warn, however, that we must not take for granted that physical existence has undergone a moral transformation and is about to administer that exact justice which the human heart demands of God. Nature tends to preserve the species and through the species the individual by every favorable variation, be that variation a wing wherewith to fly or vision wherewith to aspire. There may be many among the unworthy who may survive should we escape the doom depicted, and many innocent and saintly may perish among the guilty should mankind as a whole make the wrong decision. Then again it is theoretically possible that there may occur some stellar catastrophe, of which we at present have no inkling whatsoever, which may put an end to the drama of human life completely before the expected last act can be played, and before man has time to brace himself for the awaited climax. Nevertheless, whatever may be the balance of forces beyond the reach of man's moral will, those within his reach may well prove the decisive factors in his doom or his salvation.

God and the Reality of Evil

Yet if we forego belief in a miraculous special providence that naturally brings inevitable recompense for every deed, good or evil, and if we accept the rather grim and halting role, however important, which nature plays in sustaining and encouraging the moral development of man, we cannot, as theologians, halt our inquiries at this point, or, in the light of our moral insight, be content with nature's imperfections. A deeper problem rooted in faith itself now challenges us. Whatever may be the course of God in nature, the *nature of such a god,* who permits this evident gap between the actual world of his creation and that ideal and eternal realm in which he functions as the source of all possible goodness, of all as yet unrevealed values, of all love and justice and holiness, of all things not only as they actually are but as they all ought to be—is the question at hand.

Evasive Solutions

The greatest sin one can commit against both logic and morality is to seek to distort the reality of actual evil into some form of unreality, to say for instance that it must be unreal because it is only the negative of the good.

The physical forces and calculations by which the saboteur blows up a bridge are no less real than the forces and calculations that went into its construction. Construction may be called real and positive, destruction no less real though it be negative. So it is with the everlasting conflict between good and evil. The good deed and the evil deed, kindness and cruelty, love and hate, justice and injustice, are equally real factors in shaping human life and destiny even though evil may be defined as seeking a satisfaction which negates and rejects the good.

There is also the inclination to bypass the reality of evil by applying to it another name, as though when we call it by a word less harsh we exorcise its horror. So by many individuals evil is always spoken of as error. It is classed among life's miscalculations. Now, an error requires only correction whereas sin calls for repentance and atonement. It is never a mere miscalculation of the mind, despite the familiar Socratic dictum; it is also and always a misdirection of the will. The correction of the error in the bill I received is one thing, but my will to pay it, or to abscond with my possessions, is quite another. Mere error cannot so easily be equated with guilt. Dr. Robert Oppenheimer, who is not, I believe, in any formal sense religious, speaking of the atomic scientists shortly after the second World War is reputed to have said "We go about with a sense of guilt and do not know how to redeem ourselves." These terms are borrowed from the theological thought that differentiates sin from error. It may be true that sin is also a kind of error, but mere error is by no means equivalent to sin.

Even the evil of pain and suffering is sometimes ascribed to an aberration of the human mind and hence something that can be relegated to the domain of mere appearance and denied actual existence. Should it be true that to suffer from a burn is only to think we suffer from a burn, the pain involved is equal in either case, and the reality of that pain is precisely the evil in question. We may have recourse to therapy either psychiatric or physical to overcome the pain. We may even find good reason justifying the existence of evil, but even the best of reasons will not make evil good.

If you suck the reality from evil, what is left of the reality of the good save an empty shell. An act of mercy which relieves no suffering and can ameliorate only *seeming* sorrow is itself only seemingly good, for actual it becomes good for nothing. It is not a question here, whether pain is subjective or objective, whether when suffering from a toothache a man shall locate the pain in his tooth or in his consciousness.

(Personally, I should say that the pain is in my tooth, and both the tooth and its pain are mine. If the tooth is extracted, neither the tooth nor the pain are any longer mine and I suffer neither. If the nerve is anesthetized, I would say the ache is no longer in the tooth and therefore I do not suffer it. But when, for any reason, I have a toothache, the pain which I suffer is in my tooth and I or my consciousness or myself are painfully aware of it. Consciousness is the state of awareness, not the locale of that which I am aware. If I had no awareness I could not discuss the locale of any pleasure or pain or whether or not it were real. I am self-conscious, that is, aware of myself as the percipient, and of the object of which I am the percipient. The object is never merely in my mind. So I am aware of myself as the sufferer, and of the pain which I suffer, but the locale of the pain is not in my mind but somewhere in my aching flesh.)

The truth that there is suffering which cannot be attributed to human sin must be extended beyond man. There is suffering even on the part of creatures to whom no guilt can possibly be imputed. The innocent beast caught in a forest fire also calls to Him "Who heedeth to young ravens when they cry." The children whose flesh was seared by the atom bomb which fell on Nagasaki and Hiroshima, who were not old enough to utter a battle cry in any language or capable of reacting, for good or evil, to the legacy of ancestral guilt uncovered at Pearl Harbor—their pain was also real.

The Necessary Basis for Moral Values

You remember, we had previously hinted as to what is at the root of the whole problem of moral evil. It is expressed in the simple question, why did not God, who can do everything, make all men good? Let us see if we cannot approach the solution of this puzzle by submitting the question itself to critical analysis. Unless we define what we mean by 'goodness' and what we mean by 'goodness in the making,' we shall never see the light. Let me put it this way: What goodness can a man have who has been *made* good? Would there be any virtue in a goodness which is the result of unyielding necessity? We know very well why we admire the good men or women among our friends. They are people who, we believe, have through their own free choice preferred kindness where their own interests might have suggested cruelty. They are people who, we believe, having the same passions of lust and hate that sometimes move us, and having faced the alternatives of good and evil, have chosen the way of love and mercy rather than that of lust and greed. We admire the good man just because, though free to do evil, he has chosen the path of righteousness. Only virtue rooted in freedom can have any essential merit—can be really good. Our first answer, therefore, is that God has not made man good because He has chosen to make him free, and thus insure the reality of his goodness. "All is in the hands of God save the fear of God," reads an old Talmudic maxim. If God wills righteousness on earth He must needs have endowed man with that freedom by means of which his significant acts bear the imprint of man's own volition.

We cannot extricate ourselves from this dilemma. Rabbi Akiba, one of the greatest theologians of his period, long ago stated the Jewish position in the words "Though all is foreseen, yet is freedom granted man. Though the world is judged by Divine Grace, yet all is in accordance with the deed." There is likewise an ancient legend—or cycle of legends—which points to the same spiritual situation. The legend tells us that when God wished to reveal the Torah to Israel, and to send it from the celestial realms to the lower sphere of earth, the angels in heaven protested against this act of degradation. They pointed out that if flesh and blood were to receive the Law, it would only be defiled by man's sin. God, however, turned to his ministering angels and asked them if they ever faced the temptation to steal or commit adultery or kill, and, armored by their perfect purity they indignantly denied that they could be guilty of any such act. Then God said, "The moral law is not meant for such as you who cannot sin. It is the prerogative of man who is tempted by sin but who, through the power of his will, may overcome temptation and choose the good." In many a phrase of the Midrashic literature it is hinted that God gave man a status above the angels by virtue of the fact that celestial beings are bound to fulfill the destiny for which they were created, while man has the tragic prerogative to defy God and to sin. God's own satisfaction with His world when He declared that it was "very good" is based, according to several Midrashic interpretations, on the fact that the world included the temptation to evil (the Yezer Hara), the imminence of suffering and the inevitability of death.[2] We can only understand this to mean that the world is supremely good because it permitted the emergence of righteousness and heroism and self-sacrifice.

The scientific world picture confirms the spirit of these high insights. All physical entities conform to certain patterns of conduct and behavior; these are the laws of nature which govern them. Though we are not so sure, as once we were, that a certain element of indeterminism does not even here preclude us from predicting exactly what they will do, nevertheless there is no sign that they are torn by inner conflicts of passion arrayed against reason and conscience. The beasts on the level below man are governed by their instincts to live and mate and produce their kind. When hungry, they seize their prey; when desire moves them, they seek their mate; when the time is ripe, they produce their kind—they are on another level of being. They are blessed with an essential innocence as are the angels of our legend, and therefore, they prove themselves not man but beast. It is only man who can sin, and the power to sin is the source of his righteousness. It is because all conduct for which he admits moral responsibility is a choice between alternatives, that the wrong he does is sin, and the heights he attains is saintliness.

Let us put the question then once more, why does not God make all men good? Because God chose to make them free that they might become really good. Had He not willed them to be free, to choose between good and evil, nothing that they could achieve would have the quality of moral goodness. But "He is not all-powerful," we say, "if He cannot work this miracle, if He cannot reconcile these contradictions." It is a mistake, however, to think that even the Omnipotent can fulfil a meaningless demand. For God all things may be possible, such things, too, as are forever impossible for us, but even God cannot give a logical answer to an absurd question. Let us have recourse to a classical example. The world of space is full of triangles and of squares. We can all define them and even sketch them though we may never have studied Euclid. Suppose we say that the triangles are spatial forms that have three sides and angles and the squares four sides and angles. Now, if God is infinitely greater than we are, why cannot He make triangles that have four sides and squares that have three? You will see at once that we are not asking a legitimate question. A triangle is by definition a three-sided figure and nothing else. God makes triangles and squares of such refinement and magnitude as stagger our imagination. Their cosmic dimensions can only be expressed in terms of light years. But even God cannot make a three-sided square or a four-sided triangle. The question contains a self-contradiction. We are posing an absurdity as a test of wisdom. It is the same with man. God can make man a free personality, or simply a member of the lower realms of nature. If man is free, he may do good or evil. If he lacks freedom, he can do neither.

Granting, now, that God in His omnipotence and wisdom has endowed man with that freedom which makes real the possibility of both good and evil, there is other than moral evil. There is the heritage of pain and suffering to which all flesh in varying degrees is heir. The ecstasies of life are only matched by its agonies. The more sensitive we become, the larger becomes the sphere of possible pleasure and pain. To the lover of the beautiful, everything ugly inflicts a hurt. To the merciful and sympathetic, the suffering of others in distant lands is a source of personal grief. We find happiness in the satisfaction of desire, whether the hunger of the body or the yearning of the soul. This is the meaning of happiness—desire slaked and satisfied. And yet the desire is itself a craving that is pain. The pangs of hunger are fearfully real. Upon this imbalance man has pondered from the days of Koheleth to the days of Hamlet. The essence of life among the higher animals is to be bearer of pleasure and pain.

And now the quest for four-sided triangles appears on another trail. We ask, why did not God, all-merciful and all-wise, make all life immune to suffering? The very writing of these lines recalls a consoling cliché frequently heard in funeral sermons 'nothing can hurt him now.' It is an accurate description of death but not of life. Living tissue, especially for the animal world, has this as its identifying characteristic—it is sensitive to pleasure and pain, it reacts against pain and toward pleasure. It learns to avoid the fire because it has suffered the burn. It develops the techniques of love to overcome suffering. Sensitive living tissue, whenever it first appeared, was something utterly new in the history of the cosmos, something more wondrous than all the dead expanse of heaven with its burning stars, something more marvelous than the chemistry of the dust and the symmetry of the crystal, something more delicate than the finest tempered watch spring—tissue that can suffer and rejoice because it is alive and can, through joy and suffering, learn the nature of its environment and how to subdue it to its will.

Let me repeat, in all humility, that I do not know why God made the quivering tissue of the sore-tried flesh. God perhaps could have made a universe without life. But despite His omnipotence and His mercy and His wisdom, He could not have made a conscious living being without making the possibility of pain as real as that of pleasure. When we ask that God create a world immune to sin and suffering, though we have seen that it is tantamount to the death wish insofar as it would be a world anchored to the level of the inorganic, the demand itself may not be self-contradictory.

It would puzzle us to explain why or by whom, since

no consciousness exists which could inquire as to its origin, such a creative process be ascribed to God at all.

We have also the right to demand of God a better world than now we have. In that case our demand is not only logical but thoroughly moral. God demands it too through the moral will implanted in the human heart. Conscience is given the everlasting task of transforming whatever is on any level of existence into what ought to be. It reflects the pressure of God's continued creativity against the limits of mere existence. It is meant not merely to accept suffering but to assuage it through compassion, to establish justice in place of power, to reveal holiness in the midst of animality, to establish truth in place of superstition. The human spirit is the instrument of God in His continued creativity in nature and history. The human spirit and the Divine spirit are allies in this cause.

The logical self-contradiction in the question we have asked lies in the fact that we fail to realize that the better implies the reality and actuality of the good. We can ask intelligibly for something better only insofar as we experience something that is good. To call a world from which true goodness has been excluded because evil has been made impossible, in which there can be no need for compassion or self-denial because suffering is unknown and happiness satisfies no need—to call such a world better which is not even good seems to me logically illegitimate. Only a world in which goodness is real and its function necessary, only such a world can become better. To any other kind of world the term better has no relevance whatsoever.

The Involvement of God in the Moral Life of Man

And yet we claim the right to one more protest. Granted that if freedom and life and their respective values are to be real and actual, we cannot avoid accepting the realities of sin and suffering too; yet is it quite fair that the onus of the latter shall fall solely upon the creatures of flesh and blood which God has Himself called into existence.

The lords and ladies of ancient Rome sat comfortably in their seats in the arenas and watched the gladiators fight their bloody battles. You may be sure that the lords and ladies had initiated the spectacle, not the gladiators. If we are not immune to all the pain involved in the glories of life and freedom, why should God who made us be immune? What does His mercy signify if in His omnipotence He has made Himself the author of this living pageantry in which the actors are not only expected to display nobility but also to accept with resignation whatever lot of anguish and suffering may be theirs.

If this challenge escapes our lips, it is because we have not yet freed ourselves from an idea of God which, I believe, modern thought has quite outgrown and which has never satisfied the deeper reaches of mystical feeling. It is true that we are not so childish as to think of Him as a bodily form nor are we quite so naive as to picture Him a being enthroned in some stratosphere beyond the clouds. But old habits of thought are not easily cast off, and for many men, when off their guard, God still leads a ghostly existence of His own beyond the confines of finite space and time. He has somehow brought His creatures into being, and these are the pawns with which He plays the game of destiny on the checkerboard of the universe.

According to the view of God which we have been developing, we can no longer place the human spirit and the divine spirit in detached and separate realms of being. They enfold one another and are opposite poles in a spiritual field of force created by their interaction. This apparent paradox constitutes the final insight we make our point of departure. "God lives in man and (since He also transcends the being of man) man lives in God" as the mystics have it, and all that befalls mankind is also a phase of the divine life. Outside of God there is nothing.

The expression for God so commonly found in Jewish literature, The Place of the World, is interpreted by the Talmudic rabbis, by St. Paul, and even by Spinoza, to mean that the whole world has its being within the life of God, as God ever manifests his presence within the world. Wolfson quotes Spinoza to the effect

> "Like Paul, and perhaps also like all ancient philosophers. . . . .I assert that all things live and move in God; and I would dare to say that I agree also with all the ancient Hebrews as far as it is possible to surmise from their traditions."[3]

In this connection he likewise calls attention to the Hymn of Unity which is included in the Jewish liturgy and which reads

> "Thou encompassest all and fillest all; and since Thou art all, Thou art in all. . . .Thou art not separated or detached from anything, nor is any place empty or devoid of Thee. . . . .Thou art and existeth in all; all is Thine, and all is from Thee." [4]

When a man can say to himself, "God is within me and I am within God," the experiences of his own life take on new meaning. His struggle against temptation becomes part of the great drama of the enthronement of righteousness. His joys become part of the ecstasy of life, the "joie de vivre" which all flesh experiences, and his sufferings and agonies and trials are not something upon which God looks down—they are a phase of the divine life. They are, in a sense, the suffering of God.

Let us make clear to ourselves that we do not mean that in God the psychology of human suffering and the mechanism of human emotions repeat themselves on an infinitely larger scale. What we do mean is that in the infinite whole, the limits to human pity and compassion are transcended. No matter how I may feel for another person or how truly my imagination can picture his suffering and my own heart make its response, the 'other' for whom I have compassion is always external to my own suffering. I remain I and he remains the 'other,' whatever may be the bond between us. I can never enter into his being to take his experiences upon myself. The 'otherness' of him is always a limit to my approach. God's compassion can be said to be perfect because all the suffering of man is not external to the divine being but is, as it were, internal to it, that is, involved in His creative love. The pity which any creature feels for his suffering fellow creature belongs to God and is a manifestation of His divine love, but the anguish which arouses that pity also belongs to God. Nothing is merely God's 'other,' each is also a facet of God's being. They all emanate from Him and are sustained by Him and are manifestations of His continued creativity.

If one should insist, as did the scholastic rationalists, that we can describe God only in negative attributes, we would still be justified in the statement that what we mean by God's suffering with man is that man's suffering is not external to God. The joys and sorrows of His creatures are momenta in the infinite life of the universe. Every finite experience is registered in some phase of the infinite reality.

The belief that human misery could not be a wanton act of God because God Himself suffers with His creatures is traced to a verse in Isaiah, interpreted according to the Masoretic text:

"In all their affliction He was afflicted,
In His love and His pity He redeemed them.
But they rebelled and grieved His Holy Spirit."
(Is. 63:9)

This passage has become the *locus* for many a homily dealing with God's compassion. In speaking of the criminal condemned to death, the Mishna does not hesitate to say, "If He who is the 'Abode of the World' thus suffers because of the blood of the wicked that is spilled, how much more surely does He suffer when the blood of the righteous flows." The suffering of the innocent is something not only imposed upon man by God, but something shared by man and God.

We have thus seen that the conception of the suffering of God is in Jewish ethics not involved in any mythological conception of the identity of the suffering Messiah with the son of God, or of the latter's incarnation in a historic personality. It is merely a necessary phase of God's compassion in its infinite depth, as contrasted with mere human pity, with its finite and psychological limits.

That the statement above, made by Rabbi Meir, is not an isolated example of this ethical point of view and its mystical insight, can be borne out by many similar expressions in various parts of the great rabbinic literature. I omit reference purposely to those more or less homiletic and romantic references to the fact that the cause of Israel is deemed to be the cause of God and that God suffers with and laments over the doom of His people. Beautiful and moving as these may be, they belong to the sphere of religious poetry rather than to that of theology. There are statements, however, so clear and decisive that they cannot be interpreted otherwise than as expressing the insight of the relation of God to the suffering of man in its most universal sense. Thus we have the observation (I translate correctly, I believe, though rather freely) that "in all the songs of thanksgiving in the Bible, the expression is used 'give thanks unto the Lord for He is good, for His mercy endureth forever.' Yet in the song sung by the Levites as they precede the armies of King Jehoshaphat, the phrase 'He is good' (Ki tob) is conspicuous by its absence. This is to indicate, as it were, that there is no joy before God at the destruction of the wicked. If then Heaven is bereft of joy, as it were, because of the death of the wicked, it is all the more certain that there can be no joy on high when the righteous perish, each one of whom outweighs (in value) the whole universe, for it is said 'the righteous is the foundation of the world.'" We can only comprehend the significance of the omission 'ki tob' if we realize that the word 'tob' in Hebrew can mean not only 'good' but also 'happiness' or 'well-being.' The song of thanksgiving with this conspicuous omission would then indicate 'give thanks unto the Lord, *though all is not well,* because God's love is eternal.' Even the destruction of Israel's enemies evokes only sorrow in heaven above.

More important still is a comment on Isaiah 66:16. Here we have a portrayal of God's final judgment upon the wicked of the earth—a bit of prophetic eschatology. It reads "For by fire will the Lord enter into judgment, and by His sword with all flesh." Now it happens that the Hebrew word 'to render judgment' has the structure of the passive voice. Seizing upon this peculiarity, R. Hannina, one of the great Palestinian Aggadists, has the boldness to exclaim, "Were it not explicit scripture, one would scarcely dare utter the thought, for it is not written that God judges all flesh with fire, but that *God himself is judged* in the penalties He brings upon mankind."[5] The Prophet Ezekiel long ago laid down the principle that God takes no delight in the death of the wicked. The passages that we have quoted merely state this in more sensitive and more positive form. God's judgment against the wicked is a judgment against Himself. He is imagined to bear in His compassion the pain of the penalties which He inflicts.

Even the sins of man, which we have seen are only an aspect of the awful gift of His freedom, must be viewed as registering also in the Divine life. We speak very glibly of the righteous as doing God's will. Every man who unselfishly, instead of indulging his own desires has in mind his duties to his fellow men, can be said to be fulfilling in his own will as an isolated individual that higher will which animates him in the search for the right.

But if righteousness is the doing of God's will, how shall we view the prevalence of wickedness, of cruelty and bigotry, and of pride and greed, of all the horrors which our generation has witnessed throughout the world and for a repetition of which the world may be again preparing. Shall we say fatalistically that here too God's will is being done? God is all powerful and cannot be successfully opposed and therefore whether all's well with the world or all's ill with the world, God's will is being done. Though all this would entail the collapse of our moral judgment, nevertheless it is easier to submit to it than to rise up against it and say, with all the love for God possible in our hearts, there are times when God is not victorious upon earth and where His will is being denied. To say whatever man does whether good or evil he is doing God's will is to loosen the props beneath the whole edifice of morality. To deny in any context of finite existence that God's will prevails is to impute a weakness to God inconsistent with our thoughts of Him as the Almighty. We seem to be impaled on the horns of this dilemma.

The difficulty arises because we fail to hold fast to the insight that ultimately God's will cannot be denied. It is He who wills the reality of righteousness and permits the possibility of evil and endows man with that spiritual freedom which enables him to exercise the prerogative of sinning. To that extent, even the wicked who defy God express God's will to freedom in their defiance. Nevertheless, man cannot avoid the consequences of the sin he chooses to commit, and we have already seen that evil is always a factor making for suffering and death, and that God's will ultimately fulfills itself because man has the power of repentance and redemption and God the power to make him face the ultimate consequences of evil.

Nevertheless, within the finite perspective in which evil prevails, God for the moment has permitted Himself to be set aside and frustrated. There is in the final song of Moses an accusing phrase which states "The Rock that bore thee didst thou forget." (Deut. 32:18). Through an ingenious play on the last word in the original Hebrew, the sentence is made to read: "The Rock that bore thee didst thou deprive of strength." The Midrash thereupon affirms: "Behold the sins of man frustrate the power of the Most High." Man's sin is God's defeat. The will toward righteousness is, by man's free choice of evil, turned aside and denied.

War and bloodshed, tyranny and chauvinism, bigotry and hate not only turn back the tides of human progress, they encompass the frustration of the divine will. The Almighty cannot be forever gainsaid because He has all eternity in which to fulfill his purpose. He is not only here and now, but everywhere and everywhen, and man himself cannot long exist in the chaos of the evil which for the moment he creates. Man will, to save himself, learn from his errors and repent, or blast himself out of

God's world with his bombs and his scientists, so that God's justice will be vindicated in man's extinction.

---

1. Edmund W. Sinnott, "Cell and Psyche," *Main Currents in Modern Thought*, Vol. IX, No. 1, published by the Foundation for Integrated Education.
2. Ber. R. 9.
3. Harry Austryn Wolfson, *The Philosophy of Spinoza* (Cambridge, Mass., Harvard University Press, 1934), p. 296.
4. *Ibid.*, p. 297. cf. infra pp. 274-275.
5. Yal. Shim, to Is. 66:17 and *Mid. Tehilim*, edition Solomon Buber Lemberg, 1891.

CHAPTER FIVE

RETRIBUTION AND THE FAITH IN IMMORTALITY

Introductory Remarks

We have seen then, how in the natural order, where man's moral life and the culture in which it flourishes have their origin and existence, morality becomes a factor making for survival and enhancing human well being for the individual and the society which it helps mold. It remains however *only* a factor and there is no point by point correspondence between virtue and man's lot upon earth. Nature in its relation to the moral life can be construed as reflecting the purpose that goodness shall be real with the reality of the finite and the actual, not merely with the reality of the perfect and the ideal. Existence, despite its fragmentary character, lends to all value an additional and enhanced value. The thinking which enables a man actually to fly, overcoming many obstacles intellectual and physical, is something more wondrous than the thought of perfect flying dwelling forever in some glorified but arid atmosphere of pure possibility.

True goodness stakes its life venturesomely on the superior value of the Good, knowing that in the course of nature's processes, evil can only lead to personal and social disintegration, whereas all the sacrifices that virtue may be called upon to make will in the course of history be allied with the constructive and positive powers that enrich life and make it more desirable. In the universe of nature, however, the perfect justice for which man may hope, from that infinite goodness to which the religious person pins his faith, fails him.

God, nevertheless, since He is immanent in nature as well as transcendent, does not impose these conditions arbitrarily upon His creatures for He is Himself determined by what He decrees. God in His compassion suffers with His creatures in all their agonizing experiences and therefore with every deed of self-sacrifice undertaken for righteousness' sake. He even permits Himself to be frustrated by the sin of man because He has endowed man with that freedom which issues from His own being and therefore enables man to defy even God.

God's justice as well as His mercy therefore can find ultimate fulfillment. For whereas God is immanent in all creation and in every creature in its weal or woe, so every creature shares not only the limitations of actual existence but also lives in the eternity of God. Every actual entity is not only a concrete individual thing, it is the meeting point for diverse possibilities. It is not only a definite individual, it is a congeries of defining universals which enter with itself into existence. Earth bound though man may be, he is endowed with an awareness which makes him realize that though he exists in time and passes with time, the essence of him has reality not only in time but also in eternity. So we come to the problem of immortality.

The problem is how, though God's creativity places man in the fragmentary world of space and time and cause, God's eternity redeems him from mere transience and enables him to triumph over time. The joy in this experience is the ultimate fact of the divine justice, the final recompense for suffering and death which on earth befalls the righteous and the wicked alike. But before we approach the problem of immortality from the naturalistic and philosophical angle, it is well that we examine the theories of divine retribution in biblical and rabbinic literature in the period before the idea of a final judgment in the World to Come came to full focus and in that later period when, though almost universally affirmed in both Judaism and Christianity, it was still overladen with colorful but irrational and mythological imaginings.

THEORIES OF DIVINE RETRIBUTION IN BIBLICAL LITERATURE

I—Justice in General

It is not our purpose to provide an exhaustive analysis of all the many and sometimes contradictory theories of divine retribution mirrored in biblical literature with all their subtle variations, but rather to note the major trends and to determine what relevance they have to one another and have, or could have had, to the actual experiences of man in ancient times.

We find in this literature a certain dogmatic optimism which crops up in repeated assertions that justice makes itself felt in human experience, no matter how dire such justice may be. This assurance asserts itself in the Torah, the Prophets, and, with certain exceptions as striking as they are rare, in the Wisdom literature.[1]

We have made it clear that the ancient Jewish point of view could not have been derived from analysis of nature and its laws—it was spun from the faith in the necessary justice of God. The dominant idea concerning divine retribution, whether in regard to individuals or nations, is that God's justice as well as His grace are unfailing and that He will give to each "according to his ways and the fruits of his doings." The righteous if they are patient and humble will know His blessings: happiness, prosperity, length of days, and joy with their children. The wicked, though they may appear to flourish for a time and though they may delude themselves with a sense of their security, are doomed to final deprivation and destruction. This doom can be averted only through the grace of God and His forgiveness which is always at the command of the sincerely penitent. By and large, this seems to have been the belief held by the vast majority of the faithful in the biblical era.

There is no sign in the Hebrew Bible, with the exception of the world-weary lament of Ecclesiastes, that earthly blessings are to be discounted as mere illusion or as not worth enjoying, and even Ecclesiastes stigmatizes the pursuit of wealth, of luxury, and the delights of sophistication as vanity only in favor of the simpler pleasures of life—to eat, drink, and be merry, and to rejoice with the wife of one's youth (Ecc. 2:24; 9:4). This should not surprise us. In every stage of human civilization, not only in biblical times, the well-to-do and the highly sophisticated were always ready to sing the praises of the simple life. In taking for granted the fact that the joys and sorrows of life are not to be dismissed as unreal or without value, the Hebrew Bible is eminently realistic.

II—*The Sins of the Fathers*

One theory, however, which suggested some reservations concerning this faith in absolute justice, and yet a doctrine as ancient as any, is that God visits the sins of the fathers upon the children unto the third and fourth generations and yet shows mercy unto thousands who love Him and keep His commandments. This served, first of all, to explain the discrepancies between the doctrine of individual retribution and the actual facts of experience. A man might be righteous and yet suffer through inherited ancestral guilt or he might be wicked and yet prosper because of the accumulated merit of ancestors long passed away. Yet it must soon have become apparent to many that a doctrine of imputed guilt inherited from generation to generation could not express the flawless justice expected of God the father of all perfection, for according to the Bible such a doctrine very early became inadequate even for the uses of human justice. Thus we find the explicit provision that children shall not be put to death for the sins of their fathers or fathers for the sins of their children (Deut. 24:16), canceling from the realm of practical justice such primitive proceedings as are recorded with regard to Achan (Joshua 7:24) or such instances of ancient Semitic usage as are recorded in the laws of Hammurabi by virtue of which in certain instances of criminal negligences children were put to death for their father's deeds.[2]

Nevertheless, however repudiated in legal practice, the doctrine that succeeding generations must suffer for ancestral guilt even as they enjoy the rewards of ancestral virtue seems to have maintained itself even after it was called into question by the ethical demand that divine justice must have an exactness beyond that possible to human law or natural consequence.

It may be said in extenuation of this doctrine that every individual is an organic part of the society which is his own, viewed vertically as well as horizontally. No man for good or ill can create the moral climate, ideational or institutional, in which he finds himself, nor does anyone refuse the blessings that have come down to him out of the past. Why then should he refuse to share the consequence of its failures and its guilt? The moral problem as it faces the individual is always how to transmit to his children a social legacy in which the fund of guilt will have been diminished and the sum of blessings enriched by his own acts.

III—Collective Guilt

A similar self-contradictory situation and yet by no means an unworthy one is envisaged in the prophetic notion of God's retribution upon the individual nation. Amos, the first of the great documented prophets, cries out "behold the eyes of the Lord are upon the sinful kingdom and I will destroy it from the face of the earth, will I not then utterly destroy the house of Israel." Most versions soften the last clause of the sentence above, so that it promises not utterly to destroy the house of Israel. This is both contrary to the context in which Israel is taken to be like 'the children of the Ethiopians' in the eyes of God and also contrary to the Hebrew idiom which should then have read "hashmed lo ashmid" instead of "lo hashmed ashmid."[3]

Modern biblical scholarship has called attention to the fact that nations other than Israel are never said to be punished for their idolatry or polytheism but only for their cruelties toward one another or to the helpless and oppressed. Only Israel, bound by covenant to God and bound by oath to serve Him, bears the burden of guilt if it turns to idolatry. With Israel, it becomes moral infidelity which God, jealous in His justice, cannot ignore. The people of the flood, however, were destroyed because the earth had become corrupt and full of violence. Sodom meets its doom because "the cry of the oppressed" had reached the ear of God. Nineveh of the Book of Jonah is forgiven when its people lay aside 'the violence which was in their hands.' The indictment of the nations which Amos pronounces is all based on similar moral grounds—cruelty, greed, injustice. It is worth observing that even the nations of Canaan which Israel was bidden utterly to exterminate are said to have justified this treatment (contrary to the general laws of war laid down in Deut. 20:10-18), not because of the gods they worshipped or the idols to which they bowed down, but because of the immoralities involved in the established cults 'for every abominable thing which the Lord hates have they done to their gods; for they even burned their sons and daughters in the fire to their gods' (Deut. 12:31). It is not *what* they worship but *how* they worship that moves God to destroy them lest they corrupt Israel. This is doubtless a rationalization of the actual ban pronounced against the whole population of Canaan during the period of the conquest (Numbers 21:1-3) but it is a rationalization with profound ethical motivation. God destroys nations for their inhumanity, not for their heresies.

What is assumed in this concept of God's judgment upon the nations is not only the social solidarity involved in the link between generations but a solidarity which binds each individual to the society of which he feels himself a part and imputes the guilt of the social whole to each individual.

The frightful doom which befell Israel and the slaughter which was to overtake Israel's oppressors or the empires which had cruelly ravaged the peoples of the earth always involved the death of men, women, and children who personally never held the reins of power or directed the course of empire. If men accepted such tragedies as signs of the justice of God, it could only have been because they had not found the way to distinguish individual from collective guilt. It is not even an easy problem for us. To say that the individual has no responsibility for the state of society in which he lives or that society is not to be held responsible for the evil wrought by the units constituting it, will satisfy the social conscience of neither biblical nor modern man. A man who can through his act or influence prevent an evil and makes no sacrifices to make his act or influence effective, or the man or woman who accepts unquestioningly the fruits of evil, the wealth or prosperity which may come in the wake of war and conquest and enslavement, cannot complain if a share of the collective guilt is imputed to him.

Nevertheless, such justice could not long satisfy those who believe in a God all wise and all just, all merciful and all omnipotent, for though the conscience and wisdom of man may not be able to determine in any particular social situation what is the exact degree of collective or of personal guilt or merit, God should and His justice should establish the difference. Though it is scarcely possible for man to distinguish between his neighbor's share or even his own share in the guilt or merit of what is wrought by the state or nation to which he belongs, God ought so to distinguish, and the blessing or disaster that befalls such a society ought to be graded for each individual according to his ways and his doings instead of striking with equal grace or fury the collective mass.

IV—The Rhetorical Questions

And so we meet in even early strata of biblical literature certain rhetorical questions which are among the great and inspired utterances of religious thought. Abraham apprised of the coming destruction of Sodom asks "Wilt thou indeed destroy the righteous with the wicked" and again "Far be it from Thee to do such a thing—to slay the righteous with the wicked so that the righteous fare as the wicked, far be that from Thee. Shall not the judge of all the earth do justice?" Moses finds himself in a situation the reverse of that of Abraham. Korah leads a rebellion. the climax of several such as would have nullified the whole work of liberation and God says to Moses and Aaron "Separate yourselves from the congregation that I may consume them in a moment." God imputes the sin of Korah and his followers to the people from which they sprang. Whereupon Moses asks "O God, the God of the spirits of all flesh, shall one man sin and wilt Thou be angry with the whole congregation?" The query here is evidently based on the theological assumption that God's providence should cover not only Israel as such, or the human species as such, or the human spirit in its universality, but the spirits of all flesh in their distributive singularity. All spirits belong alike to God and it behooves His justice to deal with each according to its merits. To impute to the collective whole the sin of the individual, or a section of the community, involves the same blurring of the concept of divine and perfect justice as does imputing the guilt of the collective whole to each individual irrespective of his personal share therein.

V—The Primacy of the Individual

The final and most outstanding repudiation of all these forms of what may be called proximate justice versus the divine attribute of infinite justice and love is more clearly put by the two prophets who beheld what they believed to be God's punitive wrath outpoured upon the people they loved. Jeremiah oscillates between heartbreaking tenderness and implacable vindictiveness in announcing the impending doom of his people already sealed. He advises absolute surrender, the bending of the neck to the yoke of the conqueror. Yet when the agony will have passed, and the chosen people which has broken the covenant will have drained the cup of its collective guilt, there will follow the establishment of a new covenant

> "I will put my law in their inward parts,
> and in their heart will I write it; and I
> will be their God and they shall be My
> people; and they shall teach no more every
> man his neighbour, and every man his brother,
> saying: 'Know the Lord'; for they shall all

> know Me, from the least of them unto the
> greatest of them, saith the Lord; for I
> will forgive their iniquity, and their sin
> will I remember no more." (Jer. 31:33-34)

The prologue to these inspiring words contains the promise of purer justice about to fulfil itself:

> "In those days they shall say no more:
> 'The fathers have eaten sour grapes,
> And the children's teeth are set on edge.'
> But every one shall die for his own
> iniquity; every man that eateth the sour
> grapes, his teeth shall be set on edge."
> (Jer. 31:29-30)

All this is in the last analysis an eschatological hope. It is to come at the end of the era in which the prophet lives and is to introduce a new era. It admits that God for Israel's sake and His own had to make a horrible example of the faithless nations, but hereafter God would resort to that personal retribution only, which is in closer harmony with His infinite justice and His perfect understanding.

More significant still is the rather sustained argument of Ezekiel on this subject. It too has eschatological touches in that it envisages complete redemption, a new heart and a new spirit:

> "As I live, saith the Lord God, ye shall
> not have occasion any more to use this
> proverb in Israel." (The proverb to which
> Jeremiah alludes.) "Behold, all souls
> are Mine; as the soul of the father,
> so also the soul of the son is Mine;
> the soul that sinneth, it shall die." (Ez. 18:3-4)

The repudiation of inherited guilt and the emphasis upon individual responsibility is based as in the case mentioned above, upon the fact that all souls, not only collectively but distributively, belong each one to God since He is the God of the spirits of all flesh and therefore the God of each soul in every generation. Wherein this teaching supersedes the statement of Jeremiah is that the urge to repentance is based on the recognition "for I have no pleasure in the death of him that dieth wherefore turn yourselves and live." The thought that retribution is God's prerogative, but that he takes no delight in its exercise, had important repercussions in later thought.

VI—Tentative Doubts

We shall eventually examine the literature in the Bible critical of the views we have hitherto expounded and eventuating in the doctrine that there may be death and suffering upon earth that is not the consequence of sin. The reader may have noticed that we have made no reference to the Paradise story or to the notion that death came into the world through Adam's disobedience. There is reason for this. As a matter of fact, the biblical story does not attribute death to Adam's eating of the Tree of Knowledge but to his being created from the dust of the earth to which he must inevitably return (Gen. 3:19). His sin, if it be a sin, deprived him of the chance of becoming immortal for God banished him from Eden for his sin, and the cherubim with the flaming sword were sent to block the way to the Tree of Life. An interpretation of the Paradise story from the standpoint of comparative mythology and of modern psychology is still a desideratum. Whatever may have been the consequence of Adam's fall, it was not a fall from virtue but a fall from innocence. Its immediate result was not death but the realization of his own nakedness—the dawn of mature sex-consciousness.

Schechter has this to say of the misadventure of Adam in Eden:

"There can be little doubt that the belief in the disastrous effects of the sin of Adam on posterity was not entirely absent in Judaism, though this belief did not hold such a prominent place in the synagogue as in the Christian Church. It is also thought that in the overwhelming majority of mankind there is enough sin in each individual case to bring about death without the sin of Adam." [4]

Moore's exposition points to the same general evaluation of the Adam story in rabbinic literature. [5] That God originally created man for immortality, a thought expressed in the Wisdom of Solomon and upon which Moore comments with some rabbinical parallels, was certainly not the concensus of opinion in Judaism and is emphatically repudiated in certain passages to which we have already alluded. [6] However, even among those prophets and psalmists who held to the doctrine that God owed and would grant exact retribution and that in the end the well-being of the righteous would reflect their well-doing, there were moods of uncertainty. We meet with reflective passages in which God is reproached with not fulfilling the justice expected of Him. In these we encounter a faith which stands midway between the common biblical view focused upon mundane life in which the eschatological hope finds fulfillment through the restoration of Israel or in the Messianic era, and that later faith in which resurrection and The World to Come play so important a part.

I have in mind such protests and affirmations as we already find in Habakkuk. The advance of the Chaldeans was only the occasion, not the sole source of these prophetic protestations.

"How long, O Lord, shall I cry,
And Thou wilt not hear?
I cry out unto Thee of violence,
And Thou wilt not save.
Why dost Thou show me iniquity,
And beholdest mischief?
And why are spoiling and violence before me?
So that there is strife, and contention ariseth.
Therefore the law is slacked,
And right doth never go forth;
For the wicked doth beset the righteous;
Therefore right goeth forth perverted." (Hab. 1:2-4)

> "Thou that art of eyes too pure to behold evil.
> And that canst not look on mischief,
> Wherefore lookest Thou, when they deal treacherously,
> And holdest Thy peace, when the wicked swalloweth up
> The man that is more righteous than he;" (Hab.1:13)

Habakkuk receives an answer which promises no comfort in the present:

> "And the Lord answered me, and said:
> 'Write the vision,
> And make it plain upon tables,
> That a man may read it swiftly.
> For the vision is yet for the appointed time,
> And it declareth of the end, and doth not lie;
> Though it tarry, wait for it;
> Because it will surely come, it will not delay.'
> Behold, his soul is puffed up, it is not upright in him;
> But the righteous shall live by his faith." (Hab. 2:2-4)

The lesson to be learned is that the righteous must not abandon faith in divine justice but must be willing to wait for 'the appointed time' when that justice will become fully manifest.

The final words ending the prophetic canon, whether or not they were written by Malachi, strike a similar note.

> "Then they that feared the Lord
> Spoke one with another;
> And the Lord hearkened, and heard,
> And a book of remembrance was written before Him,
> For them that feared the Lord, and that thought upon His name.
> And they shall be Mine, saith the Lord of hosts,
> In the day that I do make, even Mine own treasure;
> And I will spare them, as a man spareth
> His own son that serveth him.
> Then shall ye again discern between the righteous and the wicked,
> Between him that serveth God
> And him that serveth Him not." (Mal. 3:16-18)

This reference to the special day that God creates implies again no relinquishing of the faith that God will ultimately do justice upon earth but an indefinite postponement, until the time be ripe when all men will see the fruits of His justice.

In Psalm 102 which is called 'A Prayer of the afflicted, when he fainteth, and poureth out his complaint before the Lord,' the final hope of the sufferer is expressed in these words:

"Of old Thou didst lay the foundation of the earth;
And the heavens are the work of Thy hands.
They shall perish, but Thou shalt endure;
Yea, all of them shall wax old like a garment;
As a vesture shalt Thou change them, and they
   shall pass away;
But Thou art the selfsame,
And Thy years shall have no end." (Ps. 102:26-28)

In this psalm, the sufferings of the individual are integrated with the sorrow of an exiled people. Originally, however, I am convinced that the national element constituted the content of a separate hymn. Here, the whole panorama of earth and sky are thought to pass away that God may deal anew with His creatures.

Perhaps the high-water mark of such reflection upon the prosperity of the wicked, and their effect upon the individual, is found in the psychological self-revelations contained in Psalm 73. The case is simply stated;

"But as for me, my feet were almost gone;
My steps had well nigh slipped.
For I was envious at the arrogant,
When I saw the prosperity of the wicked."
(Ps. 73:2,3)

The Psalmist describes the prosperity of the wicked despite their defiance of God
"And they say: 'How doth God know?
And is there knowledge in the Most High?
Behold, such are the wicked;

And they that are always at ease increase riches."
(Ps. 73:11,12)

Then in his disillusionment, the psalmist exclaims:
"Surely in vain have I cleansed my heart,
And washed my hands in innocency;
For all the day have I been plagued,
And my chastisement came every morning."
(Ps. 73:13,14)

The mood remains until he enters the sanctuary of God and then he realizes that God's justice must be infallible and the triumph of the wicked but deceptive and transitory. Thereupon follow the significant words which, with reawakened interest in dreams so characteristic of modern psychology, are particularly appealing.

"As a dream when one awaketh,
So, O Lord, when Thou arousest Thyself, Thou
  wilt despise their semblance.
For my heart was in a ferment,
And I was pricked in my reins.
But I was brutish, and ignorant;
I was as a beast before Thee." (Ps. 73:20-22)

When God's justice finally overtakes them, the psalmist seems to say, the wicked and all their works will appear like dream images which, upon awaking, we dismiss as without substance. Then follows the hope of a final transformation:

"Nevertheless I am continually with Thee;
Thou holdest my right hand.
Thou wilt guide me with Thy counsel,
And afterward receive me with glory.
Whom have I in heaven but Thee?
And beside Thee I desire none upon earth.
My flesh and my heart faileth;
But God is the rock of my heart and my portion
  for ever.
For, lo, they that go far from Thee shall perish;

Thou dost destroy all them that go astray from
  Thee.
But as for me, the nearness of God is my good;
I have made the Lord God my Refuge,
That I may tell of all Thy works." (Ps. 73:23-28)

The question always remains, to what does the adverb 'afterward' in the verse above refer? (In Hebrew it is exactly the same word as in Job 19:26 where it is translated 'after'). It need not here mean after death and most probably does not have that connotation. It refers in all probability to that final climax of judgment which remains the hope of the righteous despite their present experience.

VII—The Skeptical Classics

In the midst of this vast sea of biblical faith, little islands of skeptical realism occasionally rear their heads which evoke our admiration by the fact that they have maintained their position despite the onrushing currents of religious ardor and the sluggish but eroding calms of conventional opinion.

It should be noted that the doubt expressed both in Ecclesiastes and in Job is not of the existence of God. It does not seem to have occurred to the reflective thinker of the biblical era that God could be dispensed with. On the contrary, we are occasionally told "The fool saith in his heart there is no God" but Wisdom even in its moods of doubt and rebellion takes God for granted and even in despair addresses its challenge to God Himself.

Chesterton has somewhere called attention to the fact that only in ages of faith can such rebellion be called heroic. The modern sophisticate who denies God has, of course, nothing to fear from the god whose existence he has denied. At most, he may have to forego publishing his doubts in deference to public opinion. But he who believes in God the Almighty and then undertakes to accuse Him of misgoverning the world of His creation, of failing to discriminate between right and wrong, must have been prepared to marshal all the forces of his soul in support of the truth.

True monotheists could not take refuge in the pagan view that perhaps God must reckon with demonic forces which even a beneficient deity sometimes fails to overcome. The god whom they worshipped could plead no such external pressure in extenuation because they acknowledged no such limitation to his power. Their lament concerning the sad lot of man which parallels certain Egyptian and Babylonian sources [7] is overshadowed by the urgency which they, as monotheists, are under to explain how a God who must be all powerful and all good can yet betray the hopes and expectations of those who fear Him.

The thesis which finally emerges in this literature is that though God may be just when He judges, there is suffering which cannot be traced to the retributive justice of God. It must, under God, have some other function which baffles the wisdom of man. The prose legend of Job with its majestic prologue glorifies the attitude of the suffering saint. Suffering is a trial, not a penalty, in his case. God permits the trial in order to convince Satan (and perhaps carping public opinion on earth as well as in heaven) that the righteous will not deviate from his righteousness and will not deny or blaspheme God whatever be his lot. It thus becomes a tribute to the authenticity of righteousness that God sometimes brings sorrows to the righteous whereby he may prove his spiritual mettle even to himself. In this section of the Book of Job are embedded two moving declarations of complete faith—first

> "Naked came I out of my mother's womb,
> And naked shall I return thither;
> The Lord gave, and the Lord hath taken away;
> Blessed be the name of the Lord." (Job 1:21)

and secondly,
> "Shall we receive good at the hand of God,
> and shall we not receive evil?" (Job 2:10)

The influence of these passages is attested by the fact that they have found acceptance in the very liturgy of sorrow both Jewish and Christian.

The Book of Job proper is, of course, the celebrated and splendid poem which the great artist has inserted in the framework of the prose narrative. Job of the poem does not accept his fate in silent equanimity. The argument of the friends that in some sin of Job, or in some warning against intended sin, lies the secret of Job's suffering, invokes in Job the great denial. God has crushed him for reasons he does not understand. If God would only disclose his failings, he would be happy to bear the burden of his guilt. As it is, he is convinced that God is aware he has done no evil that would deserve the vast sea of suffering in which God has plunged him, and from which he can see no escape but death.

> "O earth, cover not thou my blood,
> And let my cry have no resting place.
> Even now, behold, my Witness is in heaven,
> And He that testifieth of me is on high.
> Mine inward thoughts are my intercessors,
> Mine eye poureth out tears unto God;
> That He would set aright a man contending with God,
> As a son of man setteth aright his neighbour!
> For the years that are few are coming on,
> And I shall go the way whence I shall not return."
> (Job 16:18-22)

> "But as for me, I know that my Redeemer liveth,
> And that he will witness at the last against the dust;
> And when after my skin this is destroyed,
> Then without my flesh shall I see God;
> Whom I, even I, shall see for myself,
> And mine eyes shall behold, and not another's."
> (Job 16:18-22)

The latter lines are somewhat obscure. The meaning of the declaration "I know that my Redeemer liveth" can perhaps better be rendered "I know that my vindicator liveth" and the phrase "then without my flesh shall I see God" might be taken to mean "then bereft of my flesh shall I see God." The verses are not an expression of hope but rather of despair. Job reproaches God with the fact that when it will be too late as far as he is concerned, God will admit that the sufferer was right. If the lines just quoted are not an interpolation as many think, then we must take for granted that there is some parallel here between the phrase "And when after my skin this is destroyed" and the passage in Psalm 73:24

"Thou wilt guide me with Thy counsel,
And afterward receive me with glory."

They both reflect a faith in some cosmic catastrophe which may be pre-biblical and antedate the prophetic eschatology. [8]

Moreover, Job has too high an opinion of the moral integrity of God to believe that God can be cajoled by flattery or be pleased when men distort the truth to win His favor.

"Hear now my reasoning,
And hearken to the pleadings of my lips.
Will ye speak unrighteously for God,
And talk deceitfully for Him?
Will ye show Him favour?
Will ye contend for God?
Would it be good that He should search you out?
Or as one mocketh a man, will ye mock Him?
He will surely reprove you,
If ye do secretly show favour." (Job 13:6-10)

"And Job again took up his parable, and said:
As God liveth, who has taken away my right;
And the Almighty, who has dealt bitterly with me;
All the while my breath is in me,
And the spirit of God is in my nostrils.
Surely my lips shall not speak unrighteousness,
Neither shall my tongue utter deceit;
Far be it from me that I should justify you;
Till I die I will not put away mine integrity from me.
My righteousness I hold fast, and will not let it go;
My heart shall not reproach me so long as I live."
(Job 27:1-6)

Job therefore tells God the truth and holds fast to his own integrity (Job 31). He insists to the end that nothing he has done can account for the agony God has brought upon him. This is at least one case where suffering has no relevance to guilt and Job sees no reasons to believe that there are not many such.

> "I am innocent—I regard not myself, I despise my life.
> It is all one—therefore I say:
> He destroyeth the innocent and the wicked.
> If the scourge slay suddenly,
> He will mock at the calamity of the guiltless.
> The earth is given into the hand of the wicked;
> He covereth the faces of the judges thereof;
> If it be not He, who then is it?" (Job 9:21-24)

In the opinion of many scholars, the Book of Job proper ends with Chapter 31. There is nevertheless solid authority against this view. It is my personal opinion, however, that it is correct. The words of Elihu, while they add some new points of view to that of the friends, nevertheless are only variations played upon the conventional theme that there is some inevitable connection between suffering and sin.

The majestic poem in which God is made to speak out of the whirlwind, while it bears no relevance to the theophany which may be hinted at in Chapter 19, and answers no question addressed to God by Job, and whether or not it is a later interpolation—is meant to suggest a new approach of Wisdom to the problem of human suffering. In the unparalleled Wisdom Song in Chapter 28, the creative wisdom of God is declared to be "hidden from the eyes of all living." The wisdom with which God has endowed man is "to fear the Lord and shun all evil." In this final section of the Book of Job as at present constituted, God overwhelms him with some of the mysteries of creation, none of which man can penetrate, "Where wast thou when I laid the foundations of the earth?"

The general effect of these verses is to suggest that when dealing with the suffering of the righteous one must look not only to the punitive justice of God but to His creative wisdom. If men knew the secrets of that wisdom, they might also understand the function of suffering. Since however, this divine wisdom is not within our comprehension, it may be better to remain silent in the presence of God the Creator.

At any rate, Job declares that having gazed upon the glories of God in His creative majesty, he realizes that "Therefore have I uttered what I understood not, things too wonderful for me which I know not." God rebukes the friends of Job with the significant words "Ye have not spoken of Me the thing that is right as my servant Job has." There is no insistence upon the necessary relation between sin and suffering on the part of God, and as for Job, we have only a confession of his ignorance but no recantation of his innocence.

Ecclesiastes, whether it is a unit including conventional and prudential advice in a general framework of skeptical reflection as Dr. Gordis maintains, or a composite admitting certain pious interpolations, brings us face to face with a mood of boredom and despair; boredom with the world because "all is vanity" and "there is nothing new under the sun," there is no end to the recurring cycles repeating themselves without climax or direction, and despair because the righteous and the wicked, the wise and the foolish meet essentially the same fate. The author is not lacking in pity but is quite void of indignation. He has, on the other hand, the detachment of the scholar and observer. The book seems very modern in temper and according to some scholars already shows the effect of Greek thought. Kaufman[9] however believes that though the form and idiom appear to be rather late, the problems and the point of view go back to that humanistic pre-biblical reservoir of wisdom from which Job and Proverbs stem, transformed only by Jewish monotheism. Professor Max Margolis in his little book *The Hebrew Scriptures in the Making*[10] already calls attention to the fact that the adage pronounced by the wise women of Tekoah (Sam. II. 14:14) already strikes the keynote of the theme with which Ecclesiastes deals

> "For we must needs die, and are as water spilt on
> the ground, which cannot be gathered up again;
> neither doth God respect any person;"

This sort of bitter-sweet pessimism is at least as old as the dogmatic optimism which Wisdom so often manifests.

In our book, it is stated more articulately and in more sophisticated terms. Note for instance

> "For that which befalleth the sons of men
> befalleth beasts: even one thing befalleth
> them; as the one dieth, so dieth the other;
> yea, they have all one breath; so that man
> hath no pre-eminence above a beast; for all
> is vanity. All go unto one place; all are
> of the dust, and all return to dust." (Eccl. 3:19, 20)

Or more emphatically,

> "There is a vanity which is done upon the earth:
> that there are righteous men, unto whom it
> happeneth according to the work of the wicked;
> again, there are wicked men, to whom it
> happeneth according to the work of the
> righteous—I said that this also is vanity." (Eccl. 8:14)

And

> "This is an evil in all that is done under the
> sun, that there is one event unto all; yea also,
> the heart of the sons of men is full of evil,
> and madness is in their heart while they live,
> and after that they go to the dead." (Eccl. 9:3)

Koheleth advises, as we have already seen, that man take advantage of all the simpler joys of life which God grants him and that he live his life within the bounds of conventional respectability

> "Be not over-much wicked, neither be thou
> foolish; why shouldest thou die before thy
> time? It is good that thou shouldest take

> hold of the one; yea, also from the other
> withdraw not thy hand; for he that feareth
> God shall discharge himself of them all."
> (Eccl. 7:17,18)

The fact that there is suffering and happiness that have no special relation to moral good or evil must have troubled more men than the few who assumed the responsibility of authorship. Psalm 131 is a case in point. This is usually taken to express the faith of a simple soul not harassed by speculative problems. The opposite is the case. It reveals a soul torn with conflict which because it could find no answer retreats into faith and makes the confession

> "Surely I have stilled and quieted my soul;
> Like a weaned child with his mother,
> My soul is with me like a weaned child." (Ps. 131:2)

One would like to know what was in the Psalmist's heart before he succeeded in quieting his soul.

VIII—*The Ethical Function of Suffering and Martyrdom*

There is one further thought in biblical literature which seeks an explanation of the suffering of the righteous not in the mere negation of the idea that suffering and sin are necessarily bound together, but in a positive affirmation which may be called a philosophy of martyrdom and ascribes a redemptive function to the sorrows and woes of one elected to be the "Servant of the Lord."

This thought finds expression in the so-called Servant Chapters of the Second Isaiah which begin in Chapter 42 and reach their moving climax in the 53rd chapter. The first reference is in 42:6-9

> "I the Lord have called thee in righteousness,
> And have taken hold of thy hand,
> And kept thee, and set thee for a covenant on the people,
> For a light of the nations;

> To open the blind eyes,
> To bring out the prisoners from the dungeon,
> And them that sit in darkness out of the prison-house.
> I am the Lord, that is My name;
> And My glory will I not give to another,
> Neither My praise to graven images.
> Behold, the former things are come to pass,
> And new things do I declare;
> Before they spring forth I tell you of them."

It continues with verses 18 and 19, introducing the question "Who is blind but my servant" and continues to describe "A people robbed and spoiled, they are all of them snared in holes. And they are hid in prison-houses; They are for a prey, and none delivereth, For a spoil and none saith 'Restore.'" (22) In chapter 42 the prophet addresses 'Jacob My Servant' and 'Israel whom I have chosen' and bids him not be afraid, never to forget, and never to abandon hope (42:1, 21-28).

The following lines, wherein the servant addresses the distant isles and describes his own lowly condition, and God addresses the servant and assigns him his glorious task, are among the most eloquent and significant passages in prophetic literature.

> "Listen, O isles, unto me,
> And hearken, ye peoples, from far:
> The Lord hath called me from the womb,
> From the bowels of my mother hath he made mention of my name;
> And He hath made my mouth like a sharp sword,
> In the shadow of His hand hath He hid me;
> And He hath made me a polished shaft,
> In His quiver hath He concealed me;
> And He said unto me; 'Thou art My servant,
> Israel, in whom I will be glorified.'
> But I said: 'I have laboured in vain,
> I have spent my strength for nought and vanity;
> Yet surely my right is with the Lord,
> And my recompense with my God.'

And now saith the Lord
That formed me from the womb to be His servant,
To bring Jacob back to Him,
And that Israel be gathered unto Him—
For I am honourable in the eyes of the Lord,
And my God is become my strength—
Yea, He saith: 'It is too light a thing that thou
  shouldest be My servant
To raise up the tribes of Jacob,
And to restore the offspring of Israel;
I will also give thee for a light of the nations,
That My salvation may be unto the end of the earth.'
Thus saith the Lord,
The Redeemer of Israel, His Holy One,
To him who is despised of men,
To him who is abhorred of nations,
To a servant of rulers:
Kings shall see and arise,
Princes, and they shall prostrate themselves;
Because of the Lord that is faithful,
Even the Holy One of Israel, who hath chosen thee."
(Is. 49:1-7)

Sometimes, as in the lines we are about to quote, it is difficult to discern whether the prophet means to identify himself with the servant or is only speaking on behalf of the servant:
"The Lord God hath opened mine ear,
And I was not rebellious,
Neither turned away backward.
I gave my back to the smiters,
And my cheeks to them that plucked off the hair;
I hid not my face from shame and spitting.
For the Lord God will help me;
Therefore have I not been confounded;
Therefore have I set my face like a flint,
And I know that I shall not be ashamed.
He is near that justifieth me;
Who will contend with me? let us stand up together;
Who is mine adversary? let him come near to me.
Behold, the Lord God will help me;

Who is he that shall condemn me?
   Behold, they all shall wax old as a garment,
   The moth shall eat them up." (Is. 50:5-9)

and again,

   "Who is among you that feareth the Lord,
   That obeyeth the voice of His servant?
   Though he walketh in darkness,
   And hath no light,
   Let him trust in the name of the Lord,
   And stay upon his God." (Is. 50:10)

For the climactic 53rd chapter, I have taken the liberty to avail myself of the version found in Dr. Finkelstein's book on *The Pharisees* [11] where he himself admits indebtedness to Torrey's reconstruction of the text:

"Behold, My servant shall prosper,
   He shall be honoured and greatly exalted.
   For as much as many were appalled at him
   For his face was marred more than any other;
   And his visage than the children of men,
   So shall the mighty ones be startled at him,
   Kings shall be silent before him,
   For what had not been told them they shall see,
   What they had not heard, they shall understand.
   'Who had believed what we report?' (they shall say)
   'And to whom was the Lord's arm revealed?'
   For he grew up as a slender shoot before us,
   As a root out of the arid ground;
   He had not form nor charm, that we should notice him;
   No beauty that we should admire him.
   He was despised and forsaken of men, a man of sorrows and acquainted with pain;
   As one from whom men hide their faces he was despised, and we esteemed him not.
   Yet it was our woes that he bore, and our sorrows that he carried;

> While we accounted him punished, smitten of God,
>   and afflicted.
> But he was wounded for our transgressions, bruised
>   for our iniquities;
> On him fell the chastisement that made us whole,
>   and with his stripes were we healed.
> All we like sheep had gone astray, we had turned
>   each to his own way;
> And the Lord laid on him the penalty, charged upon
>   him the guilt of us all." (Is. 52:13-53:6)

But the suffering of his Servant is not to be in vain. The Lord assures him:

> "When his life shall make atonement for sin,
>   He will see his seed, will prolong his days,
> And the Lord's purpose will prosper in his hands.
> He will see the fruit of his mortal travail,
>   In knowing himself true will be satisfied;
> My servant will bring many to the right,
>   For he will carry their sins." (Is. 53:10-11)

We gather from all this that the prophet who has assigned to the servant the tremendous task of bringing salvation to the ends of the earth, of making his voice heard in the distant isles, of bringing the world to God and establishing God as King over all mankind, is convinced that it is his willingness to suffer and endure which will finally enable him to accomplish his mission.

Whether the suffering servant of the 53rd chapter is identical with the ideally glorified Israel of the earlier chapters, or whether the servant here is a sort of composite picture of individual sufferers and martyrs who had experienced the horrors of the destruction and the frustrations attendant upon the restoration, we do not know.

It should be noted that the suffering servant here is never explicitly called Messiah. The Messiah in biblical literature is never, as a matter of fact, described as a Redeemer or Saviour. It is God who is the Redeemer and the rule of the Messiah is among the fruits of redemption. Nevertheless, the New Testament has appropriated this passage as depicting the redemptive office of Jesus in his messianic capacity, and later Jewish literature, perhaps under the influence of certain sectarian sources, shows traces of a faith in a suffering Messiah.[12] Most interpreters of these chapters both ancient and modern, who have approached the subject matter independent of Christian dogma, tend to agree that the servant depicted here is Israel in its suffering and martyrdom.

The degree of uncertainty, however, has recently increased. It has been suggested in the light of the findings of the Dead Sea scrolls, and especially in view of the sectarian writings glorifying the Teacher of Righteousness, that these chapters of Isaiah may prove to be very late or that there may be at least a connection between the 53rd chapter and some actual leader and martyr such as the sectarian documents contemplate. Let me call attention particularly to what has been said concerning the Dead Sea scrolls by Edmund Wilson first in the columns of *The New Yorker* (May 14, 1955) and more recently in slightly expanded form in his book *The Scrolls from the Dead Sea*.[13] The above is a remarkable piece of reporting insofar as it portrays for the layman, or for one who cannot keep abreast of the detailed scholarship now focused upon these problems, the whole enterprise of their discovery and the questions it is now raising for biblical students and archeologists.

> "Now, one of the most impressive pieces of evidence that can be adduced from the Old Testament in support of the claim of the Christians that the advent of Jesus as Messiah had been prophesied in the ancient text is, of course, the chapter (53) of Second Isaiah that speaks of a Suffering Servant, 'despised and rejected of men, a man of sorrows,' who has been 'wounded for our transgressions' and yet by whose 'stripes we are healed.' If this is not Jesus, the Christians have asked, who can it possibly be? The scholars have proposed Israel, the unknown Second Isaiah himself, the real Isaiah, or Jeremiah. None of these seems satisfactory, and Dupont-Sommer has suggested that Second Isaiah may date from

171

a period as late as that which is dealt with in the literature of the sect. These later chapters of Isaiah had long been assigned to the Babylonian Exile, two hundred years later than the original Isaiah, and it had already been admitted that still later additions were possible. Why, now asks Dupont-Sommer, could these passages not have been written after the death of the Teacher of Righteousness? And 'now that the alert has been sounded,' he says, 'many passages of the Old Testament must be examined with a fresh eye. Wherever it is more or less explicitly a question of an Anointed One or of a Prophet carried off by a violent death, how is it possible to avoid asking whether the person indicated is not precisely our Teacher of Righteousness?' "[14]

We are not called upon, in this connection, to venture an opinion either as to the composition of the Book of Isaiah or whether the suffering servant be Israel in its collective affliction or some individual teacher and martyr. The important matter for us here is that we are face to face with the thought that the righteous who serve a great cause or a great truth must be prepared for suffering and self-sacrifice if they wish that cause or that truth to be ultimately triumphant.

This spiritual insight seems to me to be the climax of the biblical discussion concerning suffering and retribution. It points out that not only is suffering not always an instrument of punitive judgment designed to chastise the sufferer, but that God imposes it and the servant accepts it that he may bear witness to some faith which can bring healing, liberation, and salvation to humanity at large.

THEORIES OF DIVINE RETRIBUTION IN RABBINIC LITERATURE

I—Complexity of the Problem

Western scholarship is quite aware that in the Apocryphal and pseudo-epigraphic writings not admitted into the biblical canon by Jewish authority, and above all in the New Testament scriptures and the writings of the Church Fathers, there are views concerning divine retribution, immortality, and the World to Come, as well as the function of suffering and martyrdom, that differ greatly from the so-called Old Testament writings. The Christian sources often introduce points of view that claim to have fulfilled and surpassed what in the Hebrew Bible was supposed to have been only promise and prophecy.

What on this subject is original and novel in the rabbinic sources which parallel the literary productions noted above is not so clearly recognized. This is due, as we shall presently see, to an overabundance and to a paucity of material presented for our consideration in the great compilations of Mishna, Talmud, and Midrash. English readers are therefore all the more deeply indebted, first to the splendid essay in the First Series of Schechter's *Studies in Judaism* called "The Doctrine of Divine Retribution in Rabbinic Literature" and to the various chapters dealing with this and cognate subjects in his *Aspects of Rabbinic Theology*, as well as to George Foot Moore's luminous and discerning volumes on *Judaism in the First Centuries of the Christian Era*. These works all stress the variety of views with regard to retribution held in solution in the vast rabbinic literature and make no attempt to distinguish the more profound and original from the vast bulk which merely retrace certain patterns inherited from the past or contain variations all on the same level of naïvete but differing in imaginative or emotional content.

We can accept with confidence Schechter's general evaluation of the position of rabbinic Judaism, as a whole, when he observes

> "Thus Judaism has no fixed doctrine on the subject. It refused a hearing to no theory, for fear that it should contain some germ of truth, but on the same ground it accepted none to the exclusion of the others."[15]

Schechter seems inclined, however, to attribute this reluctance or inability on the part of the rabbis to develop the logical implications of a particular position or to exercise their minds on theological subtleties, to an inherent naïvete and a simplicity of character which made them more or less indifferent to possible inconsistencies.

Professor Moore in one of his notes makes the illuminating observation

> "The subtleties of the Rabbis were mainly in the sphere of observance, those of the theologians of the Church in that of correct beliefs, or to express it more accurately of intellectual apprehension. The one is called 'legalism,' we might name the other 'creedalism;' both Rabbis and Church Fathers were convinced that they were showing men exactly how to conform to the revelation of God."[16]

Professor Moore is quite aware that, for Judaism, divine revelation or Torah had a scope larger than law and, for Christianity, a significance broader than mere creed. He is correct, however, in that rabbinic Judaism always seeks some consensus of authoritative opinion with regard to law or practice and does not, as a rule, seek such consensus of opinion with regard to differences of creedal interpretation. True, it takes for granted the unity of God, the belief in Creation and Revelation, in the Election of Israel, in providence and therefore in divine grace and retribution in this world or the World to Come. This is evident from the fact that we often find judgments excluding from the community of the faithful those who would deny or reject these fundamentals. Nevertheless, there is no proof that the dialectic subtlety which the rabbis displayed in the field of law utterly failed them in the field of theology even if we must give the palm for abstract metaphysical speculation to the Greeks.

Schechter does go out of his way to demonstrate the essential rationalism of rabbinic argument in its main field despite the fact that rabbinic literature is full of folk tales of miracles and wonder stories concerning great saints and teachers. Miracles, however, were never invoked to bolster arguments.

".... We are told in I Corinthians (1:22), that 'The Jews ask for signs as the Greeks seek for wisdom.' As a fact, however, in the whole of Rabbinic literature, there is not one single instance on record that a Rabbi was ever asked by his colleagues to demonstrate the soundness of his doctrine, or the truth of a disputed Halachic case, by performing a miracle. Only once do we hear of a Rabbi who had recourse to miracles for the purpose of showing that his conception of a certain Halachah was the right one. And in this solitary instance the majority declined to accept the miraculous intervention as a demonstration of truth, and decided against the Rabbi who appealed to it. Nor, indeed, were such supernatural gifts claimed for *all* Rabbis. Whilst many learned Rabbis are said to have 'been accustomed to wonders,' not a single miracle is reported for instance of the great Hillel, or his colleague, Shammai, both of whom exercised such an important influence on Rabbinic Judaism. On the other hand, we find that such men, as, for instance, Choni Hammaagel, whose prayers were much sought after in times of drought, or R. Chaninah b. Dosa, whose prayers were often solicited in cases of illness, left almost no mark on Jewish thought, the former being known only by the wondrous legends circulating about him, the latter being represented in the whole Talmud only by one or two moral sayings."

Schechter sums up the discussion with a significant statement

"Signs, then, must have been as little required from the Jewish Rabbi as from the Greek sophist."[17]

He likewise admits that the impression we receive that the rabbis were not interested in following through an idea in prolonged theological discussion may sometimes have been due to the fact that in the course of compilation, certain sources have been lost. (This loss might be explained both by the fact that the compilations had a pragmatic rather than a theoretical aim, or that many of the issues involved in such arguments were no longer relevant and perhaps not understood when the compilations were made.)

> "I will allude only here to the well-known controversy between the school of Shammai and the school of Hillel regarding the question whether it had not been better for man not to have been created. The controversy is said to have lasted for two years and a half. Its final issue or verdict was that, as we have been created, the best thing for us to do is to be watchful over our conduct. This is all that tradition (or the compiler) chose to give us about this lengthy dispute; but we do not hear a single word as to the causes which led to it, or the reasons advanced by the litigant parties for their various opinions. Were they metaphysical, or empirical, or simply based, as is so often the case, on different conceptions of the passages in the Scripture germane to the dispute? We feel the more cause for regret when we recollect that *the members of these schools were the contemporaries of the Apostles; when Jerusalem, as it seems was boiling over with theology, and its market-places and synagogues were preparing metaphysics and theosophies to employ the mind of posterity for thousands of years.*"[18]

Beside the significant philosophical debate to which Schechter alludes in the above, it should not be forgotten that the schools of Hillel and Shammai are said to have engaged in two other controversies dealing with theology. One of these raises the question whether heaven or earth were created first,[19] the second, whether the 'idea' of each day's creation came into existence the night prior thereto, or whether idea and creation were simultaneous. It is generally admitted, meager as is the material presented to us, that these discussions bore some relation to contemporary debates in Greek schools concerning the relation of the Platonic realm of ideas to actual existence.[20] Now, if the report of one of these controversies mentioned above, as it is recorded in Er. 13b, is correct, then it becomes clear that such discussions were at the time viewed with utmost seriousness for we are here informed that at the end the participants actually did take a consensus of opinion as was then the custom in Halachic discussion.

We shall not attempt to review the material so aptly expounded in Schechter's essay on "Divine Retribution in Rabbinic Literature" but only to select such portions as are not mere echoes of biblical thought and to examine them with a view to their logical and theological foundations.

II—The Paradox of Human Mercy as it Clashes with God's Justice

In the biblical as well as in the rabbinic literature, there was never a doubt that the 'zadik' or the 'hasid' felt it his duty to feed the hungry, clothe the naked, comfort the suffering, and champion the underprivileged (the stranger, the widow, the orphan) no matter what was his opinion of the relation of human suffering to divine punishment. In rabbinic literature, the naive acceptance of this paradox seems not to have been so universal. Judaism had to justify itself in the face of that pagan civilization, Greek and Roman, of which it was at these times, in extent, a mere enclave. We are, therefore, told that Tineius Rufus, who, as Dr. Finkelstein points out, won immortality through his friendship with Rabbi Akiba, is said to have brought the contradiction inherent in such a situation to the attention of Rabbi Akiba who as we know represented the essence of Pharisaic thought and life. The argument ran somewhat as follows: "If your God loves the poor, why does He not abolish their poverty?" To this Akiba replies, "That there may be some act by which we may redeem ourselves from the judgment of hell." "On the contrary," the pagan replies, "The very fact that you are prepared to help the poor should convict you of guilt. Let me present a parable. Imagine a king of flesh and blood who, being wroth with his servant, condemns him to the dungeon and commands that none shall give him food and drink, and imagine a man who despite that King's decree has mercy upon the sufferer and gives him the needed sustenance. Will not the wrath of the king light upon this presumptuous subject? You are such presumptuous subjects for you call yourselves the servants of God as it is said 'For the children of Israel are my servants.' And yet, through your charity, you interfere with the course of His justice." Rabbi Akiba is said to have answered him, "Let me cite you a parable in return. This can indeed be likened to a king of flesh and blood who was angry with his son and felt compelled to consign him to the dungeon and withhold food and drink. Will not the king, however, be inclined to reward the stranger who showed mercy to his child? This is our point of view; for we do not think of ourselves only as subjects. We think of ourselves as His children, as it is said 'Children are ye unto the Lord your God.' "

There is nothing naive or simple minded in Rabbi Akiba's position. He contrasts the pagan with the Jewish point of view on the basis that God is not only our King but our Heavenly Father and though it may be His prerogative to chastise His children, He is nevertheless pleased when the latter are kind to one another.

Akiba's argument follows not only congruently but logically from a position of his reiterated again and again, especially for polemical purposes. Among the several beatitudes attributed to Akiba in Abot, there is one which reads "Beloved are Israel who are called children of God. Boundless love was made known to them when they were thus designated." We meet likewise with a remarkable statement by the same authority in Mishna Yoma, a tractate which deals with the elaborate ritual of the atonement day and the part that both priest and people play therein. "Happy are ye O Israel! In whose presence do ye seek purification? And who is it that purifies you? It is your Father in Heaven, as it is said 'It is I who sprinkle upon you waters of purification that ye be pure' and again 'the fountain of Israel's purification is the Lord Himself.' As the waters purify the defiled so the Holy One blessed be He purifies Israel."

We are allowed to surmise that there must have been more statements of the same kind accredited to Rabbi Akiba. He draws from his general position, with precise logic, an attitude contrasted both with paganism as he viewed it, and with the developing Christian theology which he could not but view as heretical. The divine King, he seems to say, unlike the deified emperor, is also the Father, and though it be His prerogative to punish, it still remains the duty of the children to love one another. All Israel alike are called children of God and hence no one individual can claim to be 'the only begotten son of God.' And finally it is not the Messiah who redeems from sin but God himself, the Eternal Father. The prayer which begins "Our Father Our King" and which plays so important a part in the liturgy of the synagogue during the penitential days is only an expanded version of a supplication uttered by R. Akiba on the occasion of a public fast

"Our Father Our King
We have sinned before Thee.
Our Father Our King
We have no king beside Thee,
Our Father our King
Have compassion upon us."[21]

All these father passages weave a logical and consistent pattern characteristic of an important aspect of Akiba's theology.

It is evident that rabbinic thought had become sensitive to some of the contradictions inherent in the biblical position and to the criticisms these evoked in the minds of thoughtful non-Jews. There are other important currents in rabbinic thought which display a deepening awareness of the problems involved and which approached these with an attitude both of wider experience and greater sophistication than we find in the Bible.

III—Immortality and the World to Come

In the rabbinic period as in the biblical period, there

were some who held the view that there is no inevitable connection between sin and suffering and death, but they differed from the biblical writers in that they could venture the general negation "The reward of a good deed cannot be looked for in This World." For in the rabbinic literature, in the Apocryphal writings, and in the Gospels, the Pharisaic faith in resurrection and the World to Come had in various forms taken firm hold. However, only that there is a World to Come seems to have met with universal acceptance. What the relations were between resurrection, the World to Come and the Messianic era, what exactly were the functions of Paradise and Gehinnom, display almost every possible variation upon the general theme. We shall not concern ourselves with these, nor shall we inquire as to the causes and the sources of this vivid theodicy of which there are at best only faint glimmerings in the biblical literature.

We are mainly in search of those currents in rabbinic literature which demonstrate the logical and theological basis for this radical change of position. We meet with a statement, for instance, to the effect that "This world is but an ante-chamber to the world to come. Prepare thyself in the ante-chamber that thou be permitted to enter the banqueting hall." The author of this otherworldly point of view turns out to be both a realist and an idealist. His name was Rabbi Jacob and he insists that "There is no good deed commanded in the Torah and promising a reward for its fulfillment which does not imply the Resurrection of the Dead. Man is told to honor father and mother, 'that thy days may be long and that it may go well with thee' and likewise not to take the mother bird and the young together from the nest but to let the mother go free (Deut. 22:6) 'that it may be well with thee and that thou mayest prolong thy days.'" The Rabbi then tells the story of a father who bade his son bring him some doves. The son prompted by filial love and obedience fulfills the good deed as prescribed but falls from the perch to which he had ascended and dies. "What then of the length of days or the happiness promised this young man? Events such as these go to show that the 'length of days' here promised can refer only to a *world that is long without ending* and the 'well being' here promised to a *world that is good without blemish.*"

This point of view in its drastic realism is far more moving and more radical than anything found in biblical literature. It points out that not only do the righteous sometimes suffer in the natural course of their lives, but that in the very act of doing good, and contrary to the folk adage that no one is ever injured on a mission of mercy, man often meets with misfortune and death. Morality may be a dangerous thing. This is evidenced not only in the life of the martyrs but in the simple annals of daily living where man can suffer and die because nature seems indifferent to the quality of his acts. What is most remarkable is the bold reinterpretation here advocated of all the glowing promises so often found in the Bible. How different from the ardent but dogmatic faith and optimism of the psalmist who can confidently assert

> "A thousand may fall at thy side,
> And ten thousand at thy right hand;
> It shall not come nigh thee.
> Only with thine eyes shalt thou behold
> And see the recompense of the wicked."
> (Ps. 91:7,8)

Here then we find a naturalistic and self-consistent delineation of the facts of human experience side by side with the hopes of the human spirit which make faith in some form of immortality a logical necessity. The fulfillment of divine justice, if there is such a justice, must reach beyond the limits of our transient existence.

This faith evidently did not lead to any gloomy view of what life on earth has to offer man but rather to the conviction that there is something glorious in the fact that right and goodness must be achieved at some cost. The same teacher exclaims elsewhere "Better is one hour of repentance and good deeds in this world than all the life of the world to come but better is one hour of bliss in the world to come than all the life of this world." This amounts to the confession that the world of actual existence has greater *value* than life in that 'Other World' but that the bliss experienced in and through that 'Other World' exceeds whatever lure this world may offer.

IV—*Above the Desire for Reward or Fear of Punishment*

It is well known that the Pharisaic faith in immortality, resurrection, and the World to Come was taken over not only by later Judaism but by Christianity and Islam, and the hope for heaven and fear of hell consequently entered largely into ethical motivation. On the higher level of religious thinking, however, it was always felt that deeds done under the spell of such hopes or fears leave a taint upon the moral life. This is especially the case in rabbinic literature. The feeling seems to have prevailed that if there exists a divine justice, then this must realize itself on earth or in heaven, but on the other hand, wherever the will to righteousness exists, it must attest its genuineness by disinterested service without hope of personal reward or punishment. The faith in immortality aims not so much to comfort man as to justify God. It comforts man only indirectly in that it assures him that there is a pure and perfect justice which he serves when he does God's will.

It is characteristic of rabbinic Judaism that the great moralistic compilation included in the Mishna and known as Abot or Ethics of the Fathers almost begins with the words 'Be ye not like servants who serve the master in expectation of a reward but be ye like servants who serve the master understanding that they are to receive no reward and let the fear of heaven rest upon you.' In this case, the fear of heaven is exactly equivalent with the love of God. It is the fear of offending that which we most dearly love.

Sentiments expressing similar views are too numerous to be mentioned here; yet we cannot leave the subject before calling attention to another clear affirmation of the attitude that promised reward must never enter into the calculations of conscience.

This statement which is so often quoted that it has become almost normative, displays sardonic wit as well as nobility of mind. The first Psalm begins with a triumphant assertion

> "Happy is the man that hath not walked in the
>   counsel of the wicked,
> Nor stood in the way of sinners,
> Nor sat in the seat of the scornful.
> But his delight is in the law of the Lord;
> And in His law doth he meditate day and night."
> (Ps. 1:1,2)

It continues with the delineation of the bright destiny of the righteous who is compared to a green and fruitful tree and is assured that "In whatsoever he doeth he shall prosper." The wicked, of course, must expect the opposite of all this, for "The way of the wicked shall perish." The rabbinic commentator insists that the righteous glorified in this Psalm is one of whom it can indeed be said that "His delight is in the law of the Lord," and this means that when he fulfills a commandment he finds pleasure in the commandment itself and not in the reward promised for its fulfillment. He who delights in the latter cannot truly be called righteous.

All this so manifestly overlooks the spirit of the whole Psalm that one cannot but feel that the author of the statement was perfectly aware that his interpretation was quite divorced from the literal meaning of the verses to which he referred. We often find in rabbinic literature that a rabbinic homily is not so much intended to interpret a verse in scripture as to correct an impression which the literal meaning of the verse might convey. To these men, the administration of justice was left to God, but only one who gave to goodness disinterested service was deemed to be serving God in righteousness.

A similar instance of such perverse or adverse interpretation is in reference to the biblical lines we have already quoted "I was young and now am old, yet have I not seen the righteous forsaken or his seed begging their bread." The verse is so interpreted as to read 'yet have I not seen the righteous bereft of his faith even though his children must beg their bread.' They are never 'forsaken' by the faith which has all along sustained them even though they be reduced to abject poverty.

Thoughts such as these dominating rabbinic literature made it possible for one of the later saints in the midst of his prayers to exclaim "I have no wish for Thy Paradise, nor any desire for the bliss in the world to come. I want Thee and Thee alone."[22]

The logic which permits this exalted and austere conception of righteousness to emerge out of a sacred literature rich in promise and threat is best illustrated in another Hasidic epigram. We are told of one of the Hasidic masters, that he was once watching with rapt attention the performance of a tight-rope walker. When his disciples asked him what it was that riveted his gaze to this foolish performance, he answered, "This man is risking his life and I cannot say why, but I am quite sure that while he is walking the rope he is not thinking of the fact that he is earning one hundred goolden for what he is doing; if he did he would fall."[23]

V—Beloved is Suffering!

There is an anonymous Boraitha variously quoted in the rabbinic literature[24] which reads as follows: "Those who are persecuted but persecute not in return, those who suffer offence but give none, who hear themselves reviled yet reply not in kind, who act only through love and who rejoice in suffering, of these Scripture truly says 'And those who love Him are as the rising of the sun in his might.' (Judges 5:31)." Here the last verse of the Song of Deborah and the last half of that verse, a song which exults over victory in battle, is made to be the bearer of experiences and moral insights accumulated not in a succession of victories but in a long history of suffering. It was meant perhaps to save the song from encouraging that heroic but mistaken zealotry which from the time of Gedaliah had proved so futile and disastrous. Lines such as the above, somewhat paralleled in the Sermon on the Mount, are often compared with Stoic pride in being able to rise above pain and sorrow. Thomas Carlyle in "Sartor Resartus" however has noted a difference which he defines according to his faith as a Christian, "Small is it that thou canst trample the Earth with its injuries under thy feet, as old Greek Zeno trained thee: thou canst love the Earth while it injures thee, and even because it injures thee; for this a Greater than Zeno was needed, and he too was sent. Knowest thou that *'Worship of Sorrow'?*"[25] As Jews we would be compelled to paraphrase Carlyle's lines so as to read "For this a people other than the Greek was needed. A people more schooled in sorrow." He is right, however, in pointing to the difference. To be able to embrace pain with joy is quite different from merely accepting it with indifference or contempt.

If the quotation above were the only utterance of its kind inculcating love and viewing sorrow as a source of joy, it might be dismissed as the vagary of some individual saint. We hear, however, the almost triumphant phrase "Beloved is suffering" again and again in the rabbinic literature out of the mouths of teachers in successive generations. Indeed we find[26] a whole anthology of such phrases as hail suffering in terms of love and for a variety of motives. Suffering is said to outweigh sacrifice as a mode of atonement and purification. One Rabbi declares "Beloved to God is suffering for the glory of God rests upon him who endures such suffering with love." All the best gifts—Revelation, the Land of Promise, and the World to Come—Israel has earned only through suffering endured.

Schechter in the essay mentioned above refers to the sources with sufficient fullness. What is important, however, is that the phrase itself expresses the conviction that suffering has its source not only in divine justice but in divine grace, and thus asks man to accept his trials not only in resignation but with corresponding love.

Most of these lofty homilies seek biblical foundation in the words of Job "Shall we not accept the evil at the hand of the Lord as well as the good?" or in certain phrases describing the 'Servant' in Isaiah 53 or in the adage 'Him whom the Lord loveth he chasteneth' or 'As a father chastises his son so the Lord chastises those who fear Him.' Yet these are only biblical pegs for thoughts and sentiments not yet expressed in biblical literature. The chastisements of love here are not truly chastisements at all. They flow not from God's punitive justice nor even from His creative wisdom alone, but out of God's love itself. They constitute a sort of moral opportunity which God holds out to man and which man should embrace with gratitude.

If this attitude must not be confused with Stoic fortitude so must it not be identified with mere masochism. It is not even necessarily bound up with voluntary asceticism. One need not inflict pain upon oneself or refuse to overcome it, in order to appreciate its moral value when one must needs suffer it. The logical consequence for the individual of these views of suffering combined with faith in divine retribution and compensation is summed up in the following passage which has become practically normative in Jewish religious thought, "If a man observes that sufferings come upon him, let him examine his conduct. If he examines his conduct and can honestly find nothing to warrant his pain then let him be sure that these are the chastenings of love."[27] It is a high thing to demand of man. It is vaguely related to the conclusion at which we had already arrived on other grounds, that the capability of suffering, or experiencing both pleasure and pain, is a mark of the higher forms of life. For the individual, then, it may become the supreme opportunity of proving to himself his own moral stature.

What may be as difficult as the courageous endurance of suffering is the self-examination which is to precede it. Saintly men are very punctilious about this. Schechter relates the story of several such great sufferers. One attributed his suffering to the fact that once as he was riding on the way a poor man asked him for alms and he delayed until he had dismounted. In the meanwhile the man collapsed and died. The instant of delay was to him a mortal sin which haunted him all his life. A judge and teacher in Israel having searched his deeds in the very hour of his martyrdom avers that once he might have delayed a decision and justice delayed is like justice perverted. A story even alleges that the compiler of the

Mishna—saint and scholar that he was—attributed an affliction of which he suffered to the fact that once a calf had sought refuge from the slaughterer beneath the folds of his mantle and he had callously bidden it go to its doom. The saints with that hypersensitiveness which makes them saints are more than likely to find some act of theirs for which their suffering serves as compensation, but as for the most of us, I believe that the exhortation of Carlyle, if I may be permitted to quote him once again, is quite in place: "Now consider that we have the valuation of our own deserts ourselves, and what a fund of Self-conceit there is in each of us,—do you wonder that the balance should so often dip the wrong way, and many a Blockhead cry: See there, what a payment; was ever worthy gentleman so used!—I tell thee, Blockhead, it all comes of thy Vanity; of what thou *fanciest* those same deserts of thine to be. Fancy that thou deservest to be hanged (as is most likely), thou wilt feel it happiness to be only shot: fancy that thou deservest to be hanged in a hair-halter, it will be a luxury to die in hemp." We are justified in stating that this heroic attitude towards suffering was generally accepted at least as an ideal because among the qualifications, ethical and intellectual, demanded for the acquisition of Torah, the above attitude is especially mentioned. The Torah student must be capable of welcoming suffering with love.[28]

VI—Suffering and Natural Necessity

Schechter does not fail to touch upon those rare affirmations in which the suffering and especially the martyrdom of the righteous is attributed to that impotence of God which is nevertheless rooted in His own omnipotence. There is for instance the reply which God is said to have made in a dream to a great sufferer who asked how long he would be bidden to endure his anguish. The answer was "My son, will it please you that I destroy the world for your sake?" An allusion is likewise made to the legend telling us that when Moses was granted a glimpse into the future he beheld both the splendors of Akiba's teaching and the cruel death meted out to him.

He asked God "Is this indeed the glory of Torah and its reward?" God is said to have answered him "Be silent, this I have determined." Finally we are reminded of the poetical and mystical martyrology in the liturgy of the day of Atonement in which again God pleads with the sufferer to accept his hard decree lest God be compelled 'to turn the world back to primal chaos.' Schechter's summary of the whole matter is contained in the following

> "One might perhaps suggest that these passages when examined a little closer, not only contain a rebuke to man's importunity in wanting to intrude into the secrets of God, but also hint at the possibility that even God's omnipotence is submitted to a certain law—though designed by His own holy will—which He could not alter without detriment to the whole creation."[29]

From the philosophical point of view, however, it amounts to the recognition that natural necessity and the moral imperative both derive from God. God cannot constantly intervene in the laws of nature without nullifying the cosmos, the physical world of His creation.

For the first time in Jewish thought what approximates to the Greek view of the unity of nature is evoked to modify the prevailing view of the perfect justice of God. Schechter rightly observes "It is only in this light that we shall be able to understand such passages in the Rabbinic literature as that God almost suffers Himself when He has to inflict punishment either on the individual or on whole communities . . . the Shechinah laments even when the criminal suffers his just punishment."[30] There is no escape from this conception of God suffering with man in His compassion if we realize that God has created the physical universe as the scene of man's moral self-realization. All this we have treated at greater length before. What should be remembered in relation to the present discussion is that God's confession that He cannot always help the righteous in their immediate need without destroying the world is a foreshadowing of that scientific point of view which Greek thought was first to develop but with which modern thought must wrestle if it is to understand the moral life of man and continue to hope in the ultimate triumph of the human spirit.

IMMORTALITY

I—Statement of the Problem

The most common form of the question concerning immortality is usually this, do you believe in life after death? Or, somewhat elaborated, do you believe that any human being has ever experienced life after death? Now, it must be apparent that no man could ever have experienced life after death since no man could ever experience death after life. We must cease to think of death mythologically if we are ever to conceive of immortality rationally.

II—The Mythology of Death

By the mythological view of death we mean that idea of death which holds it to be an actual experience through which one passes from life upon earth as an existent organism to some extra-mundane existence which we call immortality. Now, death cannot possibly be an experience either enjoyed or suffered or merely endured somewhat as the shades in Hades were thought to experience death. For to be conscious of new experiences means not to be dead but to be very much alive and since we cannot experience a state of death after life has ceased to be, the experience of life after death is also impossible. Either we must deny immortality or approach the problem from a different angle.

The defenders of immortality might say our question was a careless one. We should have asked, do you believe that the *soul* experiences life after death? Only the soul lives on after death—but not, of course after its death, but only after the death of the body. It itself knows no death. Let us then admit there is no life after death but only the deathlessness of the soul. Within that immortal existence the life and death of the body are vital experiences. The trouble with this rather easy solution is that, though it claims to disregard the mythological idea of death, it substitutes for it a purely mythical conception of the relation of body and soul which would satisfy neither modern science nor, as we shall see, the ethical motivation for the belief in immortality. The idea of the separate existence of the soul is in the Jewish tradition earlier than the idea of resurrection (witness the story of the Witch of Endor) and was met in later biblical thought either by the significant silence of prophetic literature concerning the ancient death myths, by the occasional devastating skepticism of the Wisdom literature (Job 10:18, 14:10, 14; Ecc. 3:25, 9:5) and in post biblical literature was supplemented by the eschatological view of resurrection and the World to Come when body and soul together would partake in a glorified life after the final judgment.[31]

In modern science, the dichotomies which science and philosophy had long suspected of being the result of illegitimate abstraction have been more or less resolved. Thus space and time taken separately are now believed to be abstractions from a continuum known as space-time which is neither empty space nor empty time but might be called the field of existence. Alexander has given it further metaphysical properties and calls it the matrix of all existence or 'pure motion' in which moving things and changing qualities arise. The idea of space-time as pure motion gives it a creative aspect since moving things and changing qualities rise in the course of this pure motion. Now in the space-time continuum we were wont to think of two separate aspects of matter, mass and energy, playing their respective parts as things interact in space and time. I still remember a definition in one of my school books which spoke of matter as having extension and energy being matter in motion. Today the mathematical physicists tell us that mass is energy and energy is mass, that matter in mass is frozen or organized energy and nothing else, they are not two contradictory essences. There is only the matter of energy and the energy of matter.

Philosophically, I believe body and soul must be similarly conceived. There is only the soul of my body and the body of my soul. By the soul I mean the subjective pole of that which is called a human organism, and the body is the objectification in nerve-cell, brain, and muscular movement of that soul as it relates itself and communicates with entities other than itself. I can think of no individual soul without the organism of which it is the soul, or any individual thing without a soul or inner essence which is its meaning to itself. There is no facade of actuality without inner depth, like movie sets where doors on elaborate housefronts lead only to the great outdoors. The purely inorganic analyzes into drops of organic spontaneity, the atom and the electron. Living things all seek their subjective ends. To man, these are not only well-being, but values and ideals. The notion, however, of the soul as a kind of ghost or even as a fragment of divinity which somehow has got to inhabit and to animate the lowly flesh is neither scientific nor is it in the best Jewish tradition. Both matter and soul are in the great creation story the work of God. He breathes life into the matter which has come into being through His divine word and wisdom. Neither has any origin save in God, whereas according to both Plato and Aristotle there is posited a primal substance or that which is called the Void or the Receptacle, which is outside of God but co-eternal with Him. The body derives from this non-divine realm. Only the soul is necessarily immortal since its connection with the body is a descent into a lower level of being, and the death of the body is the soul's redemption.

From our point of view, the contrary is true. The cosmic process involves not the descent of the spirit but elevation of matter. As the energy of the universe assumes more complex forms of organizations, it rises to higher levels of being and displays aspects of reality in an ascending scale of values—the dynamics of the inorganic, the protoplasmic sensitivity of living tissue with its comparative independence of the environment and lastly self-conscious awareness and reason, memory, imagination and will—all that we call soul in the individual being and in the spiritual climate of human culture. But these aspects of reality thus emergent and exemplified in individual things are in themselves not things though they give character and value to existent things and define their place in the scale of being. They are universals of quality and value. They are, like all universals or essences, phases of the overall structure of reality and thus permanent possibilities for things in actual existence everywhere and at all times. We may not know how many human beings now exist or may exist or whether or not the whole human race may perish from the earth, but this we do know, that wherever and whenever a living organism shall arise with bone and flesh and brain structure like our own, it will be a self-conscious minded organism sharing not alone in the qualities which characterize inorganic and organic entities but displaying qualities of subjective awareness of selfhood, of spirit, of soul, which define its humanity.

The mythological thinking against which we have given warning is really what Morris Raphael Cohen used to refer to as the "Fallacy of Reification"—of regarding as a thing what may be more than a thing, since it is an essential qualification or function of many things but which is not by itself a separate existent thing. Thus all stones have weight but weight is not a thing that has entered the stone at some time in its history. It is just the magnitude of the stone's inertia. So long as a stone remains a stone, it has this property which it shares with all physical entities including even the most ethereal dreamers and poets. So soul or mind or subjective awareness is not a thing which has entered the body and exists there in temporal or spacial relation with it. It is not inside or outside or before or after the body, it is the soul of the body as the body is the body of this or that soul, or as the weight is the weight of the stone and the stone a stone of a particular weight. It would not be a stone if it had no weight and the body would not be a living human organism had it not a soul.

The soul may, therefore, be deathless as is every essence but it is not an immortal *thing*, a center of experience apart from the body by virtue of which it can experience and survive the body's death and therefore be said to have life after the death of the body. Before and after refers only to things and events, not to things and their defining essences. There are no time intervals between a thing and its essence, that pattern of universals which makes it just that thing and no other. When I say that a thing must first be possible in order that it shall become actual, I do not imply that possibility is an actual thing preceding the thing for which it provides the possibility. We would then have to ask how came possibility to become possible. What we state is simply that reality is such that a thing must logically be possible if it ever has become or will become actual. The blueness of Gainsborough's famous picture "The Blue Boy" will not perish if the canvas is destroyed; it will still be visible in the sky or in other canvases painted by other artists for it is not a thing which existed either before or after the famous masterpiece. Blueness is simply an ever recurrent quality which may appear anywhere and at any time under certain conditions of existence. It is the reality of blueness which makes "The Blue Boy" possible.

III—The Reification of Death

Those who most emphatically deny life after death are no less prone to construe the situation mythologically. They are likely to lament that all life ends in death, in nothingness, in not-being. There is therefore only life before death, not after death. The fallacy here lies in treating nothing as though it were something. Something in which life spends its last days. Nothingness is just nothingness and not-being simply has no being at all. The not-being of any particular thing is merely the being of something else. I may be writing upon a table because it certainly is not a chair. What the table is not I can only define by describing a chair and other pieces of furniture or other objects of which I have knowledge. The being of the latter is what the table is not. To speak of death as though it were a state of being into which life passes after the state of being we call living has come to an end is pure mythology.

The fact of the matter is that birth and death, or the

coming into existence and the passing of any living things, are the limits between which life is lived. The limiting events, birth and death, beginning and end, are never within the series of events which they limit. We cannot experience life after death, as we have seen, because we cannot possibly experience death after life. All experience means living, even that of dying. The poets and mystics have often spoken of life as a perpetual dying. This may be true even scientifically since the energy of any structure begins to disintegrate the moment it has come into existence, and in its disintegration it plays its part in the actual world. We expend energy in all that we do. It behooves us to remember that he who feels himself dying, sometimes in anguish wishing himself dead, is still very much alive. Life knows only the experience of living, and all experiencing is a sign of life. As long as we are alive, said Epicurus, death does not exist for us, and when death comes, we no longer exist.

Is death therefore unreal? A mere illusion that haunts the mind of man? By no means. Can we in this age which has witnessed beyond all other ages the mass production of death cast it aside as mere illusion? Was he blind to actual experience who said "A generation goeth and a generation cometh though the earth standeth forever." Are the love of life and the fear of death sentiments to be dismissed as trivial in the history of human progress? Was the piercing lament of David without significance for human love "Absalom my son, my son, would I had died in place of thee." No, I am afraid we walk each day as living beings in the valley of the shadow of death and one of life's great problems, no matter how long life may be prolonged, is how to live with the certainty of death without permitting this certainty to rob life of its beauty and its joy. All that I wish to emphasize is that it is no argument against immortality to say that no one has ever returned to tell us of life after death since no one has ever returned to tell us of death after life. Yet despite this fact, we do not doubt the reality of death though it is clear that only the living could experience death if death were an experience, since all experience is the stuff and substance of actual life.

My father, for instance, could never have experienced his own death and therefore a life subsequent to his own death, but both my father's life and his death are real aspects of my living experience—momenta in my own life's history. I knew him as a living person, an object of love and veneration. I felt myself subject to his command, instruction, and his censure, or his praise. I saw him with my eyes, heard him with my ears, touched him with my hands, and then after a brief illness his body was bereft of life, could no longer communicate with me, and at last disintegrated and returned to dust. He was no longer an actual object in my environment but a cherished memory, and only through the channels of memory does he now communicate with me. Something had perished out of the world of my experience, I had experienced its perishing. The world was still crowded with natural phenomena and populated with living beings but they were all *not he*. They spelled his not being. His being and his not being, his life and death, were within the sphere of my living experience. This is the reality of death. The death of another which enters into our own life. I cannot repeat too often that death has no reality save as an experience in some continuing life. Only in the perspective of some living observer does death become an actual experience. Death is a phase of life and not the reverse.

Those who deny the reality of ultimate purpose, and value either with the tentative probing of Koheleth or the wine-soaked sentimental melancholy of Omar Khayyam or the triumphant desperation of modern materialism, all describe existence as having emerged by chance out of nothing and vanishing into eternal night. Cosmologists like Eddington often speak of the continuous increase of entropy in the physical universe till the arrow of time ceases to point. When time ceases, space also ceases to have meaning. Today we know that space is filled with time and time with space and they are both abstractions from a continuum called space-time, something for which there are no descriptive adjectives but only mathematical symbols. Not only does matter come to an end with space and time and they with it, but matter itself is no longer regarded as solidified extension but its very mass is only organized energy and in the disintegration of its energy matter ceases to be.

What then happens? We must always beware lest, having abandoned the gods or heroes of ancient mythology and the colorful cosmologies in which they played their parts, we build new myths which we imagine to be rational only because the gods have been banished, and we clothe with substance terms borrowed from science instead of from religion.

The idea that the whole universe of actual existence in time and space can be translated into nothingness at a particular period of time is simply mythological thinking. It is on the same plane as 'creatio ex nihilo' where ex nihilo is meant to exclude even God—which is never the case in religious thinking. For if it is impossible that all substance shall emerge out of nothingness, it is equally impossible that all substance shall lapse into nothingness. Some astronomers now posit continuous creation to save themselves from this dilemma. The fact of the matter is that should the whole physical universe come to an end, the end to which it comes will not be succeeded by nothingness for nothingness has no reality either before or after something. It is so easy to say that after a time there can be just nothing, were it not for the fact that that which comes after must be in time and therefore something. *If it has a date, it is an event.* Before and after have no significance except as temporal or logical designations. The end of time and physical processes in time and space are relative only to a larger realm of being. The end of time can only be within God's eternity for time and space must be conceived as in God, not God in time and space. In His non-temporal or supra-temporal existence is every beginning and every end whether of the individual or the whole universe of actual existence. Thus the end of an individual or a whole universe must not be sought as an event within the history of the universe, or in some nothingness which follows that history, for then we elevate the nothing into something related in time to what goes before and therefore demonstrating continuity rather than dissolution. The end of the universe can only have reality in that eternity of being within which all times are contained and are transcended.

IV—Time as Possibility and Time as Actuality

We must not confuse mathematical space and time, or space-time, as a *possibility* for all existent things and events in nature with the space-time as experienced by, and integrated into, the course of events. Thus when we analyze space and time intervals into points and instants which themselves have no dimension and say that a line, no matter how short, is drawn through an infinity of points and that a time interval, no matter how brief, endures through an infinity of instants, what we really mean is that for each particular event in nature, each enduring or persistent thing, the line offers an infinity of possible locations and that even the briefest moment of time offers an infinity of possibilities for the 'now' of any event. We dare not take it to mean that the infinity of points makes it possible that an infinite series of actual finite events or entities can be correlated with the points or instants in the space or time under discussion. This would be contrary to all that we know of the physical universe. Time intervals and space intervals are all finite, each offering an infinity of possibilities for the coming into existence or perishing of an event.

Every natural fact or object or process has extension and endurance. The points and instants of mathematical time have no extension whatever. They are therefore not existent things but possibilities for existence. They have the indisputable reality of all universals or essences of defining possibilities of order among the concrete multiferous things in actual existence. An infinity of actual entities, each without extension, occupying an infinity of mere points and instants in space-time would leave us no extension whatever and therefore no actuality.

The inability to understand the difference between essential time and space and the way time and space enter into the existence of actual things has led to the well-known antinomies which were to prove that time was an illusion. The only illusion is that space and time are themselves actual things. Actual time is not only between things, measuring their respective limits and establishing their sequence, it is also within things, making possible their endurance and persistence.

The here-now of any actual event, no matter how long or short its duration, is not a non-extended instant. It contains within itself a past and future out of which it builds the actual present of its existence. An event is not only in time, but we may say, with some metaphysical exactness, that 'it takes time to be an event.' Every natural entity, every drop of actual existence, appropriates unto itself possibilities inherent for it in space and time and makes of them an actual here-now in which the significance of all time and space is exemplified.

V—*The Nature of the Here-Now*

The actual existence of anything is always in such a here-now, in the actual present in which a thing experiences its persistence as well as its transience. The past as such has no actuality. Indeed, it may be defined as that which was but is no longer actual, and the future as that which never arrives[32] or never becomes actual, and if the present is only the dividing line between the two, then actuality itself becomes an illusion. For every 'now' is, in such a definition, only a non-extended something between what is no longer and what shall never be in actual existence, and all three are equally bereft of actuality.

The situation, however, is quite different. The past is actual since it lives in the present of every experiencing subject. It conditions all present experience. Every mote of matter is in part what now it is because of all that affected it and entered into its being in time past. Its past is actually mirrored in its present structure. I am now what my memories are, what my character and habits have shown themselves in my past acts to be. The human organism has, of course, inorganic memories like the crystal and organic memories registered in every cell and tissue, and unconscious memories as well as conscious memories all entering into what now I am and constituting the only basis for what I may become. When we speak of what now I am being mirrored in memories, we include, of course, racial memories and traditions as well as recorded history though I may share these with others beside myself. The past is actual insofar as it plays its role in the living present. Moses on Mount Sinai, Columbus discovering a new world, are phases of the existential present in which I live insofar as what now I know myself to be requires their existence. They have actual existence here and now as they help constitute my living present, no matter what date I ascribe to them. The past may then be said to be a projection in time of all that is determined and settled in the present experience of an enduring subject. Whatever is a fait accompli must be in the past. Whatever cannot be undone must be accepted, before, in the realm of the present, action is possible. Nothing in time or eternity can undo the discovery of America. There is no such thing as undiscovering it no matter how men may differ as to its ultimate destiny. The carboniferous age still exists in the coal mines out of which we dig our fuel. We may tell its story as something in the past, but we are impelled to reconstruct that past because it is something which enters into the living present. Whatever is necessary to account for the structure of a fossil bone or a piece of pottery now under observation becomes the geological and anthropological past. There would be no actual past were it not for the bone or the potsherd. The point we are making is that the past remains actual within a present experience as whatever determines some present event or object to what it is. The past insofar as it is not only presupposed but actually known stands revealed in individual memory, in social tradition, in recorded history, as well as in organic structure. It remains actual only as it plays a part in some here-now of actual experience.

VI—*The Future as Actual*

If the present, the enduring present, gives actuality to

the past, so the present likewise vouches for the actuality of the elusive future. It is true that it never arrives. We can never live in the future, but we can and do live *for* the future. To be an event, we have seen, takes time, and as the present takes the past into itself and in human imagination gives it forth in the form of history as a tale of 'once upon a time' against a map of abstract time in which dates are set down rather than places, so the present, the here-now in which we live, projects a future out of that aspect of actual being which is not yet determined or complete.

If the past cannot be undone, the future always calls for doing. If whatever is fait accompli must be in the past, opportunities for further fulfillment and novelty belong to the future. It is the temporal realm of opportunity, the perpetual land of promise beyond the horizon of the present and yet in the direction toward which the present is steering. Through what the present now *is,* it pays tribute to the reality of the past and endows that past with actuality. Through what the present may *become* it pays tribute to the reality of the future and endows it with actuality. Every phase of an individual being and every being in actual existence and all processes in which beings play their part are something and are becoming something. Every infinitesimal bit of matter or energy is in part an effect of causes that have played upon it and becomes itself a cause creating new effects. For it to be an effect, the past is required; for it to be a cause, the future is evoked. The effective cause is always in the past, the final cause is ever in the future. Tomorrow never comes. It is always today. But what we are today involves all the yesterdays that have gone, and what we do today or plan today or dream today or desire in the present will create the histories of all the tomorrows yet to come. Ah, you will say, but tomorrow never arrives. Yes, it never arrives because it is already present, not in what today is, but in what today is striving to become or achieve. It is because every event is in part both determined and self-determined and determinative of other events that this is true. Because there are always in experience things which cannot be undone and always the urge to do what has not yet been done, man has mapped the chart of possible time which stretches from the past into the future but can live only in that present which weaves both past and future into the now of actual existence.

VII—Time and Eternity

There is no universal here-now for the whole of space-time. The universe never is at any one instant of time, and therefore the old argument for predestination, which supposes a perfect observer witnessing the pageant of the whole universe and noting the location and velocity of every atom thereof at any particular instant of time, is quite outmoded because it presupposes a situation which does not exist. The whole of time would consist not alone of the sequence of an infinite series of instants or an indefinite series of events but of every possible and actual perspective in which these could be viewed. In other words, it would include every here-now and the actual past and future which radiate from each.

This is known as the principle of relativity with regard to time. There is no absolute simultaneity. Two events happening at the same time in one frame of reference, that is, in space through which an observer travels with a particular velocity, might be successive events in another and so the reverse. They would lie in different perspectives. "At the speed of light" says Arthur Clarke, "time ceases to exist, the moment now lasts forever."[33] The whole of time is, therefore, as it became obvious, not within time. It can have no beginning or end as we have already noticed. But it is a whole made up of an infinity of perspectives which themselves have no temporal relation to one another. There are no time intervals between perspectives any more than there are space intervals between space perspectives. If a tile appears as a perfect rectangle to one looking down at it from above and is diamond-shaped to one who glances at it obliquely, it is futile to argue which is its true shape. It is simply a portion of space which in one perspective is square and in the other is diamond-shaped. It does not occupy more of space in the one image than in the other. There is no additional space, a sort of neutral territory, between the diamond and the square. And so it is with time perspectives. The whole of time is therefore not a temporal affair but a phase of God's eternity. Let us for a moment represent the sequence of events, as it appears in any time series, as follows:

n . . . . . d' c' b' a b c d . . . . . n

In this diagram (a) is an actual present, the here-now of some particular thing and what is simultaneous with it. We shall, for purposes of simplification, take no account of the overlapping of events which always takes place in every natural history. Now, if it is true that events forming a sequence in one time perspective may be simultaneous in another, let us symbolize this fact on a vertical line. Instead of writing (a), (b), (c), the sequence of events in one perspective in which (b) follows (a), we shall put (b) beneath (a) to show they are now viewed as simultaneous. In the perspective of (a), (b) is still subsequent so that the whole situation might be sketched as follows:

n . . . . . d' c' b' a b c d . . . . . n
n . . . . d' c' b' a b c d . . . . . . n

to one not pinned down to either perspective but viewing them both at the same time, which no finite creature could. If there is a perspective in which (a) and (b) can be simultaneous there is also one in which (b) and (c) can possibly be contemporaries. We could continue this indefinitely and then our symbol for all possible time perspective would be as follows:

```
                         n
                         .
                         .
  n . . . . . . . .d' c' b' a b c d . . n
  n . . . . . . .d' c' b' a b c d . . . n
  n . . . . . .d' c' b' a b c d . . . . n
  n . . . . .d' c' b' a b c d . . . . . n
  n . . . .d' c' b' a b c d . . . . . . n
  n . . .d' c' b' a b c d . . . . . . . n
  n . .d' c' b' a b c d . . . . . . . . n
                         .
                         .
                         n
```

so that in essence whether or not there are such actual experienced perspectives, every event has not only its place in the temporal sequence but in the non-temporal. There are no time intervals between things that are exactly contemporary, and there are no causal relations between them. If the baby awoke at exactly the same time the telephone began to ring, the ringing of the telephone could not possibly be the cause of the child's awakening. Each thing in a temporal sequence may be caused by another, but all things together cannot possibly be caused; they can only be created as well as the time sequence and the causal chain in which they are linked. Insofar as these are actual events, they have their existence in the created world. Insofar as they are not actual, they are phases of possibility or essences and they then belong to that larger whole, that more inclusive reality in which both possibility and existence, the universal and the particular, have their relevance to one another.

When we call that reality God, we may lay ourselves open to the same criticism we had previously leveled against others—we too are engaging in mythological thinking when we call that whole of reality, the unity of all being, God. Even Morris Raphael Cohen seems inclined to admit the legitimacy of some kind of absolute:

> "Complete nature cannot reveal or exhibit itself in any moment or interval of time as far as that mo-

ment excludes other moments. But in so far as the meaning and content of each 'here' and 'now' necessarily involves some essence or character that is more than merely here and now, we have a point of view in which the whole of time is included. The point of view to which the whole of time and space has a meaning may be called the eternal (as distinct from the everlasting, which applies to what endures in time and space). It is true that in no moment or interval of time can we grasp or see as actually present to us the whole content of time and space which we call *the* universe. But in knowing the meaning of any fragment as a fragment we know the direction of completion. In this sense there can be no valid objection to the assertion that a knowledge of the absolute is involved in any true knowledge of phenomena."[34]

I am reasonably sure that he would hesitate to call the absolute, God, or apply to it the term One because it may be confused with numerical unity. Samuel Alexander, wrestling with the problem of space-time, has this to say,

"The world which is Space-Time never and nowhere came into existence, for the infinite becoming cannot begin to become. It could only do so in a larger Space and Time and at the order of some cause exterior of it.
In like manner Space-Time is in no case a unity of many things; it is not a one. For that implies that it can descend into the field of number, and be merely an individual, and be compared as one with two or three. The universe is neither one in this sense, nor many. Accordingly it can only be described not as one and still less as a one, but as the one; and only then because the quasi-numerical adjective serves once more to designate not its number but its infinite singularity; or, as is more clearly still expressed by calling it substance, that it is not so much an individual or a singular as the one and only

matrix of generation, to which no rival is possible because rivalry itself is fashioned within the same matrix."[35]

The author was most probably not aware that the term for the oneness of space-time or substance, which he prefers, is precisely the one most frequently met with in rabbinic theology (echad umeyuchad), the One and Singular or the One and Unique.

James Feibleman, who makes the unity of all being a necessary and primal postulate, nevertheless points to the fact that since such a postulate is pre-logical, it tends to gather mythological properties and would be named God. This is not said in any derogatory sense for in an earlier work by Friend and Feibleman, we read the following,

> "It is very evident from our language that we believe there must be an ultimate beyond experience. Here we are on ambiguous ground; since we are immediately estopped from describing such an ultimate by the synthetic, symbolic, and abstract character of all human thought and discourse. In short, this ultimate is unknowable; yet this unknowable can be indicated partially and representationally by language, although the description of its essence is limited to the verb, to be, without predicate. But we might call it the synthesis of all syntheses, the concretion of all abstractions, and the significance from which all symbols derive significance. It is the oneness which includes all possible units in its unity; any attempt to conceive of it in space and time must be futile."[36]

Later in the same work, there is an assertion with which Maimonides and the medieval scholastics would find themselves largely in agreement,

> "God can only be described by saying what He is not; and the negative always asserts something else; this is in effect a double negative, which affirms. But such logical procedure yields only the most abstract

possible description. The negative approach to God is therefore unsatisfactory, for it speaks abstractly about the most concrete fact. Yet it is the only logical approach; consequently theology is foredoomed to be a barren affair. Rationally God is but a logical postulate.
The existence of God cannot be proved. Yet without this ad hoc theory nothing is rationally demonstrable. He cannot be rationalized because He is the irrational basis of rationality."[37]

I would correct the final sentence in the above to read "He cannot be rationalized because He is the supra-rational basis of rationality" and I would add that He cannot be *impersonal* since all personality actual and possible spring from His being. If He is not a person, He must be supra-personal. He cannot be immaterial for all the energy of matter, all the forces of nature are revelations of His power, but He must be incorporeal for every natural thing or body contains only a limited amount of nature's energy and has limited and finite extension in space and time. Each of God's attributes is negative, but it is always the negation of some natural limit and is therefore a double negative pointing to a fullness or plenitude of being inexpressible in words. Thus even the late Professor Cohen who constantly aims his darts against obscurantism and mystification nevertheless makes the following significant admission,

> "If this doctrine that our universe thus contains something fundamental to which we may point but which we cannot fully describe be called mysticism, then mysticism is essential to all intellectual sanity. Language ceases to be significant if it cannot indicate something beyond language."[38]

Man is not therefore guilty of mythological thinking when language is consciously used in this sense and it is in this sense that devotional literature applies to God the multiplicity of metaphors pointing to His relevance to human experience and human values. We can indeed describe Him as King, as Judge, as the Portion of My Cup, as the Holy One, as the Light of the World, as the Abode of the Universe, as the Life of all Worlds, as Our Father in Heaven, provided we acknowledge that He is in reality none of these but cannot, to the human spirit, be less in value than all of these.

God is eternal and non-temporal in the sense that all times are within His being because the wholeness of time can be contained in no time or epoch no matter how vast. In God all times and all lives contained therein are contemporaneous as well as successive. When a man dies, he no longer exists in the time perspective in which he passed his life, but he never ceases to be in that eternity in which the past and future of every perspective is forever present in the being of God.

This view of the relation of God to all things in time expresses a pantheism (emphasis is placed on theism rather than on pan) more beautifully and completely described in certain lines from the Shir Hayichud or the Song of the Unity.

> "All that was at first
> And all that at last shall be
> All the creatures and all their deeds
> And all their spoken words and thoughts
> From beginning to end
> Thou knowest them all
> And thou forgettest not
> For thou art co-present with them. . . .
> There is nothing so secret that it is hidden from thee
> Events of the future and of the past
> With thee are they one. . . .
> For thou art from eternity to eternity
> They are all in thee as thou art in them all."

We meet with some form of this faith in all the high religions of the Orient. It is recurrent in Jewish tradition. There is a trace of it in the first lines of the 90th Psalm. It finds expression in the familiar rabbinic designation for God's omnipresence, "The Place" (of all things) explained to mean "The Holy One Blessed be He is the place of the universe, not the universe the place of Him." It is found in the rationalizations of the mystic's feeling of the world's oneness with God both in the writings of the German Hasidim as we have discovered in the poem above, and in the theosophy of the Kabbalitst.[39] It is very like the "Substance" of Spinoza as Wolfson points out, and it is not too distant from the conception of God advanced more recently by Samuel Alexander in *Space, Time and Deity*. If I understand the latter aright, the whole of Space-Time which is not *in* Space-Time is the body or substance or being of God, and deity is its ever emergent quality. To my mind, some such form of pantheism is the only way in which scientific and historical truth can be held to be congruent with faith in God.

VIII—Immortality as an Actual Experience

The fact that man knows that the past lives only in the presence of his felt experience and that the future together with the past exists actually only in that present—where what a man is, and what he strives to become or to achieve, unite to define his character and moral status—means that man experiences his own immortality. He feels that there is something about him that triumphs over time. The past never really escapes him; the future never actually outruns him, for they are welded together in the everlasting 'Now' of every actual experience. He is not mere driftwood afloat upon the surface of time's current but, paradoxical as it may seem, though he moves with the current, he knows himself also as the channel that directs its flow. He thus wins the assurance that however brief his life may appear upon the chart of any time perspective, however swiftly the generations may follow one another in the inevitable succession of historical events, yet each separate life and each moment of every life must be forever present in the now of God's eternity where the whole past and future abide in essential simultaneity. The point that I am making is that the knowledge of *any* past and future in the actual inner life of an individual involves an awareness of the eternal as well as of the temporal.

Let it be clear that when we speak of the awareness of the eternal or the infinite, we do not mean eternal and infinite awareness which can only be ascribed to God. We point to a temporary and fleeting glimpse within a particular frame of space and time of that which points to something beyond Space and Time and helps make even our temporal experience more intelligible.

IX—Moral Consequences

The question must now be put as to the moral consequence of such a view of immortality as we have been developing. In God's eternity, all things in actual sequence are also essentially co-present. They remain possibilities for actualization. The experience of immortality, it would then appear, is the experience within ourselves of that situation between the actual past, present, and future, which enables us to conceive of the fact that nothing completely perishes out of that wholeness of being which we know as God. Past and future, in their wholeness, are with Him equally present as they are partly present in every here-now of our own awareness. God does not have to recall the past—"Before the throne of His glory there is no forgetting."

The fact nevertheless remains that what is eternally with God is every finite life as it was lived with its meed of joy and sorrow, achievement and failure, comradeship and isolation. There is involved no extension of the finite personality to embrace other than finite and mundane experience. There are no experiences acquired after death in addition to those that make up the history of life upon earth. All that we have been saying is that every life which once came into existence remains forever a phase of God's being. Immortality has not transformed it or prolonged it. How can such immortality, without heaven or hell beyond the grave, without the soul's capacity to enjoy or suffer either, did such heaven and hell actually exist, serve as an incentive to righteousness. The answer is this—the truly righteous do enjoy their immortality and they enjoy it here and now. They do not receive their reward in the World to Come, their joy in the World to Come is their reward. They know even as they are dying that what now is dying, and will in the course of time surely be dead, nevertheless lives forever, not in any time, but in that here-now where the whole of the future meets the whole of the past in God's eternity. The wicked, I think it can be shown, are psychologically incapable of sharing in that joy.

Let me for a moment recall the story of the man who was planting a carob tree that would only yield fruit after seventy years. When asked why he expended all this futile labor since he could never hope to see the tree in its fruitage, his answer was "I find a world with carob trees which my fathers planted for me so I plant for my descendants." [40] Did the man who so vividly felt himself a link between the generations act for the sake of the joy his children would experience by partaking of the fruit in the decades after his death? Such a conclusion would not express the whole truth or even the most significant truth in the situation at hand. You remember that in discussing the egoistic and altruistic poles of motivation, we pointed out that far from being able to identify the moral impulse with one or the other they are often indistinguishable. The good man acts not only to bring happiness to others but because he himself can only find happiness in doing the good and in contemplating the joy and well-being his deed may bring to his fellow man. So the man who plants the tree finds his own joy now, in the living present, through the assurance that he is satisfying the needs of his children in some future yet to be when he will no longer be alive to taste the fruit of his own planting. *His joy in the future is an experience of the present, not of the future.* So the good man will rejoice that nothing that is good is ever lost but that the doer and his deed, his travail and his triumph and all the happiness wrought by the champions of truth and righteousness throughout the ages have their place forever in the timeless resplendency of God who is timeless only because all times are in Him as He is in all times.

Only the righteous can experience this joy. Only he

identifies himself in his goodness with every act of mercy and justice performed on earth, with all the goodness that is his legacy from the past, (the "Merit of the Fathers,") with all the righteousness and truth to be wrought in the future as man advances toward his Messianic goal. They are all projections of his own intent, they are all the fulfillment of his own passion. The Good is one and harmonious. However small the individual's contribution may be to the sum of human righteousness, he will never for one moment admit that there can be too much of justice and holiness in the world. Through God he communes not only with eternal and perfect goodness in the ideal and universal sense, but with all the individuals who in time past or in eras yet to come bear the yoke of God's Kingdom in the joy of victory or in the pangs of frustration and suffering. This naturally includes all the loved ones he has known and all the comrades who march behind him or go before him that help to shape the moral destiny of man. He knows that even in life through God he is near to all of these as they are near to him, that being present with God he is present also with all who have ever lived in times no matter how remote. The total value or essence of each individual life is forever conserved in the timeless eternity of God. We must bear in mind that the total value and essence of each individual life is something more and not less than the individual life itself.

Socrates, Feibleman (Ontology) somewhere remarks, is an actual individual, but the total value of Socrates (to himself I presume and to all the world) is an essence, that is, a possibility for actual existence, something that is part of the overall structure of reality, a phase of the fullness of God's being. The total value of Socrates as essence would include not only the meaning of Socrates to himself in his own self-consciousness and to all the contemporaries who lived with him or were in touch with him or learned from him, but would include every effect of his life and thought and teaching upon future generations and upon the history of human thought in general. As an individual person, he has died out of the perspective of Space-Time and circumstance in which we chart his life. But our chart is relevant to a particular frame of reference. There is always a frame of reference actual or hypothetical in which he or his thoughts and deeds occupy the Here-Now of some present experience.

We have taken exception to the doctrine of the immortality of the soul as it is commonly understood because it implies the actual existence of the mind apart from the body. If, however, we allow ourself the liberty to interpret 'soul' to mean the total value or essence of any individual and understand that the essence of any particular and concrete thing in existence also involves the essence of its particularity and individuality, which latter are universals—then we can indeed affirm belief in the immortality of the soul. Every individual thing or fact or event, as we have suggested, involves a subjective and objective pole. The essence of a human individual, however, involves mind and body, inner self-consciousness and outward act—in short it involves the meaning and significance of the whole person. Therefore, though I would not exclude the term immortality of the soul, if correctly understood, I would prefer to say that I believe in personal immortality. When we pass judgment upon the essential character and worth of any human being, of his place in our lives and in human history, we are doing very much what God is said to be doing in the act of resurrection—putting body and soul together and judging them as one, for only together do they constitute the individual, transient and immortal, responsible for his deeds.

I would here call attention to an important reservation which we have failed to make explicitly but which obviously is to be understood in all these discussions. We have spoken of the righteous and the wicked as though they were mutually exclusive. As a matter of fact, all religious literature recognizes that very few human beings are wholly either one or the other "There is none righteous upon earth who doeth good and sinneth never." Almost all that we have said concerning the righteous or the wicked should be qualified in the following manner—Insofar as a man is wicked or insofar as a man is righteous he will suffer or enjoy his immortality as a living and present experience in the world of actual existence.

Proceeding now with our argument, let me again state that to the wicked such joy as the righteous experiences in his immortality is denied. He is doomed to live the "Life of the hour" rather than the "Life everlasting." He averts his eyes from both heaven and hell and says to himself "If it were done when 'tis done, then 'twere well it were done quickly." To get the deed over with and forgotten by God and man is his primal hope. He cannot in his lifetime possibly take satisfaction in the reflection of his own wickedness in hearts other than his own as the righteous contemplate with joy the flowering of love and justice everywhere. The murderer must seek escape not only from the pangs of his own conscience and from the vengeance of the just, but from the murderous instincts in the hearts of his comrades in crime lest they shed his blood as he has shed the blood of others. The thief cannot hope for the triumph of thievery throughout the world lest his treasure be snatched from his hand the moment he has acquired it. The cruel tortures which others inflict upon their victims cannot increase the malignant satisfaction a man has felt in his own acts of cruelty. He knows he may be the next victim. One who has given love can hope to enjoy love given in return whereas one who has wrought evil must continually dread that the identical evil he has practised recoils upon his own head. In this way, this wholly objective and realistic way, conscience tends to rob evil of its joy. This is so because evil provides a satisfaction that is *incongruous not only with the universal Good but with universal evil.* It cannot entertain the hope, for its own sake, that the evil done might become a prevalent and all pervasive pattern for conduct.

If a man could say "I rejoice in the rising tide of evil, in the pleasures experienced by all the wicked, I pray for their success even though my life and happiness are threatened by the cruelty and greed and lust of wicked men other than myself"—if he were capable of so thinking, and thus surrendering his own satisfactions for the happiness of others, he would never have been capable of the wicked deed in the first place. For this is the essence of goodness—it denies a transitory and private desire that it may contribute, even through self-sacrifice, to a more enduring well-being, to a social good shared in ever widening circles. Immortality itself thus cannot redeem wickedness from its essential isolation.

Nevertheless, every individual life that affects and is affected by other lives has an essential value. Even the wicked deed that is freely willed exemplifies in its rebellion against the good, the creative freedom which makes the choice between good and evil possible in man. Even the sinner thus pays unwilling tribute to the reality of holiness. His will, too, though misdirected, remains a phase of that moral freedom through which the saints achieve their glory. Every life capable of moral decision has moral value whatever be the nature of its separate deeds. Even those who are deprived of the joy of their immortality, insensate beings, because they have no awareness, or the wicked who are only aware of their freedom to sin, must through God's grace partake of it. All souls, we may well say, dwell forever "beneath the wings of the Shechinah" but only the righteous in every hour of their lives enjoy "the perfect bliss" which this entails, the assurance that all the loved ones they have known and all the righteous throughout the ages are forever with them. They are not lost in the sea of the infinite nor present only in memory; their lives as lived in time and space, their actual influence on human destiny remain *essentially* unchanged in God's eternity—in that whole of time where whatever is experienced in sequence abides in essential simultaneity. The exclusion of the wicked from this realm of joy constitutes their hell, as the participation therein on the part of the righteous constitutes their paradise.

In the familiar memorial prayer of the synagogue (el male rachamim) the souls of the righteous and the pure in heart are described as "Shining with the brightness of the firmament." The allusion is to the promise in the Book of Daniel (12:3) "And they that are wise shall shine as the brightness of the firmament; and they that turn many to righteousness as the stars for ever and ever." This hope is to find fulfillment after the resurrection, and this passage is perhaps the only one in the Bible affirming clearly and indubitably the faith in resurrection and immortality. In our memorial prayer it is the souls of all the righteous and the pure who shine like the eternal stars. This poetic imagery can therefore serve as an apt, if metaphorical, rendering of the thoughts we have attempted to expound metaphysically.

Another feature of the memorial service that is wholly congruent with our view of immortality, though the words are violently wrenched from their original context, is the hope that the soul be "Bound up in the bond of (eternal) life" and that the Lord may become the soul's inheritance. This sentiment stems from the wish expressed on behalf of David by Abigail "May the soul of my Lord be bound up in the bond of life with the Lord thy God and the souls of thine enemies, them shall He sling out as from the hollow of a sling." By a particularly bold stroke of imaginative interpretation and adaptation, the phrase 'to be bound in the bond of life with the Lord God' has come to stand for the soul's status after death and has even been cited in support of the profoundly mystical concept that the souls of the righteous have their abiding place beneath the Throne of Glory.[41] Our denial of the mythological views concerning heaven and hell finds confirmation, strange to say, in a flash of mystical insight revealed in a Hasidic story. It is said of Moshe Teitelbaum that he desired to enter the paradise of the Tannaim (where were regaled the masters of the Mishnaic period). In a dream, after he had undergone certain ablutions, the angels guided him to the desired haven of his soul's quest.

> "There he saw one of the masters sitting with a fur cap on his head and studying the tractate called 'The First Gate.' There the path stopped. Rabbi Moshe was surprised. 'That can't be paradise!' he cried. 'Listen, child', said the angels, 'you seem to think that

the Tannaim are in paradise, but that's not so; paradise is in the Tannaim.' "[42]

1. Some striking instances of this general point of view are the following passages: The great admonition in Lev. 26:3-46; Deut. 29:9, 30:10; and 32:1-43; Psalms 1, 34, 37 (note particularly 'I was young and now am old yet have I not seen the righteous forsaken or his seed begging bread'), 92:7-10, 13-16; Proverbs 3:1-10; Job 4:1-11, 5:3-5, 11-27.
2. See Heinrich Miller, *Die Gesetze Hammurabis* (Wien: Alfred Holdr, 1903) in reference to the text of Exodus 21:31.
3. Dr. Shalom Spiegel, Professor of Medieval Hebrew Literature at the Jewish Theological Seminary of America in New York, first called the writer's attention to this construction.
4. S. Schechter, *Some Aspects of Rabbinic Theology* (New York: The Macmillan Company, 1910), p. 188 text and notes.
5. George Foot Moore, *Judaism in the First Centuries of the Christian Era* (Cambridge, Mass.: Harvard University Press, 1927), Vol. I pp. 475-477.
6. cf. p. 177 supra., and Schechter, *Aspects of Rabbinic Theology*, p. 266.
7. Ezekiel Kaufman, *Toldot Haemunah Hayisraelit*, Vol. II (Tel Aviv, Israel: Dvir Co., Ltd., 1952) p. 602 and Robert Gordis, *Koheleth—The Man and His World*, Vol. XIX (New York: Bloch Publishing Co., 1955) p. 3.
8. cf. supra pp. 208, 209.
9. Ezekiel Kaufman, *op. cit.*, p. 646.
10. Philadelphia: The Jewish Publication Society of America, 1922.
11. Louis Finkelstein, *The Pharisees* (Philadelphia: Jewish Publication Society, 1940) Vol. II, pp. 485-486.
12. Friedman, Pes. Rabbati, pp. 160-163.
13. Edmund Wilson, *The Scrolls of the Dead Sea* (New York: Oxford University Press, 1955), pp. 90-91.
14. There is even reference to a variant to Is. 52:14 which would indicate a kind of 'anointing' of the servant (p. 92).
15. S. Schechter, "The Doctrine of Divine Retribution in Rabbinic Literature" *Studies in Judaism* (Philadelphia: The Jewish Publication Society of America, 1911), First Series, pp. 213-214.
16. George Foot Moore, *Judaism in the First Centuries of the Christian Era* (Cambridge, Mass.: Harvard University Press, 1927), Vol. III, p. 60.
17. S. Schechter, *Some Aspects of Rabbinic Theology* (New York: The Macmillan Company, 1910), pp. 6-8. The italics are those of the present writer.
18. *Ibid.*, pp. 8-9. Italics are those of the present writer.
19. Ber. R. 1, 21.
20. For this and related materials see Norman Bentwich, *Hellenism* (Philadelphia: Jewish Publication Society, 1919), p. 255.
21. Taanit 25b.
22. S. Schechter, *Studies in Judaism* (Philadelphia: Jewish Publication Society, 1938) Second Series, p. 181. Also Martin Buber, *op. cit.*, p. 267.
23. Martin Buber, *op. cit.*, p. 174.
24. Shab. 88b, Git. 36b, and the tractate Der. Er. Chapter II.
25. Zeno was not a Greek. He belonged to the Phoenician population of Citium in Cyprus. Wolfson nevertheless points out that the tradition of his school was thoroughly Hellenic. Bentwich, however, remarks that "probably it (stoicism) possessed an original infusion of Semitic thought."

26. Sifre, p. 75a and b.
27. Ber. 5a.
28. Abot. 6 (a chapter appended to the original Mishna).
29. S. Schechter, *Studies in Judaism,* First Series (Philadelphia: Jewish Publication Society, 1911), p. 228.
30. *Ibid.,* p. 228 and supra pp. 185-188.
31. San. 91a.
32. J. W. Friend and J. Feibleman, *Science and the Spirit of Man* (London: G. Allen and Unwin Ltd., 1933), p. 28.
33. Arthur Clarke, "The Planets are Not Enough" *Saturday Review,* November 26, 1955.
34. Morris Raphael Cohen, *op. cit.,* pp. 155-156.
35. Samuel Alexander, *Space, Time and Deity* (London: Macmillan Co., 1927), pp. 337, 339.
36. J. W. Friend and J. Feibleman, *op. cit.,* p. 28.
37. *Ibid.,* p. 316.
38. Morris Raphael Cohen, *op. cit.,* p. 164.
39. The impression one receives from these writings is that the En Sof (the undifferentiated infinite) is not itself God. Indeed it is sometimes equated with the Hebrew Ain or not-being. The God of Zohar is the Infinite in His self-revelation through the ten attributes viewed as potencies (not personalities). These potencies in gradation reach down to the mundane realm of actual existence. Here man plays his part not only as the end product but as a participant in the whole process helping by his deeds to activate the higher realms upon which his being depends.
40. Taan. 23a.
41. Shab. 152b.
42. Martin Buber, *Tales of the Hasidim, The Later Masters* (New York: Schocken Books Inc., 1948), p. 190.

CHAPTER SIX

MORALITY AND RELIGION

Must Man Believe in God to be Moral?

Our treatment of the character and significance of the moral life has taken for granted the truth of certain religious postulates or at least their relevance to an understanding of our subject. We have in many instances given the impression that the moral situation can best be stated in theological terms and have therefore not hesitated to do so. Indeed, most of the illustrative material we have employed has been deliberately culled from the sacred literatures of the great religions and especially from the literature of that biblical and post-biblical Jewish tradition which on its highest levels has most clearly formulated the doctrine of ethical monotheism.

The question naturally arises at this final stage of our discussion, do we believe that the good man must also be a religious man—that to lead a moral life a man must accept the religious doctrines we have woven into our theory of ethics? More briefly put: To acknowledge the authority of the Good must he also acknowledge the authority of God? We can put this negatively and ask, can a man deny the reality of God and still so conduct himself that men will be unable to deny the reality of his genuine goodness?

Suppose we know nothing of a man's religious faiths or doctrinal attitudes, but in our social relations with him discover him to be full of the love of his fellow men and capable of great sacrifice for what he believes to be just and right and true, would we alter our opinion of his virtue because we later discover him to be without faith in God, or even because he was truly convinced that religious faith and feelings are vestiges of primitive superstitions from which man will eventually have to liberate himself to achieve complete humanization?

Must There be a God if Goodness is To Be?

Those of us, like myself, who are unwilling to repudiate goodness in those who lack faith, must be sure that they understand the implications of this attitude before they preen themselves upon their modernity or upon their tolerance. The assertion that a man may be good without faith in God must never be taken as tantamount to the assertion that a man could be good if there were no God. The latter statement may be based on a logical fallacy even though the former be true. We hold that it is based upon such a fallacy, that the phenomena of the moral life, if they are held to be real and not illusory, logically require the postulate that reality in its wholeness be more than material and mechanical, that the cosmic process which produces the mind and personality of the ethical individual with all his possibilities for good or evil, points to a source that, as we have seen, can only be described if not as personal then as supra-personal rather than infra-personal. Even that fleeting glimpse of perfection which is granted man in the conviction that nothing is so good but that it can be better —a person, a culture, society, a civilization—reveals that fact that Infinite Possibility is as real as finite actuality. It is something which can never be found within existence because every stage of existence can only be a finite fragmentary actualization of what could be or might have been, or ought to be and may yet be. Man's potentialities are potentialities to bring into existence what must always have been possible in the realm of ideas and universals, of qualities and values awaiting actualization. They are real through that aspect of God in which His being transcends mere existence.[1]

To expose the fallacy that God is unrelated to moral experience is one of the tasks of that ethical philosophy which we have been tentatively expounding. We go a step further, however, as has already been suggested, and affirm that all true goodness anywhere and in any person, whether that person be or be not insensitive to the logical implications of his acts, is living testimony to that immanent and transcendent power whose creativity stands particularly revealed in the moral individual or within the human society that is groping to live by what ought to be rather than by what is, by what is better rather than by what is good, by what is 'The Good' as distinguished from those momentary and egocentric goods which must ultimately be rejected as evil. He, therefore, though he sins and works evil, so long as he perceives the distinction between good and evil, affirms by his very sin that he lives in a world which is not merely a realm of natural necessity but of spiritual values in which the possibility of sin itself is the empirical evidence of the actuality of freedom.

In this sense, we believe that without God the moral life would be inexplicable. *Man requires God to explain himself to himself* in all those aspects of his nature wherein the physical universe which has brought him into being now enters with him into a realm of moral values, ideals, and aspirations. In this sense, every moral advance expresses the will of God for man. It is the further projection of the line indicating the direction of the cosmic process. *Conscience therefore does speak with the voice and authority of God to man through man.*

Revelation and the Moral Imperative

At this point, modern thought both affirms and parts company with the doctrine of revelation as hitherto defined in the great authoritarian religions. In the sacred literature of these religions it is said that at a certain point in history or in the career of a chosen or especially endowed individual, the Prophet, the Enlightened One, the Saviour, God breaks through the natural barriers of physical and psychological necessity and miraculously makes known His will through a voice or a word or a vision of sudden illumination. What was spoken by that voice, what was conveyed by the word, what was seen in the vision, remains everlastingly true and authoritative.

Where we part company ought be fairly evident at this stage of our discussion. Except in the sense of the wondrous and the mysterious in nature and history, we cannot allow miracle, the obtrusion of the supernatural between natural phenomena or natural processes. Just because God is immanent in the whole of nature and in the whole realm of existence, we cannot conceive Him as breaking through from without. Those who hold such views are usually called modernists as distinguished from fundamentalists. This distinction cuts across denominational differences. Almost all the organized religions of today are divided between the two camps. Yet the terms are unfortunate. I would be the first to admit that even modernity may be in error and that ideas which we call modern may prove to be merely ephemeral. On the other hand, any idea, modern or ancient, which is true is necessarily fundamental to some system of ideas based upon it or deduced from it. When we read the sacred literature of other faiths, we do not hesitate to relegate to the sphere of folklore and folk imagination the wonder stories surrounding their founders. We cannot live by a double standard of truth. If we apply the rational standards of historical evidence to Greek or Egyptian or Sanskrit literature, we dare not fail to apply them to the literature we hold sacred. If we fail to do so, we blur the distinction between the credible and the incredible. If God spoke to Moses in miracle and we hold such miracle to be possible, then there is no standard by which we can deny that God may have similarly spoken to some Greek hero, to some Egyptian priest, to some Oriental sage. We have lost all standards of credibility.

Furthermore, no literature can in itself be 'sacred.' Every literature is an expression of the genius of man and therefore shares the fallibility of its source. If we call it 'sacred,' it is only because our sincere faith, that which our conscience and our reason holds to be true and authoritative, finds supreme or unique expression therein. We do not accept it as true because it is a 'Sacred Literature,' we deem it a sacred literature because the faith and the obligations which our judgment compels us to accept as true, found their primal expression therein. It is only insofar as this is the case that the modern mind can accept such a literature as 'Sacred.'

In similar manner, there is no sacred history as distinct from a secular history. This distinction arose out of that double standard of historical truth to which we have already alluded. Sacred history was, in my childhood, a history in which the laws of historical evidence played no part. Everything could happen in sacred history because God willed it. Our critical faculties were only invoked in other domains of historical research. The triumph of biblical criticism was not in its particular findings—whether or not the Pentateuch is a unit, whether or not it consists of three main documents or is a mosaic of a multitude of sources, whether Deuteronomy precedes Leviticus or Leviticus precedes Deuteronomy—its triumph consists in the admission that all history is a natural process. The history of an idea, the history of a culture, the history of life, are all phases of the natural history of man. Hence, if we would know the truth, we must apply the general laws of historical evidence in order to reconstruct that history. A history becomes sacred history only because it is the natural history of faiths and institutions which our conscience and moral judgment holds to be sacred, not because there is anything holy distinguishing the historical process itself.

The Abnormal not to be Equated with the Untrue

The psychological experiences to which we have alluded may indeed be the bearers of the word of God, again depending upon the value attributed to them by our moral judgment. If, however, our reason will not permit us to accept the voices, the visions, the miraculous illuminations, as objective fact, as authentic history, but to view them only either as figments of folk imagination or as extraordinary yet subjective psychological experiences including perhaps hallucination, we must not permit such judgment to affect adversely our acceptance of the affirmations they contain. Reason does not deal only with judgment arrived at by means of logical inference. The subconscious foreshortenings of such processes, which we call insight or intuition, also claim our critical but impartial examination.

We must not be guilty of the reverse of a very ancient error. There were certain primitive societies in which not only was the prophet a madman, but every madman was regarded as a prophet. Truth was sought at the mouth of those suffering from all sorts of aberrations because their extraordinary speech and behavior seemed to well from the reservoirs of the supernatural.

We the civilized and the sophisticated are likely to make the opposite error—to believe that a thing must be false or at least tainted if it comes to our attention through processes other than normal. The psychological process, like the historical one, is never either true or false. It is only the judgement that emerges which may be true or false. It is quite possible that certain abnormalities of mind and body, though the physician calls them pathological, may produce a heightened sensitivity to certain truths which others not so sensitized will be unable to perceive. A shallow rationalism is likely to dismiss the epistles of St. Paul or the writings of the Koran with the glib statements that their authors may have been epileptics. As a matter of fact, the epistle to the Corinthians loses none of its moral grandeur on that account. Isaiah when he saw God sitting upon a throne surrounded by Seraphim may indeed have been suffering an hallucination, but the praise he heard the Seraphim chanting, "Holy, Holy, Holy is the Lord of hosts, the whole earth is full of His glory is still a truth which the reason and conscience of man can accept. The humanistic and artistic values in the writings of Edgar Allan Poe or Robert Louis Stevenson are none the less real though the one may have been an alcoholic and the other a victim of tuberculosis. A mystical experience of any kind, no matter how intense or convincing to one who undergoes the experience, does not in itself vouch for its own validity, but neither can a critical reason dispel as invalid or unworthy the poetry or the logic involved in the mystical experience just because the experience was that of a poet and a mystic rather than that of a professor of logic. In other words, like the historical process, so the psychological process can neither deny nor affirm the validity of a particular judgment for the conscience and reason of man. By whatever process ideas are communicated to us, they must ultimately submit to the judgment and reason of those to whom they are communicated.

Therefore, however we may disagree with ancient doctrines of revelation, and however far afield our rationalism may take us from the fundamentalist's interpretation of Sacred Literature, revelation may still prove to be a fact, not a miraculous historical fact but a rational metaphysical fact. Creation and Revelation indeed may be twin metaphysical truths none the less rational because they are born out of religious experiences. Neither has a history. We have already observed that all history is this side of creation. We may go further and point out that no truth has a history, only the idea and the quest for truth has a history. There never was a time when two plus two did not make four. The truth about the origin of life was the same at the time of Moses as it was at the time of Darwin. Our knowledge of the truth had a history, and Darwin doubtless knew some facts which were unknown to Moses. Only God knows the whole truth of anything whether that thing be an atom or a human genius or a star.

We are likely here to wander into error because we are accustomed to speak in laudatory terms of 'creative thinking' as though the creative thinker by his thinking thereby creates a truth. Creative thinking is such thinking as enables man better to perceive the truth. The negative form of the statement that all truth is revealed is that no truth and no value was ever created by the human spirit. It was only discovered by the human spirit. And this brings us face to face with one of those linguistic peculiarities that nevertheless indicates the necessary path of correct thinking.

'Reveal' and 'discover' are different words for the same fact viewed in different perspectives. What is 'uncovered' stands 'revealed' and what is revealed is uncovered. No one believes that Columbus created America by discovering it. One can wholeheartedly admit that every truth which man knows is a discovery by man, determined by his mental endowments, his experiences, the cultural environment in which he finds himself; nevertheless it is equally true that the process by which man discovers truth is the process by which God reveals Himself to man. Revelation and discovery are two poles of the same situation—the divine and the human. The Bible, therefore, if it is an achievement of the Hebraic spirit, may still be a divine revelation but only insofar as it is bearer of truths which our conscience and moral judgment hold valid for faith and conduct.

Revelation and the Eternal Verities

If, as has already been said, the mind of man can, as in biblical phraseology, be called the 'Lamp of God,' we may indeed perceive that God reveals Himself to man *through man,* as the latter snatches glimpses of truth from the abysmal obscurity of the unknown.

We are often told that modern thought does not permit us to affirm that there is such a thing as *ultimate* truth, that there is no *eternal verity,* either in science or in morals. The contrary is true. *All verity is eternal.* In truth we come face to face with eternal wisdom.

The attitude deprecating eternal verity often springs from the fact that, in the popular mind and sometimes in the confused philosophic mind, the theory of relativity is interpreted to mean the theory of the relativity of truth. It is nothing of the kind. It tells that certain dimensions of reality—time, space, velocity, mass, and energy—can only be expressed in quantities relative to one another. They have no independent values. If the theory be true, however, then the truth of such relativity is eternal. The truth finds expression in the mathematical formulae defining these relations. If I say that a palm tree is very tall, the truth is that it is tall when compared to a rose bush but not so tall when compared to the mountain at whose foot it stands. The truth is that long and short, high and low, are universals of relationship rather than of quality or value. This ought not blind us to the fact that it is eternally true that if the rose bush measures five feet and the palm tree measures fifty feet, the latter is taller than the former in the framework in which these measurements hold. Truth, therefore, is never relative and never changes. Our conceptions of what is true may undergo change. We confuse the epistemological problem, how we get to believe that something is true, with the metaphysical problem of what is the nature of truth.

In this sense, a primitive society may have different ideas of the requirements of justice than a more civilized and developed society. The social situation has changed. Man may have become more sensitive to the demands of justice than he was in his savage state, but the distinction between justice and injustice has not changed one iota. The just man at the time of Abraham was as different from the unjust as he is today. There is no sign whatever that the ethical generalizations mirrored in the Ten Commandments or in the Golden Rule or in the prophetic diatribes or in the virtues listed by the Greek moralists were ever held to define vices rather than virtues. What has undergone transformation is our understanding of what specific acts are involved in the pursuit of justice or the scope in which the moral imperative demands their fulfillment. Murder was always evil though perhaps it was sensed to be evil only within the family or the clan. It required the widening horizon of human experience to admit its relevance to the whole of humanity. We may at some future time have to decide whether or not it is a sin to kill a Martian. It will depend on how far we accept these planetary strangers as human beings. If we do so accept them, the truth that it is wrong to kill will apply to them as it does to all our fellow men. In other words, if the theory of relativity is true, and, of course, only insofar as it is true, it was as true when Noah rode the ark as in the days of jet propulsion. If the love of man is a virtue, it was virtue from the beginning of history though man may only have just discovered it to be so. There are no verities save eternal verities and all verities are eternal.

The Relation of Religious Faith to the Moral Life

We had previously expressed it as our opinion, that man can be good without faith in God. We nevertheless refuse to commit ourselves to the affirmation that man can be good without God. Even in the light of the former statement, it by no means follows that religious ideas play no part in sustaining the moral life of man. We are not now interested in those phases of religion, aesthetic and emotional, involving some sort of symbolism and discipline. Many psychologists would be willing to admit that these may be both wholesome and inspirational. I am referring now to religious ideas, to theological postulates like the god-idea. I cannot hold that there is no connection between the righteous life and the right idea which makes the righteous life a logical imperative for thinking man, which makes it a rational pursuit rather than an irrational habit. Whatever may be the truth in the alleged connection between primal hunger (economic necessity) or sexual love (the Freudian discovery) and the conscious activity and life of mature man, they do not exclude the fact that civilized man is dominated by ideas. Hunger and sexuality, man possesses in common with the beast. In directing his life according to his ideas of what is true or good, he demonstrates his uniqueness. The prominent psycho-analyst whom we have previously quoted and to whose writings I react sometimes with approval, sometimes with irritation, has this to say as to the direction of man's evolution:

> "The end to which man studies himself cannot be other than to realize the full potentiality of his being and to conquer the *triad of limitations* fate or God or destiny or sheer accident has imposed on him. Human beings are enclosed by an iron triangle that forms for their race a veritable prison cell. One side of this triangle is the medium in which they must live; the second is the equipment they have or can fashion with which to live; the third is the fact of their mortality. All effort, all being is directed upon the elimination of the sides of this enclosure. If there is purpose to life, that purpose must be to break through the triangle that thus imprisons humanity into a new order of existence where such a triad of limitations no longer obtains. This is the end toward which both individ-

ual and species function; this is the end toward which the race strives; this is the end which gives meaning and substance to life."[2]

Further on, in describing the essence of man's humanity, he makes the interesting observation, the truth of which is confirmed on every stage of human development,

> "High ranking, however, among the various peculiarities of man that enable us to diagnose him human is one which has been remarked upon many times. It is one which is central to the thesis of this book, and also one which, if it exists at all among other species, exists in such attenuated form that its presence can only be assumed on the basis of deduction from behavior. Stated broadly, this distinctive characteristic is the capacity—indeed, the tendency—for man to relate his existence not only in accordance with the impressions received by his senses, not only with the stimuli thrust upon him by the physical world, but also by those impalpable mental formulations called ideas . . . . .Fortunately, we here need not pause to argue over the definition of ideas, but merely to note that, whatever they are, men live by them."[3]

The error which Dr. Lindner makes is in failing to see that, if it be true that God has laid down the limits, then if there be a God, He has also implanted in man the power to break through these limits in his quest for truth and self-realization and thus has given to life a value which without the limits and without these powers it would not possess.

Let me here call attention to an article by Professor F. S. C. Northrop to which we have already referred.[4] The article deals with the then recent investigations by Warren S. McCulloch and Walter Pitts, and with the work in cybernetics of John Von Neumann and Norbert Wiener and certain others in the same branch of research. Professor Northrop reaches the following conclusion,

"The traditional argument of the dualists and idealists—that purposeful teleological behavior cannot be accounted for by means of scientifically verified psychology and neurology because the latter sciences give no basis for memory, universals, and purposes —and the argument of the early modern naturalists, mechanists, and their sociological followers to the effect that purposeful teleological activities and the theoretical ideas defining human goals are mere epiphenomena of no causal significance, representing mere pseudorationalizations after the fact, because again such factors are incompatible with mechanism and a scientifically verified theory of human nature, therefore apparently rest upon a common confusion and a false premise. This false premise is that teleology and mechanism are incompatible."

They are not incompatible but neither are they identical. The purposive apparatus is the apparatus for the initiation and fulfillment of purpose even as the sensory apparatus is the means by which we perceive the color red. But the red which we perceive is not in the brain but in the mind possessed of the sensory apparatus, and the quality of redness is not in the mind but in the rose. That mechanism can allow for the emergence of purpose and goals is, however, an important truth. It shows that the mechanisms of nature provide for the fact that man is governed by ideas.

Nature No Longer Regarded As Mechanical

We can make ourselves much more intelligible if we confine the term mechanism to that which is machine-like. The machine was well known to man long before the science of mechanics. The machine is a tool more or less simple like the wheel or infinitely complicated with many wheels and cogs. It was always a tool to serve man's purpose, and the triumph of the machine lay in the fact that it became a more and more efficient tool to serve the productivity of man. The calculating machines, marvellous as they seem, are no more than such machines wrought to fulfill the purposes conceived by those who designed them. They have not the slightest resemblance to the human mind and personality. If one of these astounding robots, instead of correctly computing the complicated figures they are asked to digest, or successfully deducing the correct inference from a series of propositions fed them by their masters, should only once rise up and cry out 'let be with your nonsense, I prefer composing a symphony' there would be some slight approach to human personality. When a machine shall undertake to challenge its master as Job challenged God, it will show some similitude to the independence of human individuality. It is much more dependable than a human being and therefore vastly inferior to the human being that made it so dependable.

That there is a physical apparatus, a biological mechanism of which thought and purpose avail themselves, there can be no doubt. The fact that this should be so is no longer as incomprehensible as it was, and that for the simple reason that matter itself is no longer thought to be merely mechanical. Its elementary particles show unpredictable spontaneity or, better still, matter is conceived of as being both wave-like and corpuscular, both determined and indetermined. Were the laws of matter purely mechanical, we would then be justified in speaking of teleological and non-teleological mechanism, or purposive and non-purposive mechanical phenomena. What is purposive and advances to a goal is the thinking, feeling, self-conscious human organism of which certain mechanical aspects are mere abstractions from the whole, which is not and never was purely mechanical. Matter insofar as its behavior is predictable and insofar as it can be manipulated by man for his purposes is mechanical. Insofar as the material universe is more than these, it cannot be described as a mechanism.

What is of importance to us in both the statement of Dr. Lindner and that of Professor Northrop is that ideas do govern man. Since the materialist cultures which have sought dominance in our time, both fascist and communist, have placed emphasis upon ideological orthodoxy and have persecuted deviating heresies with vindictive passion, let us at least not make the mistake of undervaluing religious ideology in the life and culture of mankind.

Theism and Humanism

What the god-idea means for the moral life of man, how it gives both rational lucidity as well as objective reality to man's moral striving, I think can best be perceived if we state their connection negatively.

That awareness and freedom of will, through which alone man imputes moral responsibility to himself and praise or blame to others, becomes an illusion if we accept the point of view that the universe is or could be a blind mechanism. Such a view would put the saint and the sinner on the same level, the champion and servant of what is good with him who works evil, for men would then be governed not by self-determining volition but by causal compulsion. Spinoza's view with regard to volition was that we deceive ourselves in consequence of our ignorance of causality. Moral responsibility now becomes the primal illusion (unless one can find some way of escape as Spinoza did in providing for blessedness through right thinking rather than right willing), and man lives under the dominance of a psychological aberration which has no relation to reality. If the decision between what is and what ought to be is of no significance because only what is has actual existence and what ought to be is never an empirical fact—what becomes of the reality of our moral life? To the theist, the world as it truly ought to be is as real as the world that now is. Whether we do what ought be done or fail to do so, the ought, that is the obligation or moral imperative, remains as eternally true as the actual outcome of our wills. Reality to the theist includes both the world of God's creation as now we find it and those real possibilities for making it better which we either reject or accept.

Goodness is a universal of value rather than of form. It is never an existent *thing* because it can be shared by many things and can enter into many actual situations

231

in which the individual and society may find themselves. The universal goodness helps define many existent things —good men, good institutions, good rules of conduct— but the whole of goodness, since it is a universal, is never in actual existence. For should man on any level of being cease to seek the better rather than the good, it would mean the end of the process of moralization, and the distinction between good and evil would lapse into nothingness. Where no possible act could increase the love and justice in the world, it would be folly to expect men to 'do justice and love mercy.' These would have no real function to fulfill.

The search for the good and the better requires two postulates to make it intelligible. First, the whole of goodness is never in actual existence and, secondly, the possibilities of goodness are never exhausted—there is an infinite well-spring of the good upon which man can draw if but he wills. Now, this can never be other than God as the plenitude of all value, the essence of all holiness. He is that infinite unity of all being through whose creative will the possible is made actual but who always transcends the merely existent insofar as He remains the continual abode of what yet may be possible. All the universals of quality and relation, of form and value, are phases of His divine being, and through His creativity they enter the realm of existence and become relevant to the world of empirical fact.

Suppose the moral good and the concept of duty and moral value are mere illusions, have no roots in the objective nature of reality but are nevertheless ideas which sustain man and enable him to walk undismayed amid the surrounding darkness, can man not live and does he not largely live by such illusions? The answer is most emphatically no; not if he knows them to be illusions. A naive person may indeed by accumulated habit, social momentum, or critical incapacity, hug to his heart illusions which give him both comfort and inspiration and which may even guide his step on the path of conduct which may win the approval of his fellow men. No honest person, however, can long live or guide his life by ideas which he himself knows are mere illusions—such knowledge saps their vitality.

I was once told a story by one of my teachers of a hard headed farmer who wished to test the truth of the maxim that faith can move mountains. And so one day he stood facing the grim heights that set a boundary to the sweep of his fertile meadows and closing his eyes stood for a few moments in religious concentration. When again he opened his eyes, he beheld the mountains all unchanged. He shook his fists at them and exclaimed 'I was not deceived. I knew all the while you would still be there.' Now, whether faith can or cannot move mountains, it should be evident that a man cannot possibly be possessed at the same time of efficient faith and the gnawing skepticism which denies that faith. Faith in reason, of course, has helped men again and again to remove mountains so that today it is just an engineering trifle, but the point I wish to make is that man may indeed live a moral life under the false impression that such a life is rational, but he will not long live it once he is convinced that it is not rational. The abandonment of theism in some form will lead inevitably to a materialist ideology which may end not only in indicting bourgeois morality but in stating that all morality is mere bourgeois preference, or in not only condemning slave morality as unfitting superman but in asserting that all morality is mere slavishness from which superman must emancipate himself.

Especially does the faith in God and in a divine purpose enter into man's evaluation of himself and his fellow man as the destined servant of divine goodness, as the bearer of the moral imperative, as the creature who knows himself, even in his sin and rebellion, possessed of a spark of that creative freedom which is God. He is not then merely an earth bound creature of the flesh but something potentially holy, an image and reflection of God. Looking back over the cosmic process which gave him birth, on the advance from matter to protoplasm, from protoplasm to living organism, from life to mind and spirit, he can then truly say "for my sake was the world created." Now, you may insist, should he know such faith to be unfounded, would he not still remain a noble and heroic figure doomed to futility but still the heroic protagonist of a lost cause without hope and without self-deception?

Never was a loftier or more eloquent affirmative answer given to this question than the one contained in Bertrand Russell's essay "A Free Man's Worship."[5]

"Amid such a world, if anywhere, our ideals must henceforth find a home. That man is the product of causes which had no prevision of the end they were achieving, that his origin, his growth, his hopes and fears, his loves and his beliefs, are but the outcome of accidental collocations of atoms; that no fire, no heroism, no intensity of thought and feeling can preserve an individual life beyond the grave; that all the labours of the ages, all the devotion, all the inspiration, all the noon-day brightness of human genius are destined to extinction in the vast death of the solar system, and that the whole temple of man's achievement must inevitably be buried beneath the debris of a universe in ruins—all these things if not quite beyond dispute are yet so nearly certain that no philosophy which rejects them can hope to stand. Only within the scaffolding of these truths, only on the firm foundation of unyielding despair can the soul's habitation henceforth be safely built . . . . . To him alone in the world with which he is acquainted, this freedom belongs . . . .Brief and powerless is man's life; on him and all his race the slow sure doom falls pitiless and dark. . . . .for man condemned today to lose his dearest, tomorrow himself, to pass through the gate of darkness it remains only to cherish ere yet the blow falls the lofty thoughts that ennoble his little day. . . . . . ."

Once we turn our eyes from the fascinating horror of this picture of a universe in wrack and ruin and shut our ears to the stirring cadences which sing the dark fate of man and all his bright hopes, we may in more serene mood ask ourselves whether we are not face to face with certain contradictions which in some form or other we have already encountered and which may eventually lose their sting because of their familiarity.[6]

To man at least, we are told, belongs the freedom to cherish in the face of lowering night the lofty thoughts which ennoble his little day. Let us then ask, is it more scientific and logical to say that the freedom and purposiveness of human striving, the reality of which man at least is justified in believing, has its ultimate roots in overall blindness and accident, than to say that what in our experience seems opaque and therefore a matter of mere chance and blind accident may have as its high purpose to evoke in the will of man those values and that spiritual reaction which will enable him to erect the mansion of his soul upon despair itself?

At any rate, it is man's faith in his essential and unique freedom, and that alone, which would make it possible for him proudly to fly the brave pennant of his innate nobility, in the midst of shipwreck and disaster. Should he ever lose that faith and regard moral freedom and moral worth not as guiding lights but as mere will-o'-the-wisps, he would soon tire of high striving. He will surrender then to the pathos of his position and slowly sink into the murky slough of self-pity. Man would then be no longer heroic but only pathetic. There is a vast difference in these terms. The saint, the prophet, the martyr, even the knight errant are never pathetic figures in the history of the human race. They are heroic. They struggle and suffer for what they deem to be of real value. Don Quixote, fighting windmills, is a glorious hero so long as he really believes that they are giants. Should he acquire the mind of Sancho Panza and realize that he is charging windmills, he would cease to be the heroic madman and become the pathetic fool.

Man unrelated to God, the victim of blind and irrational forces, is doomed eventually to realize how pathetic is the role he is called upon to play. To suffer for the sake of righteousness becomes then a pathetic gesture. To love one's neighbor as oneself will not long bear fruit when we know that the neighbor we are bidden to love is as essentially worthless as we who are bidden to love him. Only as man knows himself to occupy a high and unique status will his obligations be high and many, and only the feeling of God within us can confer such status. None other than a theocentric world can provide the elements for an anthropocentric morality. It requires faith in God to sustain a triumphant humanism.

1. cf. supra p. 62 "Can We Experience Perfection?"
2. Lindner, *op. cit.*, p. 4.
3. *Ibid.*, p. 91.
4. See p. 107.
5. Bertrand Russell, *Mysticism and Other Essays* (New York: Longmans Green and Co., 1918).
6. cf. supra p. 76.

FINIS

BIBLIOGRAPHY

Books and Articles

Albright, William F. *Journal of Biblical Literature,* LVI (1937).
Alexander, Samuel. *Space, Time and Deity.* London, 1927.
Bentwich, Norman. *Hellenism.* Philadelphia, 1919.
Bergson, Henri. *Morality and Religion.* New York, 1935.
Boodin, John Elof. *Cosmic Evolution.* New York, 1925.
Born, Max. "Einstein's Statistical Theories," *Albert Einstein, Philosopher-Scientist.* Illinois, 1949.
Buber, Martin. *Tales of the Hasidism, The Early Masters.* New York, 1947.
Buber, Martin. *Tales of the Hasidism, The Later Masters* New York, 1948.
Carlyle, Thomas. "Sartor Resartus," *The Complete Works of Thomas Carlyle.* Book II. New York.
Clark, Arthur. "The Planets are not Enough," *Saturday Review,* (November 26, 1955).
Cohen, Morris Raphael. *Reason and Nature.* New York, 1931.
Epstein, Paul. "Physics and Metaphysics," *Scientific Monthly,* (July, 1937).
Feibleman, James K. *Ontology.* Baltimore, 1951.
Finkelstein, Louis. *The Pharisees.* Vol. II. Philadelphia, 1940.
Freudenberg, Gideon. "Probability and Induction in the Light of Modern Physics," *Iyyun,* Philosophical Society, Hebrew University, Vol. IV (January, 1953).
Friend, Julius W. and Feibleman, James K. *Science and the Spirit of Man.* London, 1933.
Gordis, Robert. *Koheleth—The Man and His World.* Vol. XIX. New York, 1955.
Heitler, Walter. "The Departure from Classical Thought in Modern Physics," *Albert Einstein, Philosopher-Scientist.* Illinois, 1949.
Hoyle, Fred. *The Nature of the Universe.* New York, 1950.
Jackson, T. A. *Dialectics—The Logic of Marxism and Its Critics.* New York, 1936.

237

James, William. *Varieties of Religious Experiences.* New York and London, 1902.

Kaufman, Ezekiel. *Toldot Haemunah Hayisraelit.* Vol. II. Tel Aviv, Israel, 1952.

Lecky, W. E. H. *History of European Morals.* New York, 1955.

Lindner, Robert. *Prescription for Rebellion.* New York, 1952.

Margenau, H. "Einstein's Conception of Reality," *Albert Einstein, Philosopher-Scientist.* Illinois, 1949.

Margolis, Max L. *The Hebrew Scriptures in the Making.* Philadelphia, 1922.

Mill, John Stuart. "Essay on Liberty," *Harvard Classics.*

Miller, Heinrich. *Die Gesetze Hammurabis.* Vienna, 1903.

Moore, George Foot. *Judaism in the First Centuries of the Christian Era.* Massachusetts, 1927.

Murray, Gilbert. *Tradition and Progress.* Boston and New York, 1922.

Northrop, F. S. C. "The Neurologic and Behavioristic Basis of the Ordering of Society by Means of Ideas," *Science,* (April 23, 1948).

Ratner, Joseph. *The Philosophy of Spinoza.* New York, 1927.

Russell, Bertrand. "Free man's Worship," *Mysticism and Other Essays.* New York, 1918.

Sandburg, Carl. *Abraham Lincoln—The War Years.* Vol. II. New York, 1939.

Schechter, S. *Some Aspects of Rabbinic Theology.* New York, 1910.

Schechter, S. *Studies in Judaism.* First Series. Philadelphia, 1911.

Schechter, S. *Studies in Judaism.* Second Series. Philadelphia, 1938.

Sinnott, Edmund W. "Cell and Psyche," *Main Currents in Modern Thought,* Vol. IX, No. 1.

Strack-Billerbeck. *Kommentar zum Neuen Testament aus Talmud und Midrasch-Das Evangellum Nach Matthaus.* Munchen, 1922.

Wenzl, Aloys. "Einstein's Theory of Relativity Viewed from the Standpoint of Critical Realism, and its

Significance for Philosophy," *Albert Einstein, Philosopher-Scientist.* Illinois, 1949.
Whitehead, Alfred North. *Process and Reality.* New York, 1930.
Wieman, Henry Nelson. *Is There a God—A Conversation (Wieman, Macintosh and Otto),* New York, 1932.
Wilson, Edmund. *The Scrolls of the Dead Sea.* New York, 1955.
Wilson, Edmund. "The Dead Sea Scrolls," *The New Yorker,* (May 14, 1955).
Wolfson, Harry Austryn. *Philo.* Massachusetts, 1948.
Wolfson, Harry Austryn. *The Philosophy of Spinoza.* Massachusetts, 1934.

Hindu Scriptures
Mahabharata. Bhagavad Gita or "The Lord's Song."
Biblical Sources (Quoted in the text by chapter and verse)

	Abbreviation
Daniel	—
Deuteronomy	—
Ecclesiastes	Deut.
Exodus	Eccl.
Ezekiel	Ex.
Genesis	Ez.
Habakkuk	Gen.
Isaiah	Hab.
Jeremiah	Is.
Job	Jer.
Joel	—
Joshua	—
Judges	Jos.
Leviticus	—
Malachi	Lev.
Micah	Mal.
Numbers	—
Proverbs	—
Psalms	—
Ruth	Ps.
Samuel II	—
	Sam.

Rabbinic Sources

		Abbreviation
Mishna:	Abot	—
	Sanhedrin	San.

Talmudic Tractates:		Abbreviation
	Berachot	Ber.
	Derek Eretz	Der. Er.
	Erubin	Er.
	Gittin	Git.
	Makkot	Mak.
	Sanhedrin	San.
	Shabbat	Shab.
	Taanit	Taan.

Other Rabbinic Sources:

	Abbreviation
Bereshit Rabba	Ber. R.
Midrash Tehilim, ed. Solomon Buber, Lemberg, 1891.	Mid. Teh.
Pesikta Rabbati, ed. Friedman, Vienna, 1880.	Pes. Rab.
Seder Eliahu, ed. Friedman, Vienna, 1902.	—
Sifra	—
Yalkut Shimoni	Yal. Shim.

New Testament

I Corinthians
Matthew

Liturgical

"Song of Unity" Judah the Hasid, or one of his inner circle according to Sholem. Cf. *Major Trends in Jewish Mysticism.* New York, 1946, p. 108.

INDEX*

Aaron, 151
Abigail, 215
Abnormal, the, 222
Abot, 27, 36 n. 2, 182, 217 n. 28
Abraham, 151, 226
Absolute, the, 203f.
Achan, 148
Actuality, 11, 80, 94, 110, 112, 197f. 200, 219;
  Actual, the, 10, 11
Adam, 154f.
Aesop, 5
Ain, 217 n. 39
Akiba, Rabbi, 27f., 133, 177f., 187
Albright, William F., 36 n. 18
Alexander, Samuel, 105, 190, 204, 208
Alternatives, 6, 10
Altruism, 45, 47;
  altruistic motivation, 210
America, 199, 224
American Medical Association, 20
American Scripture, 69
Amora, 29
Amos, 149f.
Antinomies, 197
Apocryphal writings, 172, 180
Arab tribes, 126
Archimedes, 22, 114
Aristotle, 35, 71, 191
Asceticism, 42f., 186
Atheist, 20
Atonement, 185;
  Day of —, 188
Authority, 19, 127;
  established —, 18;
  international —, 65;
  moral —, 34

Beatitudes, 178
Behavior: animal, 4, 62;
  standards of —, 16
Being, 100;
  Actual —, 200;
  divine —, 140, 232;
  eternity of —, 197;
  infinite —, 80;
  realm of —, 54, 56, 138, 196
  supreme —, 108, 110;
  unity of —, 66, 108, 110ff., 205, 232;

  — vs. not being, 193
Ben Azzai, 28
Bentwich, Norman, 216 n. 20
Berachot, 217 n. 27
Berachot Rabba, 32, 144 n. 2, 216 n. 19
Bergson, Henri, 2, 5
Bible, 16, 34, 50, 114, 154, 179, 181, 215, 225;
  Biblical: canon, 173;
    criticism, 222;
    foundation, 185;
    story, 28;
    thought, 44, 177, 190;
    view, 155;
    writers, 180;
    Hebrew —, 147f., 173;
    Old Testament: 173;
    see Literature, biblical
    (for Christian Scriptures, see New Testament)
Blessedness, 231
Boodin, John Elof, 98f.
Boraitha, 184
Born, Max, 96
(British) Commonwealth of Nations, 21
Buber, Martin, 72 n. 1, 4
Buddha, 71

Canaan, 150
Carlyle, Thomas, 184, 187
Causality, 92, 96, 99, 105, 110, 231;
  laws of —, 83
  causal: determination, 89;
  law, 83, 86ff., 90f.
  relations, 203;
  causation, 80, 86f.;
  beyond —, 82ff., 106
Cause, 81, 84, 100, 104, 200;
  first —, 105, 109
Certainty, 87, 92
Chance, 82ff., 92, 96, 99f., 104, 106f., 112, 195
Change, 91
Character, 35, 74ff., 124
Chesterton, Gilbert K., 159
China, 126
Choice, 6, 111, 134, 143
Christianity, 14ff., 20f., 28, 42, 146, 174, 182;

---

* Prepared by David Lieber.

Pauline —, 14;
Christian: dogma, 171;
    era, 25;
    martyrdom, 17;
    sources, 173;
    theology, 179;
Church, 14, 17, 19, 22, 103;
  — of atheism, 21;
  — Fathers, 173
Civilization, 9, 126, 148;
    Greek and Roman, 177
Claims, 24
Clarke, Arthur, 201
Clouds of Glory, 58
Cohen, Morris Raphael, 8, 192, 203, 206
Coliseum, 15
Columbus, 199, 225
Commandments, 29, 31
Common sense, 85, 92
Communism, 21
Compassion, 139ff., 146
Compulsion, 12, 231
Compulsive behavior, 4
Concrescence, 101
Conduct, 6f.;
    standards of —, 34
Conflict, 22
Confucius, 24, 27, 71
Confusion, 24
Conscience, 6, 22, 35, 52, 56, 60f., 123, 127, 129, 134, 137, 151, 182, 213, 220ff., 224f.
Consciousness, 11, (defined) 132, 137
Constitution, 20
Corinthians, 18, 223
Cosmology, 82, 97
Courage, 18
Covenant, 149, 152
Creation, 68, 81f., 99, 101f., 104, 106ff., 146, 163, 174, 224, 231;
    continuous —, 103f., 196;
    story of —, 191
    creatio ex nihilo, 102, 196;
    creative advance, 56;
    creative wisdom, 186;
    creativity, 36, 80, 111, 140, 220;
    creator, 81, 103f., 107, 109f., 164;
Crimes, 19
Cromwell, 20

Daniel, 214f.
Darwin, 114, 224
David, 194, 215
Dead Sea Scrolls, 171
Death, 75, 125, 134, 136, 143, 150, 154, 159, 161, 180f., 187, 189ff, 209, 215
Deborah, 34
Decision, 6, 10, 40, 73, 82, 101, 107, 112, 129, 214
Declaration of Independence, 20
Democracy, 29, 67, 127
Derek Eretz, 216 n. 24
Desire, 38ff., 47f., 57, 67, 125, 135f., 214
Despair, 161
Destiny, 125, 138, 183, 214
Determinism, 77f., 83, 95, 100, 110
Deuteronomy, 222;
    passages cited in connection with:
      ancestral guilt, 148;
      collective moral guilt, 150;
      prevalence of evil, 143;
      rabbinic generalizations, 26;
      retribution, 216 n. 1;
      study of Torah, 33;
      suffering of righteous, 180
Dictatorship, 20, 64
Dilemma, 143
Disney, Walt, 5
Divinity, 191;
  see also: God
Don Quixote, 235
Duty, 1ff., 24f., 36, 38, 52, 123, 127, 232;
  see also obligation, ought

Ecclesiastes, 115, 159, 164;
    passages cited: in connection with death, 190;
      praise of simple life, 147f.;
      skepticism, 165f.
Echad umeyuchad, 205
Eddington, Sir Arthur, 195
Eden, 154
Education, purpose of, 70f.
Egoism, 45ff., 59, 210
Einstein, Albert, 51, 93, 96, 114
El male rachamim, 214
Elihu, 163
Elisha, 33
Emotions, human, 139
Emunah, 31
En sof, 217 n. 39
End of days, 55f.
Energy, 86, 95, 107, 110, 118, 122, 190f., 194, 196, 200, 206
Entropy, 88, 195
Environment, 10, 60, 111, 123f., 129, 136, 191, 195

Epicurus, 194
Epistemology:
   epistemological: defect, 86;
                    idealist, 11;
                    situation, 51
Epstein, Paul, 83, 92
Equality, 29, 51
Error, 6, 67, 131, 223f.
Erubin, 177
Eschatology, 6, 142, 162;
   eschatological: ends, 56
                  hope, 34, 153, 155
Essence, 94, 101, 192, 197, 203, 211f.;
   essences, defining, 193
Eternity, 126, 146, 196, 199, 201f., 207, 209f., 214;
   eternal, 11, 81, 209;
   — ends, 56;
   — object/s, 94, 110
Ethics, 73, 114;
   Jewish —, 140;
   ethical: demand, 149;
          generalization, 228;
          Maxim, 24, 27;
          Monotheism, see monotheism, ethical;
          motivation, 150, 182, 190;
          qualifications, 187;
          sentiments, 14;
   see also good, goodness, morality, right, values
Euclid, 22, 71, 135
Evaluation, 119, 233
Event, 84, 86ff., 90, 93, 107, 112, 193, 196ff., 200, 202f.
Everett, William, 68
Evidence historical, 221f.
Evil, 1, 6, 19, 39, 45ff., 50, 56, 61, 64, 66, 76, 115, 122, 125, 137, 143, 145, 151, 213, 220, 231;
   moral —, 132, 135;
   reality of —, 130f.;
   source of —, 38
Evolution, direction, of, 227
Existence, 11, 35, 56, 66, 82, 84, 88, 93ff., 99, 106ff., 112, 114, 122, 129, 131, 137, 143, 145f., 176, 182, 193ff., 200, 203, 212f., 219, 221, 232;
   actual —, 50, 80f., 192, 198;
   extra-mundane —, 189;
   finite —, 35;
   goal for —, 11;
   level of —, 49, 119;
   possibilities of —, 100;

   realm of —, 232;
   world of —, 51f., 77
Exodus, 26
Experience, 10, 41, 44ff., 50, 54, 90, 99, 112, 115, 120, 122, 140, 147f., 159, 181, 189, 194f., 199f., 206, 208, 212, 226, 235;
   levels of —, 43;
   moral —, 219;
   mystical —, 223;
   experiences, religious, 224
Experiment, controlled, 93
Ezeckiel, 142, 153

Faith — *Passim*
   biblical —, 159;
   common —, 16;
   naive —, 54;
   religious —, 226;
   — in the reality of progress, 62
Family, 22
Fate, 110, 161
Feeling, patterns of, 24
Feibleman, James K., 84, 109, 205, 211
Finkelstein, Louis, 169, 177
Folklore, 22, 221;
   Jewish —, 56
Force, 19, 21, 86;
   field of —, 3, 90, 138
Freudenberg, Gideon, 85
Freudian, 227
Friedman, M., 216 n. 12
Friend, Julius W., 205
Fundamentalists,
   see Modernists
Future
   see Time

Gainsborough, 193
Galileo, 114
Gandhi, Mahatma, 21
Gedaliah, 184
Gehinnom, 180
Generalization, 23ff., 28, 47, 75
Genesis
   passages cited in connection with:
      cause of death, 154;
      love of mankind, 27f.
Genius, 7, 23, 70
Gittin 216 n. 24
God — *Passim*
   (defined) 10, 53, 55, 108, 232;
   attributes of —, 140, 206;
   creative restlessness of —, 35, 53;
   fear of —, 36;

grace of —, 58, 174, 185, 214;
idea of —, 11, 227, 231;
image of —, 28;
immanence of —, 35;
judgment of —, 142, 150;
kingdom of —, 19, 36, 49, 122, 211;
knowledge of —, 55
love of —, 45, 182;
name of —, 50, 207;
obedience to —, 36;
service of —, 31;
son of —, 140, 179;
unity of —, 26, 114, 174;
— absolutely free, 73;
see also: Monotheism
Golden Mean, 42f.
Golden Rule, the, 24, 26f., 226
Good, the, 1, 6, 25, 40, 43, 47f., 56, 59, 61, 123ff., 130, 134, 210f., 218, 220;
hierarchy of —s, 48;
the larger —, 47ff.;
quest for —, 60;
the truly —, 53;
system of —s, 39;
— and evil, 38, 56, 61f., 66f., 111, 115f., 131ff., 142, 166, 214, 219, 232;
— vs. the better, 45, 49, 137, 220, 232;
— vs. the best, 49
see aslo: Ethics, Goodness, Morality, Right, Values
Goodness, 1, 6, 25, 47, 61, 124, 130, 213;
see also: Ethics, Good, Morality, Right, Values
Gordis, Robert, 164
Gospel, 18, 28;
the Gospels, 180
Greeks, 114, 174;
Greek: schools, 176;
thought, 188;
view, 188
Grotius, 65
Guilt, 4, 50, 61, 122, 132, 143ff.;
inherited —, 153

Habbakuk
passages cited in connection with:
doubts of divine justice, 155f.;
mitzvot, 30
Hades, 189
Hadrianic persecutions, 21
Hakol, 114

Halachic discussion, 177
Hamlet, 136
Hammurabi, 148
Hannina, Rabbi, 142
Hannina ben Teradion, 75
Happiness, 38f., 48, 62, 66, 121f., 124f., 135, 137, 141, 147, 166, 210, 213
Hasidim, 72;
German —, 208;
Hasidic: epigram, 184;
master, 184;
story, 215
Heaven, 209, 213, 215;
fear of —, 182
Hedonistic calculus, 47
Heitler, Walter, 95
Hell, 182, 209, 213ff.,
Hellenism, Apocryphal and New Testament, 69
Here-now, 198, 200ff., 209f., 212
Heresies, 20, 150
Hillel, 24, 26ff.,
House of —, 69, 176
Hiroshima, 132
History, 9f., 13f., 22, 50, 62, 70, 111, 118, 126, 129, 136f., 200, 221ff.;
beyond —, 56;
Cosmic —, 127;
pre —, 97, 107;
natural —, 93, 104, 122;
religious philosophers of —, 14
sacred vs. secular —, 222
Hitler, 59
Hitlerism, 8
Holiness, 130, 137, 211, 214
Holy, the, 34
Hope, 158, 161, 215
Hoyle, Fred, 102f., 106
Humanism, 231, 236
Hume, David, 85f.
Humility, 26
Hymn of Unity, 139

Idea, 11, 19, 23, 224, 229;
realm of ideas, 176, 219
Ideal, 11, 187;
ethical —, 34, 48;
highest —, 36;
moral —, 38;
personal-social —, 35;
social —, 36, 48;
the —, 10;
idealism, 41;
ideals, 191, 220

Ideology
  materialist —, 233;
  religious —, 231
Imagination, 10, 39f., 43, 61, 111, 191, 200
Immortality, 40, 115f., 145f., 155, 173, 177, 179, 181f., 189f., 194, 208ff.
Incarnation, 140
Indeterminism, 83, 86, 92, 134
India, 21, 126
Individual, 3, 28f., 57, 81, 90f., 111, 127, 145f., 150, 152, 157, 186, 191, 211;
  mature —, 58;
  moral —, 220;
  right of —, 67;
  individual deviations, 89;
  individuality, 85, 93, 114, 230
Induction, 85
Infantilism, 58
Instinct, 5, 9, 13, 39, 60f.
Institutions, 19f., 66, 222
Integrity, 125, 162
Interests, 20
Intuition, 42, 223
Isaiah, 171f., 223
  passages cited in connection with:
    God's involvement with man, 140f.;
    meaning of suffering, 167ff., 185;
    mitzvot, 30;
    power of religion, 19
Islam, 182
Israel, 26, 28, 34, 133, 141, 149ff., 155, 170ff., 179, 186;
  election of —, 174
Iyyun, 112 n. 6

Jackson, T. A., 21
Jacob, Rabbi, 180
James, William, 58
Jeffrys, 85
Jeremiah, 155;
  passages cited in connection with:
    power of religion, 19
    primacy of individual, 152f.
    prophetic challenge to man, 12
Jesus, 17f., 24, 26ff., 171
Jews, 14, 16ff., 27f., 32, 34, 64, 185
Job, 115, 159, 164, 185, 230;
  passages cited in connection with:
    death, 190;
    retribution, 163;
    skepticism, 159ff.

Joel, 34
Jonah, 150
"Joie de vivre," 139
Jordan, 99, 102
Jordan, the, 71
Joshua, 148
Judaism, 14, 16f., 42, 44f., 69, 74, 114f., 146, 155, 173f., 177, 182;
  Jewish: particularism, 18;
    point of view, 14, 147, 178
    rationalism, 114;
    thought, 188;
    tradition, 190f., 218;
    universalism, 16
Judeo-Christian, 13, 20
Judges, 184
Judgment, 10, 159, 222ff.;
  final —, 141, 190;
  God's —, 142, 150;
  moral —, 24, 142, 222, 225
Jung, Carl, 21
Justice, 24 44, 48, 52, 74, 126, 128, 130f., 137, 144, 146ff., 150, 152f., 155ff., 160, 164, 182f., 186, 188, 211, 213, 226, 232;
  divine —, 146, 149, 181f., 185;
  proximate vs. infinite —, 152

Kabbalists, 208
Kaufman, Ezekiel, 164
Ki tob, 141
Kindness, 24
Kipling, 5
Knowledge, 50, 66, 80, 86, 89, 92;
  empirical —, 52;
  imperfect and partial —, 52
Koheleth, 136, 165, 195
Korah, 151f.
Koran, 223

Laotse, 48
Law, 14, 92, 127, 174;
  causal —, 83, 86ff., 90f.;
  civil —, 25;
  criminal —, 25;
  human —, 149;
  international —, 65;
  Mendelian —, 87;
  moral —, 28, 134;
  natural —, 87, 93, 114;
  physical —, 84;
  — of causality, 83;
  laws of nature, see: Nature
League of Nations, 65
Lecky, W. E. H., 14ff.

Legalism, 25
Legend, 22
Lenin, 21
Leviticus, 222;
    passages cited in connection with:
        egocentric idealism, 46;
        Jewish universalism, 31;
        love of mankind, 27;
        moral ideal, 35;
        retribution, 216 n. 1
Liberty, 20
Life, 118, (defined) 119, 135f., 138f., 142, 165, 194;
    divine —, 139;
    goals of —, 119;
    human —, 124; 127;
    lower forms of —, 44;
    moral —, 34f., 38, 76, 121ff., 145, 182, 189, 218f., 226f., 233;
    spiritual —, 44;
    stream of —, 58;
    types of —, 44;
    — of the hour, 213;
    — everlasting, 213
Lincoln, Abraham, 68
Lindner, Robert, 13, 19f., 228, 230
Literature
    biblical —, 64, 146f., 151, 166, 170, 177, 180f.;
    Egyptian —, 221;
    Greek —, 221;
    Jewish —, 138, 170;
    Rabbinic —, 25, 31, 76, 141, 146, 155, 172, 177, 180, 182ff.;
    religious —, 212;
    sacred —, 184, 218, 220ff., 224;
    Sanskrit —, 221;
    Talmudic —, 133;
    Tannaitic —, 69
Liturgy, Jewish, 139
Logic, 6;
    logical: fallacy, 74, 219;
        imperative, 227;
        implication, 79;
        inference, 6;
        order, 6;
        positivism, 102
London Times, 68
Lord's Song, 35
Love, 18, 44, 46, 48, 58, 123, 125f., 128, 130f., 133, 185, 187, 213, 218, 226, 232;
    chastisements of —, 186;
    creative —, 140;
    divine —, 140;

perfect —, 51;
sexual —, 227;
— of mankind, 27f.
Loyalty, 10f., 16f., 58, 66;
    hierarchy of loyalties, 36
Lucifer, 45
Luther, 20

Mahabharata, 35, 49
Maimonides, 42, 56, 205
Makkot, 30
Malachi, 156
Man, 2, 6, 10, 22f., 35, 38, 50, 98, 111, 116f.., 122, 127, 134f., 137, 146f., 186, 206, 222, 225;
    animal —, 10;
    destiny of —, 114;
    fate of —, 234;
    mature —, 227;
    primitive —, 10;
    rational —, 10;
    religious —, 41, 218;
    self-conscious —, 10;
    sinful —, 62;
    spirit of —, 49;
    spiritual value of —, 28
Mankind, 9, 12, 24, 27, 65, 138;
    united —, 129
Marcus Aurelius, 14, 17
Margenau, H., — 113 n. 9
Margolis, Max L., 164
Martyrdom, 41, 166, 173, 186;
    martyr, 126 171f., 181, 235;
    martyrology, 188
Marxism
    Marxian Freudian, 13;
    Marxist, 21
Masaryk, 85
Masochism, 186
Materialism, 103, 195;
    dialectical —, 20
Matter, 86, 95, 97, 103, 106ff., 110, 118, 121f., 190, 195, 200, 206, 230, 233;
Matthew
    passages cited in connection with:
        Jewish particularism of Jesus, 18f.;
        missionary ardor, 36 n. 14
Maturity
    a mature person, 45;
    mature individual, 46, 58
McCulloch, Warren S., 228
Mechanism, (defined) 229, 231
Meekness, 18

Meir, Rabbi, 31ff., 141
Memorial Service, 215
Memory, 10, 39, 111, 191, 195, 214
Mendelssohn, Moses, 85
Mercy, 24f., 44, 52, 146
Merit
    — of ancestors, 148;
    — of the fathers, 211
Messiah, 16, 55, 170, 179;
    crucified —, 16, 19;
    suffering —, 140f.;
    Jewish Messianism, 14;
    Messianic: age, 16, 56;
        era, 155, 180;
        goal, 211;
        king, 18, 55;
        vision, 127
Metaphysics, 54
Method, 85
Micah, 1, 48
Midrash, 32, 34, 143, 173;
    -ic literature, 134
Midrash Tehilim, 144 n. 5
Mill, John Stuart, 14f.
Miller, Heinrich, 216 n. 2
Mind, (defined) 119
Miracle, 23, 81f., 174, 221
Mishna, 29, 69, 140, 173, 178, 182, 187;
    Mishnaic period, 215
Mississippi, the, 71
Modernists
    vs. fundamentalists, 221
Mohammed, 126
Monisms, 78
Monotheism
    ethical —, 115, 218
    Jewish —, 164
Moore, George Foot, 154, 173f.
Morality, 2, 4, 6, 28, 68, 70, 124, 130, 143, 145, 181, 218, 236;
    bourgeois —, 233;
    "slave" —, 8, 233;
    moralists, 16f., 45, 226;
    morals, 24f., 28;
    moral: adjustments, 128;
        advance, 24, 220;
        climate, 149;
        conflict, 41;
        conviction, 35;
        danger, 45;
        decision, 41, 129, 214;
        demands, 67;
        development, 130;
        experience, 219;
        freedom, 73;

        habits, 76f.;
        ideals, 38;
        imperative, 188, 220, 226, 231, 233;
        impulse 210;
        indignation, 128;
        individual, 220;
        infidelity, 149;
        insight, 130;
        judgments, see: Judgments, moral;
        law, see: Law, moral
        levels, 126;
        life, see Life, moral;
        opportunity, 116;
        perfection, 127;
        phenomena, 35;
        principles, 22, 38;
        problem/s, 47, 62, 149;
        situation, 77;
        will, 52f., 77, 124, 130;
        world order, 114, 122;
    see also: Ethics, Good, Goodness, Responsibility, Right, Values
Moses, 143, 151f., 187, 199, 221, 224
Motion, 190
Murray, Gilbert, 69
Mythology, 154, 189, 193, 196;
    mythological: thinking, 192, 203, 206;
        view, 215
Myths, 23, 54
Mysticism
    mystic/s, 128, 194, 208;
    mystical: concepts, 215;
        feeling, 138;
        insight, 102. 141, 215

Nagasaki, 132
National socialism, 21, 64
Nature, 8, 29, 35, 43, 81, 84, 86f., 89ff., 94, 99, 104f., 108, 114ff., 122f., 129f., 137, 145, 147, 181, 197, 221, 229;
    laws of —, 93, 134, 188;
    uniformity of —, 92;
    unity of —, 188;
    — miraculously transformed, 56
Nature fakers, 5
Necessity, 6, 133;
    inner —, 73, 114;
    logical —, 110, 181;
    natural —, 5f., 8, 122, 187f., 220;
    ontological, 107;
    physical and psychological —, 220
Needs, newer and higher, 67
Nero, 59

New Testament, 27, 170, 173
New York Trbiune, 68
New Yorker, 171
Nietszche, Friedrich, 8
Nineveh, 150
Noah, 226;
    covenant with sons of —, 33
Northrop, F.S.C., 228, 230
Nothing, 106f.;
    nothingness, 193, 196
Novelty, 93, 106
Numbers, 150

Objectivity, 5
Obligation, 1ff., 21f., 24f., 31, 33f., 38, 46f., 57, 61, 76, 123, 127f.;
    higher —, 9, 59;
    highest —, 49:
    ultimate —, 22, 48;
    see also Duty, Ought
Observation, 22f., 53, 86f., 89f.;
Oenomaus of Gadara, 32
Olam, 114
Olam Hagemul, 116
Old Testament, see: Bible
Olympics, 44
Omar Khayyam, 195
Omniscience, 77, 93
One
    the One and Unique, 205
O'Neil, Eugene, 58
Ontology
    ontological fact, 86, 90ff., 108
Oppenheimer, Robert, 131
Opportunity
    realm of —, 200
Optimism, 123, 147, 165, 181
Order, 92, 110
    actual —, 11;
    cosmic —, 104;
    Divine —, 11;
    established —, 10;
    higher —, 10;
    moral —, 57;
    natural —, 122, 145;
    new —, 11, 61;
    static —, 48;
    temporal —, 115
Organism, 80
Organization
    social —, 127
Orient, 126, 207;
    Oriental: Sage, 221;
        thought, 48
Orthodoxy, 71

Other world, 182
Ought, 34ff., 130, 137, 220, 231
    see also Duty, Obligation
"Our Father Our King," 179

Pagans, 17;
    paganism, 179
Pain, 39, 62, 115, 118, 131, 135f., 138, 142, 184ff.
Pantheism, 207f.
Paradise, 39, 154, 180, 214, 216;
    — lost, 58
Paradox, 138
Past, the
    see Time
Paul, 14, 16ff., 33, 138, 223;
    Pauline: Christianity, 14;
        theology, 19
Pearl Harbor, 132
Pentateuch, 222
Perfection, 49, 53, 55, 219;
    excess of —, 60;
    idea of —, 56;
    ideals of —, 56;
    reality of —, 53;
    social —, 50;
    transcendent —, 56;
    — of character, 55
    the perfect, 145;
Personality, 206, 209, 219, 230
Pesikta Rabbati, 216 n. 12
Pharaoh, 76
Pharisees, 17f., 25, 27f., 69;
    pharisaic: faith, 180, 182;
        thought, 69, 177
"Philanthropia," 28
Philistinism, 44
Philo, 28
Philosophy, 49, 70, 190;
    a challenge to —, 62;
    ethical —, 219;
    Greek —, 114;
    — of organism, 110
Physics, 82, 86, 93f., 118;
    "physics and metaphysics," 83;
    quantum —, 85, 92f.
Pitts, Walter, 228
Place of the World, the, 138, 207
Plato, 23, 49, 191;
    Platonic realm of ideas, 176
Pleasures
    higher and lower —, 43
Poe, Edgar Allan, 223
Possibility, 11, 80, 107ff., 112, 145, 193, 197, 203, 231;

infinite —, 219;
realm of —, 11;
possibilities, 192, 198, 209;
the possible, 11
Potentialities, 126
Prayer Book, traditional, 104
Predestination, 78, 83, 201;
see: Determinism
Predictability, 85, 92, 95;
prediction, 86f., 91
Present, the
see: Time
Probability, 84f., 87, 92, 99
calculus of —, 92
Process, 17, 81, 86, 91, 107, 112, 117f., 121, 197;
cosmic, 120, 191, 219f., 233;
creative, 101, 137;
historical, 222f.
natural, 221f.
psychological, 223f.
Progress, 23, 56, 67f., 70f., 85, 126, 143, 194;
faith in —, 66;
reality of —, 62;
social —, 65
Prometheus, 23
Prophecies, 16;
prophecy, spirit of, 34
Prophets, the, 147
Proverbs
passages cited in connection with:
retribution, 216 n. 1;
value of moral life, 124
Providence, 152, 174f.;
special —, 130
Provincialism, 69f.
Psalms,
passages cited in connection with:
bright destiny of righteous, 183;
doubt as to God's justice, 157f.;
faith in cosmic catastrophe, 162;
Jewish universalism, 31f.;
pantheistic faith, 207;
Optimism, 181;
retribution, 216 n. 1;
speculative doubt, 166
Purposiveness, 120, 235;
purpose, 229f;
— divine, 233

Quality, 193

Rabbis, 32, 33, 174f.;
rabbinic: Judaism, 173, 182;

theology, 205;
thought, 28, 179
Rationalism, 223f.
Ratner, Joseph, 78
Realism, 23, 181;
modern —, 50;
skeptical, 159;
realist, 11, 102;
Reality, 3, 50f., 54, 80, 94, 97, 99, 108, 131, 145, 193, 196, 203, 211, 219, 231f.;
aspects of —, 191f.;
infinite —, 140;
physical and spiritual —, 42;
present —, 11;
structure of —, 192
Reason, 6, 10, 22, 38, 42, 54, 60f., 111, 115, 120, 123, 134, 191, 221f., 224;
critical —, 223;
flight from —, 57
Redemption, 153;
redeemer, 16, 26, 170
Reification, 193;
fallacy of —, 192
Relativity, 201;
theory of —, 225f.
Religion, 13, 15, 49, 103, 196, 218, 220f.;
an opiate, 13;
religionist, 106
Repentance, 58, 75f., 131, 143
Responsibility, 57, 61, 64, 97, 115, 150;
individual —, 153;
moral —, 73, 111, 134, 231
Resurrection, 155, 180, 182, 190, 212, 215
Retribution, 145ff., 153ff., 172f., 186;
divine —, 147, 186
see: Reward
Revelation, 20, 174, 220, 224;
— vs. discovery, 225
Reverence, 18, 32, 69
Reward, 182f., 210;
— and punishment, 115, 182;
see: Retribution
Right, 52, 126f., 142, 181;
— and wrong, 159;
see also: Ethics, Good, Goodness, Morality, Values
Righteousness, 122, 125, 133f., 139, ,142f., 160, 182f., 209, 211, 235;
righteous, the, 146f., 155
Rome, 138

Roosevelt, the Elder, 5
Russell, Bertrand, 234
Ruth, 32f.

Sabbath, 26
Sacrifice, 185, 218;
 supreme —, 126
Saduceeism, 69
Saint, the, 9, 36, 40, 42, 46, 50, 184f., 187, 214, 231, 235;
 saintliness, 34, 134
Salvation, 78, 128ff., 170, 172;
 miraculous —, 56;
 other-worldly —, 14
Samuel, 164f.
Samuel, Maurice, 44
Sancho Panza, 235
Sandburg, Carl, 68
Sanhedrin, 30, 217 n. 31
Santayana, George, 108
Satan, 160
Saviour, 220
Schechter, Solomon, 154, 173ff., 185f., 187f.
Scholastics, 205;
 scholastic rationalist, 140
Shroedinger, 98
Scientific Monthly, 83
Seder Eliahu, 33
Self, 35;
 — caused, 85;
 — conscious, 35, 98, (defined) 132;
 — consciousness, 46, 120, 211f.;
 — contradiction, 135, 137;
 — contradictory, 136;
 — control, 124;
 — determination, 84, 112;
 — determined, 85, 111;
 — Determining 88, 101
 — discipline, 125;
 — expression, 111;
 — fulfillment, 126;
 — indulgence, 42;
 — pity, 235;
 — realization, 188, 228;
 — sacrifice, 45, 75, 134, 146, 172, 214
Semantics, 105
Semitic usage, 148
Sensuality, 39
Sermon on the Mount, 16, 184
"Servant of the Lord," 166
Shabbat, 27, 216 n. 24, 217 n. 41

Shammai, 26f., **176;**
 School of Shammai, 69
Shechinah, 214
Shema, the, 25
Shir hayichud, 207
Sifra 27f., 31f.
Sifre, 217 n. 26
Simlai, Rabbi, 29, 31
Simultaneity, 201, 208, 214
Sin, 7, 9, 19, 50, 76, 115, 123, 130ff., 134, 137, 142f., 146, 148, 152, 154, 161, 164, 179f., 186, 220, 233;
 — of Adam, 40;
 sinner, 214, 231
Sinnott, Edmund W., 120f.
Social contract, 3
Socialist, 21
Society, 3f., 8f, 14, 21, 24f., 35f., 40, 42, 49f., 53, 56, 61, 70, 124f., 127, 145, 149, 150f., 220;
 actual —, 11;
 free —, 64;
 outlaw —, 7;
 Perfect —, 49;
 Roman —, 15
Socrates, 1, 211
Sodom, 150f.
Solipsism, 11
Sovereignty
 national, 66
Soul, 136, 189, 191f., (defined) 212;
 body and —, 190
Space, 81, 88, 93, 103, 135, 195;
 — time, 107, 118, 190, 195, 197, 201, 204f., 208, 211;
 — and time, 66, 100, 104, 108, 122, 138, 146, 190, 196ff., 209, 214
Spiegel, Shalom, 216 n. 3
Spinoza, 19, 78, 105, 111, 138f., 208, 231
Spirit, 40, 45, 119, 152f., 191f., 233;
 creative —, 82;
 divine —, 137f.;
 Hebraic —, 225;
 holy —, 33f.;
 human —, 35, 45, 106, 117, 124, 128, 137f., 152, 181, 189, 224;
 needs of —, 62;
 spiritual: life, 119;
 nature, 61;
 rebirth, 58,
 spirituality (defined) 42f., 45, 123
Song of Unity, 207

Status, 3f., 7ff., 22, 25, 127;
    exceptional —, 8;
    social —, 7;
    special —, 8;
    spiritual —, 9;
    status quo, 17, 20
Stevenson, Robert Louis, 223
Stoicism, 216 n. 25;
    stoic, 15
    — fortitude, 186;
    — pride, 18, 184;
    the Stoics, 28
Strack Billerbeck, 36 n. 10
Substance, 78, 105, 196, 205, 208;
    primal —, 191
Suffering, 46, 50f., 59, 62, 67, 75, 115, 122f., 131f., 134ff., 143, 154, 157, 160f., 163f., 166, 172f., 177, 180, 184ff., 211;
    — servant, 170, 172
Summun bonum, 48
Superman, 8, 233
Supernatural, 221
    — vs. supra-natural, 122
Symbolism, 227;
    symbol, 16, 19:
    symbolization, 10
Synagogue, 19, 25, 26, 104, 179, 214,

Taanit, 216 n. 21, 217 n. 40
Tables of the Law, 4
Taboo, 127
Talmud, 75, 173;
    Talmudic Rabbis, 138
Tannaim, 26, 215f.
Tao, 48
Teacher of Righteousness, 171
Teba, 114
Teitelbaum, Moshe, 215
Tekoah, Women of, 164
Ten Commandments, 16, 24, 26, 226
Theism, 231, 233
Theodicy, 180
Theology, 108, 141, 176:
    Christian —, 179;
    Pauline —, 19;
    theological: dilemma, 115;
        discussion, 175;
        doctrines, 83;
        historians, 14:
        postulates, 227;
        subtleties, 174;
        terminology, 13, 106
Theosophy, 208
Thinking

creative (defined), 224
Throne of Glory, 215
Time, 69, 78, 81, 93, 110f., 195, 197, 201f., 207, 214;
    actual —, 198;
    beyond —, 101;
    future —, 68, 70, 77, 87, (defined) 198ff., 208ff.;
    mathematical —, 197;
    past —, 68ff., (defined) 87, 198ff.; 208ff.;
    present —, 70, (defined) 198ff., 208ff.;
    sequence of —, 202f.
Tineius Rufus, 177
Titus, 1, 5
Tolerance, 17
Torah, 25f., 28, 133, 147, 174, 187;
    essence of —, 27;
    a heathen who studies —, 33
Torrey, Charles, 169
Toynbee, Arnold, 14
Tradition, 20, 26, 49, (defined) 68:
    Biblical —, 35;
    Jewish —, 35;
    Jewish and Christian —, 48
Transcendent, 11
Transference, 22, 24
Tree of Knowledge, 58, 154
Truth, 6, 24, 52f., 111, 117, 126, 137, 159, 163, 172, 211, 225;
    absolute —, 49;
    double standard of —, 221;
    metaphysical —s, 224;
    nature of —, 226;
    passion for —, 45;
    perfect —, 52f., 55;
    ultimate —, 50, 52

Unconscious, 57
United Nations, 65
United States, 20
Universalism, 33
Universals, 88, (defined) 90, 94, 112, 146, 192f., 197, 212, 219, 232
Universe, 80
Unknown, the, 53
Unpredictable, the, 85f.
Utopias, 49, 55

Value/s, 44, 114, 117, 119f., 145, 182, 186, 191, 211, 220, 231, 235;
    artistic —, 223;
    higher —, 44;
    human —, 206;

moral —, 6, 115, 128, 132, 186, 214;
scientific —, 124;
spiritual —, 83, 121, 220
truth —, 86;
scale of —, 43, 191;
transvaluation of —, 18
see also: Ethics, Good, Goodness, Morality, Right
Van Doren, 69
Vatican, 15
Verity
eternal —, 225f.
Virtue, 28, 51, 62, 66, 133, 145, 149, 154, 218;
virtues, the, 24, 28, 35, 125, 226
Volition, 24, 97f., 101, 111, 133, 231;
infra-volitional, 102;
supra-volitional, 102
Von Neumann, John, 228

Wenzl, Aloys, 99ff.
Weyl, 98
Whitehead, Alfred North, 80, 101, 105f.
Whole, the—and its parts, 79
Wicked, the, 213

Wieman, Henry Nelson, 11
Wiener, Norbert, 228
Wilder, Thornton, 23
Will, the, 6, 38, 40, 61, 76, 102, 104, 127, 131, 134, 136, 182, 191, 220;
birth of —, 62;
freedom of —, 6, 73, 78, 231;
God's —, 142f.
moral —, 52f., 77, 124, 130, 137
Wilson, Edmund, 171
Wisdom, 63, 163;
divine —, 164
Wisdom Literature, 147, 159, 165, 190
Wisdom of Solomon, 155
Witch of Endor, 190
Wolfson, Harry Austryn, 28, 139, 208
Wordsworth, 58
World to Come, 56, 116, 146, 155, 173f., 179, 182, 190, 210

Yalkut Shimoni, 144 n. 5
Yezer hara, 134

Zeno, 216 n. 25
Zohar, 217 n. 39